Ornamental Trees for Mediterranean Climates

The Trees of San Diego

Photographs and Book Design by Don Walker

Text by Steve Brigham

**San Diego
Natural History
Museum**

Ibis Publishing Company

Ornamental Trees for Mediterranean Climates
The Trees of San Diego

Copyright© 2005 San Diego Horticultural Society

San Diego Horticultural Society
P. O. Box 231869
Encinitas, CA 92023-1869
info@sdhortsoc.org

ISBN 0-934797-23-4

Library of Congress Control Number 2005935103

Cover photo: *Cassia leptophylla* (Gold Medallion Tree)

Back Cover photos (left to right, top to bottom)
  Harpephyllum caffrum (South African Wild Plum)
  Callistemon viminalis (Weeping Bottlebrush)
  Pyrus kawakamii (Evergreen Pear)
  Corymbia ficifolia (Red-Flowering Gum)
  Ensete ventricosum (Abyssinian Banana)
  Dombeya cacuminum (Strawberry Snowball Tree)
  Brahea armata (Blue Fan Palm)
  Melaleuca armillaris (Weeping Melaleuca)
  Acacia baileyana (Bailey Acacia)
  Juniperus scopulorum 'Tolleson's Blue Weeping' (Weeping Juniper)
  Cyathea cooperi (Australian Tree Fern)
  Liquidambar styraciflua (Sweet Gum)
  Jacaranda mimosifolia (Jacaranda)
  Acacia stenophylla (Shoestring Acacia)
  Allocasuarina verticillata (Coast Beefwood)
  Cercis canadensis (Eastern Redbud)

Printed in Korea

Contents

Acknowledgements

The production of a book of this depth and scope represents the efforts of many people in addition to those whose names appear on the front cover, and we are grateful for all their help. For this edition, we appreciate the generous assistance of Dr. Bruce Hubbard in preparing preliminary scans of the new photographs. We lost a great friend in our publisher, Dr. James Clements, of Ibis Publishing Company, who was enormously helpful in getting our first edition printed. For the second edition we are most thankful that Jim's wife, Karen Clements, took over where he left off and was a huge help. Additional help for the second edition was generously given by Dave Ehrlinger, Director of Horticulture at Quail Botanical Gardens, who created a new map showing the trees there. Paul Sirois, Park Arborist, City of San Diego, was a big help in updating the coding and map for the trees found in Balboa Park. We also thank Sue Fouquette for her assistance in locating trees in Balboa Park.

For the 2003 edition of this book, we are indebted to the following members of our book committee who put in many hours to make the first edition possible: Walter Andersen, Tom Piergrossi, Bill Teague and Susi Torre-Bueno. Jason Kubrock, Lead Gardener at Quail Botanical Gardens, prepared the map showing these trees at QBG. Kathy Puplava, Balboa Park Horticulturist for the City of San Diego Park and Recreation Department, with help from Lucy Warren, designed and prepared the coding for the location of these trees in Balboa Park. Dr. Bruce Hubbard prepared hundreds of preliminary scans of the photographs, and Karl Larson provided valuable computer assistance. Dr. Jon Rebman, Curator of Botany, San Diego Natural History Museum, was a sterling scientific editor, and Sue Fouquette was a great help in proofreading our text. We were extremely fortunate to have had the help of the late Dr. James Clements, of Ibis Publishing Company, who adeptly and patiently shepherded us through the publishing process and enormously facilitated our way by anticipating many details we hadn't considered; in addition, he produced the indexes of common and scientific names for the first edition.

We owe much appreciation to the backyard gardeners and public institutions whose trees are shown in these pages for taking such great care of the handsome specimens that inspired us to do this book. Finally, thanks to Donna Brigham and Dorothy Walker for patience and support while their husbands labored long hours to bring forth both editions of this publication.

The San Diego Horticultural Society is very grateful to the organizations, businesses and publications named below for their sponsorship of the second edition of this book. We applaud their support in bringing to the public the first hardbound book of over 260 of San Diego's most beautiful trees.

Sponsors

American Horticultural Society

Briggs Tree Company & Wholesale Nursery

Evergreen Nursery

Horticulture

Hydro-Scape Products, Inc.

Nowell & Associates Landscape Architecture, Inc.

Pacific Horticulture

Pardee Tree Nursery

Quail Botanical Gardens

San Diego County Flower & Plant Association

San Diego Home/Garden Lifestyles

San Diego Natural History Museum

SeaWorld San Diego

The Garden Conservancy's Open Days Program

Walter Andersen Nurseries

We are also very appreciative of a generous grant from the Stanley Smith Horticultural Trust, which was a great help in the publication of the first edition

Foreword

San Diego has a reputation as being the place where anything grows. Flip though this book and look at the amazing diversity of trees alone, everything from Australian acacias to a huge *Yucca elephantipes,* and you'll get the idea. There are Araucariaceae and Arecaceae, Proteaceae and Pinaceae, all the way to Verbenaceae. You think of a tree and it can probably be found growing somewhere in San Diego.

As soon as they arrived, the earliest settlers began experimenting with this unusually mild and hospitable climate, planting both the familiar and the completely exotic and astounding. This experimentation continues to this day, as gardeners continue to push the envelope, trying things that probably won't grow here, and certainly shouldn't, but you never know—so why not.

Of course, there's a problem with being able to grow almost anything, and that would be selecting something—one thing or perhaps two, to plant in your garden—and I suspect that will be the major use for this valuable book, though not the only one. If you live in the vast and varied San Diego area and have a spot for a tree, it's a good idea to learn as much about it as you can before you actually stick it in the ground, so look up those you're considering. The text provides valuable, often first-hand information. Since every tree in this book is illustrated, you can also simply shuffle though it, looking for a likely tree for your front or back yard.

The text will tell you how big it gets (and perhaps how long it lives since some trees are disturbingly short-lived), how tall and wide, how best to care for it. Specific street addresses are given for most of the illustrated trees so you can actually find them and see what they look like in person.

One thing I appreciate knowing about a plant is where it comes from, since that gives valuable clues to its culture, and adds to the plant's panache. Every tree in this book is so identified. My wife likes to know what family a plant is in since she looks for similarities between species, and that information is here. More than a few of us gardeners will appreciate the guide to pronouncing each tree's botanical name.

But one needn't grow trees to appreciate them. You can put on your walking shoes and head out into the neighborhood looking for interesting trees, just like some go in search of unusual birds to add to their list of sightings. You could even use this book as a sort of checklist, making notes in the margins about trees you have seen and where, noting things like the sorry condition of the sidewalk, or how lacy the shade is, or how lovely the flowers.

Finally, I suspect that more than a few tourists will discover this guide. As they drive around, visitors are going to see unfamiliar trees—and the clear photographs in the book should make identifying them fairly easy, since no botanical training or knowledge is required.

Trees are an important part of life and they should be better appreciated. Aside from providing us with much of the oxygen we breathe and many useful products, they are the background against which we live and garden, the umbrella under which we stand, the post against which we lean. As a guide to the trees of a city, this one joins the slim but prestigious ranks of similar guides to other notable California municipalities, such as the earlier *Trees of Santa Barbara* by Maunsell Van Rensselaer, or *Trees of Santa Monica* by Grace Heinz and George Hastings. My hat is off to Don Walker and Steve Brigham who put this useful book together. I think it may just be the best one yet.

Robert Smaus, former Los Angeles Times Garden Editor and host of public television's The Victory Garden.

Trees—A World We Can Look Up To

In June of 1994, Don and Dorothy Walker, Steve Brigham, Bill and Linda Teague, and Kathy Musial sat around a table in the Redwood Grove at Buena Creek Gardens and agreed to form the San Diego Horticultural Society. Many major goals for this new group were discussed on that day, and all of those goals have since been met and in fact greatly exceeded. One of the projects we discussed was probably our most ambitious—the production of a book about the ornamental trees we grow in San Diego County. Perhaps we were inspired by the tall Coast Redwood trees that sheltered us as we talked. After all, one of them had been grown from a piece of a tree that was over 1000 years old, and it's always nice to have an older, wiser person to guide you.

Trees are not only the backbone of any landscape, they are the backbone of every community. Trees provide beauty, shade, flowers, fruit, and structure that enrich our lives, and they also reduce air pollution, erosion, and energy costs. Recent studies suggest that we in San Diego County need to plant many more trees in order to have the ideal tree coverage in our urban environments, and so many cities and homeowners here are concerned these days with choosing trees. But which trees will they choose? Because of our exceptional horticultural climate, we can and do grow an astounding variety of trees from all over the world, and there is certainly a need for more information about them. If you're thinking about planting trees, this book will help you see the many choices available to you.

Originally, our plan for this book was simply to photograph and document the most outstanding specimen trees in San Diego County, and by doing so increase public awareness of our greatest tree treasures. But along the way, we realized that we could do more. As long as we were going to feature photographs of specimen trees in public view, why not include as many kinds of trees as we could? That way, the book could be used as an identification guide for nearly any tree that might be seen. And instead of just listing where these trees are, why not also provide descriptions and cultural information for each kind of tree? Ultimately, this book evolved into a comprehensive reference guide to the many kinds of omental trees we can grow in our Mediterranean climate, and it can also be used as a tree reference by anyone anywhere in the world.

Have you ever seen a tree in bloom and wondered what its name was or what part of the world it came from? Even long-time residents of San Diego County are constantly seeing trees that are unfamiliar to them, and newcomers to our area are often completely unfamiliar with most of the trees they see. This book will help you identify the trees you see, and also show you where to look for new trees you've never seen. Don spent over four years and drove over 20,000 miles in photographing the trees featured in this book. They are all real trees of mature size that you can visit, so that you can see exactly what the tree looks like when it gets big. Since the day that we agreed to do this project, Don has also spent over 2000 hours at his computer planning, designing, and producing this book from start to finish. This book is his baby. As for the tree descriptions, we decided from the beginning that this would be a book for everyone, and it is most deliberately written to appeal to any experience level.

The appreciation of the natural world around us starts with the appreciation of plants, which starts with the appreciation of trees. We hope that you will enjoy the trees in this book, and that you will find the photographs and the text both friendly and informative. Trees may not be able to talk, but they surely can inspire. They inspired us, and we hope that they will inspire you.

Don Walker
Steve Brigham
July 2003

Introduction

First published less than two years ago, our original *Ornamental Trees of San Diego* was a sell-out success. As we were hoping, this book proved that a book on the trees of a specific region can serve not only that region but also serve as a valuable reference in other parts of the world as well. That's why we've changed the title for this second edition, and we welcome all of you new readers around the world as we also welcome back our San Diego and Southern California friends.

Far from a simple reprint, *Ornamental Trees for Mediterranean Climates* is substantially different from its predecessor. Although our format remains the same, this is a larger book, with 16 more full-color pages and 31 new kinds of trees that were not in the original text. In this book, we have updated all of our botanical nomenclature to reflect the most currently accepted names in the world today, and also rewritten many of the original tree descriptions. Many new close-up photos have been added to further illustrate the flowers and foliage of the featured trees. Also updated is our Color Chart of Showy Flowering Trees on pages 141-143, which has proven to be a most helpful at-a-glance reference in itself.

This book showcases notable tree specimens of 260 different kinds of ornamental trees that grow well in the coastal and inland regions of San Diego County, California, USA. There's a good reason why so many different kinds of trees grow in San Diego – and that reason is climate. It never gets too cold here in the winter, so we can grow many kinds of subtropical trees. But it does get just cold enough to grow many kinds of temperate trees. Our summers are warm enough to please the subtropicals, but also dry enough to grow many plants from deserts and other dry regions. With all this diversity, San Diego County may be considered to be one very large arboretum. Think of this book as your trail guide to that arboretum.

You don't have to live in San Diego to grow the trees in this book, however. Most of California, the Mediterranean Sea region, and parts of Australia, southern Africa, and western South America have climates very similar to ours, and so this book is a valuable tree reference in those areas as well. In addition, a significant number of trees in this book will grow in the Pacific Northwest, Southwest, Southern, and Southeastern United States, as well as many temperate and subtropical areas throughout the world.

One of the things we like about the format of this book is the diversity of tree forms you'll see as you turn every page. And when you do, you'll realize that our definition of a "tree" here is a utilitarian one, not a strictly botanical one. For example, the 21 kinds of palms featured in this book may not have true "wood" in the scientific sense, but they certainly do function as trees in the landscape – indeed, a few of them are among the most common "trees" we grow here. Further, this book also features many kinds of large shrubs which are commonly trained as trees. This also makes sense to us, because particularly in the smaller confines of urban landscapes here, these are the "trees" you're likely to see the most, often with spectacular results.

There are of course many fine ornamental trees that may be grown in San Diego and elsewhere that are not in this book because suitably large and impressive public specimens could not be located here or did not photograph well. It is our hope, however, that adventurous planters around San Diego County will change that, so that future editions of this book might be bigger still.

We hope you like our new tree book, and find it even more useful than our first one. And remember: the *best* time to plant a tree is 20 years ago, but the second-best time to plant a tree is today!

Don Walker
Steve Brigham
September 2005

How To Use This Book

The 260 featured trees in this book are presented alphabetically by botanical name, which is the most consistent and universally accepted way of naming plants (see below). Because most gardeners are more comfortable with common names, however, the most frequently used common name in Southern California is also listed for each tree and used in the descriptive text. Also given for each tree is a phonetic pronunciation for its botanical name, the plant family to which it belongs, and the region of the world where it grows naturally.

The photographs in this book are all of real trees in San Diego County that may be easily seen from a public street or in a public park. The location for each tree accompanies each photograph, usually with a street address. As a guide to other specimens of these trees that you can visit, location codes appear at the end of the descriptive text for trees which may also be seen in Balboa Park (including the San Diego Zoo) in San Diego and at Quail Botanical Gardens in Encinitas. These codes are explained on pages 144 and 145.

This book is designed to be used by both professionals and amateurs alike. In the descriptive text for each tree, every effort has been made to avoid technical terms without sacrificing botanical correctness. The mature sizes given for each tree are as they grow in our area, but keep in mind that trees growing under difficult conditions will often be smaller and grow more slowly than those in more favorable situations. As a guide to selecting trees for the landscape, a special section beginning on page 140 includes some helpful tips plus a color chart of showy flowering trees. Although many kinds of trees in this book are widely grown here, it is important to note that there are some trees featured that are neither common nor commonly available in local nurseries. A list of sources on page 147 will be of help in obtaining the trees you want.

About Plant Names

Plant names often cause great confusion in the minds of home gardeners and nursery and landscape professionals alike. Many people prefer common names, which have the advantage of being in English (in our case), but a single kind of plant often has more than one common name and there are many common names that refer to more than one kind of plant. Although they are written in a special scientific language, botanical names are more precisely regulated, so that ideally every plant has only one "correct" botanical name. Botanical names can and do change as the study of plants advances, but they are still the most reliable way to identify a particular plant.

Every kind of tree belongs to a particular family of plants which has a Latinized name. Each tree also has a two-part Latinized name of its own (written in italics) which identifies it as a particular natural species or horticultural cross. Many trees are selected forms or hybrids that are propagated clonally, and these also have a cultivar (short for "cultivated variety") name that is not written in italics but enclosed in single quotes. As an example, the first tree featured in this book is usually called the Bailey Acacia in California (some people call it Mimosa, however, and in its native Australia it's called the Cootamundra Wattle). It is in the genus *Acacia*, and is further defined as the species *baileyana*. A selected cutting-grown form of it with reddish-purple new growth is called 'Purpurea'. This tree is in the legume plant family, which is known as Fabaceae or sometimes Leguminosae.

Perhaps the most confusing thing about botanical names is how to pronounce them. Botanical names are based mostly on Latin, but they can be derived from a number of languages, and although there are rules on which syllables are accented there is no complete set of rules for pronunciation. Conventionally, however, botanical names are pronounced as if they were in the language of the speaker. It's true that different people pronounce botanical names in different ways—to use an analogy, some say "toe-MAY-toe" and some say "toe-MAH-toe". The phonetic pronunciations given for the botanical names in this book use English vowel sounds (which means that we say "toe-MAY-toe"). But you can say "toe-MAH-toe" if you like. Don't be afraid of saying botanical names—just sound them out slowly. Who knows, it may even be fun!

Acacia baileyana
(uh-KAY-shuh bay-lee-AN-uh)
BAILEY ACACIA
Fabaceae (Leguminosae)
Southeastern Australia

The genus *Acacia* is a large group of trees and shrubs, with some 1200 species worldwide. Most of these are native to Australia, where they are collectively called "wattles." The best-known acacia in California horticulture is the Bailey Acacia from New South Wales, an easily grown small evergreen tree whose bright yellow cut flowers are called "mimosa" in the cut-flower trade. Fast-growing to 20-25' tall and wide, it succeeds in almost any soil and is quite tolerant of drought. Finely cut feathery blue-gray foliage is dense, and specimens may be trained with either single or multiple trunks. Individual flowers are in small yellow puffballs that are sweetly fragrant, and are produced in large clusters that completely cover the tree from January to March. Even a small tree can perfume a large area when in bloom.

The Bailey Acacia makes a beautiful show in the landscape at a time when flower color is most appreciated. In fact, it produces the brightest yellow flower color of any winter-flowering tree. In addition to being easy to grow, it is also one of the cold-hardiest acacias and will tolerate temperatures as low as 15°F. Well-drained soil is preferred but not essential. The foliage of the typical form of Bailey Acacia is a steely blue-gray. Two colored-foliage varieties are also grown—'Purpurea', with lavender to reddish-purple new growth, and 'Aurea', with yellow new growth—the foliage of these is showiest in the late winter and spring.   **B25,QBG**

Rancho Santa Fe Golf Club, Rancho Santa Fe

Quail Botanical Gardens

Acacia cognata
(uh-KAY-shuh kog-NAY-tuh)
RIVER WATTLE
Fabaceae (Leguminosae)
Southeastern Australia

The River Wattle is one of the finest small weeping trees for the landscape. Formerly known as *Acacia subporosa*, it is a fast-growing evergreen to 15-25' tall and wide, with a graceful, willowy foliage composed of narrow 4" long bright lime-green phyllodes (not true leaves but modified leaf stalks, a feature common in many acacias). The River Wattle blooms in the spring with fragrant pale yellow flowers. Unlike many acacias, it prefers moist soil and will grow well in partial shade, making it particularly useful for planting under taller trees or on the shady side of tall buildings.

The River Wattle is hardy to the low 20's°F. and is tolerant of most types of soil. It is easy to grow, but benefits from some early training and pruning to make an attractive specimen. Although this tree is somewhat short-lived (15-20 years), it grows to its mature size quickly. Two selections grown are 'Emerald Cascade' and 'Emerald Showers', which have particularly attractive bright green foliage.   **QBG**

3702 Del Mar Ave., Point Loma

1656 Sunrise Dr., Vista

Acacia pendula
(uh-KAY-shuh   PEN-dyoo-luh)
WEEPING ACACIA
Fabaceae (Leguminosae)
Eastern Australia

The Weeping Acacia is a beautiful small evergreen tree that just gets better with age. Grown primarily for its pendulous blue-gray foliage (yellow flowers appear only sparingly in spring), it is distinctive as one of the very few cultivated trees with weeping gray foliage. Slow-growing and long-lived, it can be an architectural centerpiece in any garden and deserves a prominent spot in the landscape. The Weeping Acacia naturally grows upright to an eventual 20-25' tall and 15' wide, but may be trained to assume a wider, more picturesque shape—with mature plants also featuring a beautifully rugged bark.

Young plants can even be nicely displayed as espalier. Individual phyllodes (modified leaf stalks that function like true leaves) on the Weeping Acacia are 4" long and 1/2" wide and are a striking blue-gray color. They densely clothe the branchlets, which hang straight down. The Weeping Acacia likes a well-drained soil in full sun, and is hardy to 18°F. Although it is not common in nurseries, it has been grown in San Diego for over 70 years. **B25,QBG**

Acacia podalyriifolia
(uh-KAY-shuh poe-duh-leer-ee-ih-FOE-lee-uh)
PEARL ACACIA
Fabaceae (Leguminosae)
Eastern Australia

There are a number of shrubby species of *Acacia* that can function beautifully in the landscape when trained as small trees. One of the most ornamental of these is the Pearl Acacia, which is popular for its silvery foliage color as well as its fragrant, bright yellow flowers. The Pearl Acacia grows quickly to 10-20' tall and 12-15' wide, with smooth gray bark and a billowy evergreen foliage of 1-1/2" long oval phyllodes. This foliage is a striking silvery-gray color and soft and satiny to the touch, and is useful as cut-foliage in floral arrangements. The Pearl Acacia is one of the earliest acacias to bloom, and is very showy from late fall into early winter when it is covered with long clusters of sweetly-fragrant 1-1/2" bright yellow fluffy flowers. Since it is often in bloom here in December, it can be useful for holiday decorations.

The Pearl Acacia prefers full sun and a well-drained soil, and succeeds in either coastal or inland climates where temperatures do not fall much below 25°F. It is very drought-tolerant, and should not be overwatered in the summer, since too much water will shorten its life. It can be most effective when trained as a patio tree, with the best time for pruning being late winter or early spring after flowering is over. **B26**

Acacia stenophylla
(uh-KAY-shuh   steh-noe-FILL-uh)
SHOESTRING ACACIA
Fabaceae (Leguminosae)
Australia

Airy and open, the Shoestring Acacia presents an unusual sight with its long and very narrow "leaves" (actually modified leaf stalks called phyllodes) gracefully weeping from an open branch structure, forming a beautiful silhouette against the sky. This is a fast-growing small evergreen tree which is quite drought-tolerant and adaptable to a variety of soils and conditions. It also can be somewhat variable from seed, so it pays to shop around for the nicest-looking plants.

The Shoestring Acacia grows to an eventual 25' tall by 20' wide—faster with regular watering but slower (and smaller) in very dry sites. Pale green to gray-green phyllodes are drooping and up to 16" long by just 1/4" to 1/2" wide, with 1/2" creamy-white flowers appearing in clusters in late winter. This tree casts a light shade that permits a greater variety of plants to be planted under it. With age, the Shoestring Acacia can become a bit more densely foliaged, depending on the individual plant. Early training for a good branching structure will make for a more beautiful tree as it matures. The Shoestring Acacia is tolerant of heat and is also cold-hardy to 20°F. **QBG**

358 Pacific Ave., Solana Beach

Private residence, Rancho Santa Fe

Acacia xanthophloea
(uh-KAY-shuh   zan-tho-FLOE-ee-uh)
FEVER TREE
Fabaceae (Leguminosae)
Southeastern Africa

No visitor to the San Diego Wild Animal Park can ignore the magnificent Fever Tree that grows near the main gift shop, for it is indeed among the most remarkable trees in San Diego. The most striking feature of this unusual African native is its beautiful yellow-green bark which dominates the tree from head to toe (its specific name is based on Greek words meaning "yellow bark"). But its spreading branching structure invites a closer look, revealing another surprise—odd pairs of prominent white thorns all along the finely foliaged branchlets, covering the tree. You'll see many bird nests in this tree—birds no doubt feeling very protected by their thorny host!

The Fever Tree is so-named because it grows along washes and stream beds in its native land that may be home to malaria-carrying mosquitos. It grows fairly quickly to an eventual 40' tall and wide with regular watering, although it will be smaller and slower in a dry situation. The Fever Tree blooms in spring with clusters of small but sweetly scented flowers that look like little golden balls. It is tolerant of most soils and is cold-hardy to at least 20°F. **B26,QBG**

11

6781 Jackson Dr., San Carlos

Acca sellowiana
(AK-uh   sel-oh-wee-AN-uh)
PINEAPPLE GUAVA
Myrtaceae
S. Brazil, Paraguay, Uruguay, and N. Argentina

Formerly known as *Feijoa sellowiana*, the Pineapple Guava is shrubby when young but can easily be trained into a beautiful small multi-trunked tree. Enjoyable for many reasons, it bears tasty fruits, edible and ornamental flowers, and is a fine evergreen foliage plant for a variety of landscape uses. It is also tolerant of a wide variety of conditions, including temperatures as low as 15°F.

The Pineapple Guava flowers in spring with unusual 1-2" wide flowers with big central tufts of bright red stamens. The four fleshy white petals which surround the stamens are edible and taste sweet like sugar. The 2-4" long gray-green oval fruits which follow ripen in the fall with a sweet pineapple flavor— these are best picked only when fully ripe and fall from the tree on their own.

Although the Pineapple Guava is drought-tolerant, regular watering is recommended for best fruit production. If you grow this plant primarily for its fruits, you'll want to choose from several improved varieties with superior fruits which are available as grafted plants. A few of these such as 'Coolidge' are self-fruitful, but since most cultivars and seedlings fruit better with cross-pollination, planting more than one variety in proximity is a good idea. **QBG**

1430 Montgomery Ln., Vista

Acer palmatum
(AY-sir   pall-MAY-tum)
JAPANESE MAPLE
Aceraceae
Japan and Korea

The Japanese Maple is the most airy and delicate of the over 100 species of maples worldwide. It has become so popular in cultivation that there are over a thousand different forms of it grown. Although the Japanese Maple grows wonderfully in climates like the Pacific Northwest, it is more of a challenge in Southern California, where our alkaline soils and dry winds limit its performance.

In its typical seedling form, the Japanese Maple is a small, often multi-trunked deciduous tree which grows slowly to 20' tall and wide. Foliage emerges bright red in the spring, developing into 2-4" long bright green leaves that are deeply cut into 5 to 9 lobes. In areas with cold nighttime temperatures fall foliage color can be showy.

Although there are many dwarf and fancy-leaved varieties of Japanese Maple available, most of them are prone to severe leaf burn here during the summer and fall months. For us, seedling trees are much more rugged and dependable as garden plants, especially if they are given partial shade with protection from drying winds. A rich soil with plenty of organic matter and regular watering is best, with occasional heavy watering to leach out accumulated salts in the soil recommended. **B18**

Acer paxii
(AY-sir PAX-ee-eye)
EVERGREEN MAPLE
Aceraceae
Southwestern China

Most of the many kinds of maple trees are from cold-winter climates, and do not grow well in climates with very mild winters. There are, however, a few subtropical maples that adapt well to our mild coastal climates. The Evergreen Maple is successful here even in areas that do not get frost, and the fact that it is an evergreen tree is considered a plus by many gardeners.

Although it is a larger tree in the wild, the Evergreen Maple grows slowly in cultivation to around 30' tall and 20' wide. It has shiny, leathery green leaves which on young trees are 3-lobed but on older trees are nearly entire with a long tail-like tip. New leaves are pink-tinged as they emerge before the previous year's leaves drop, which is why the tree is never out of leaf.

The Evergreen Maple blooms in the spring with small greenish flowers that are followed by attractive red winged fruits. It grows in full sun or partial shade, and is cold-hardy to 20°F. It grows best with regular watering, and makes a good lawn tree. It is closely related to another Chinese species, *Acer oblongum*, and has been considered a variety of that species by some botanists. **B28**

Balboa Park

House of Pacific Relations, Balboa Park

Acrocarpus fraxinifolius
(ak-roe-KAR-pus frak-sih-nih-FOE-lee-us)
PINK CEDAR
Fabaceae
India, Myanmar, and Sikkim

The Pink Cedar is a handsome tropical mountain tree that out of bloom somewhat resembles our commonly grown Evergreen Ash (*Fraxinus uhdei*). But that resemblance ends in late winter or early spring, when the Pink Cedar produces dense foot-tall spikes of showy scarlet-red flowers just before its new leaves are produced. Uncommon in cultivation here, this tree deserves to be more widely grown.

Tall and narrow when young but eventually with a spreading crown, the Pink Cedar grows quickly at first here, but then slows to an eventual 40-60' tall and 25-30' wide. It has a smooth grayish trunk and tropical-looking foot-long leaves which are composed of pointed oval leaflets to 5" long and 1" wide that are crimson-pink when new. The Pink Cedar needs full sun and regular watering, and does not like hot dry conditions or strong winds. Best in frost-free areas, it is not reliably hardy below 30°F. Although trees are usually deciduous, they may remain evergreen in very mild winters. **B29**

13

Aesculus californica
(ESS-kew-luss kal-ih-FOR-nih-kuh)
CALIFORNIA BUCKEYE
Hippocastanaceae
California

Native to dry slopes and canyons in California's Coast Ranges and Sierra Nevada foothills, the California Buckeye is a very drought-tolerant small tree. Usually multi-trunked, it grows to 20-30' tall and wide with moderate watering but can be smaller if it is seldom watered. This is a deciduous tree that holds its leaves until October if watered in the summer but may shed its leaves as early as late July here if not watered at all.

The California Buckeye has smooth gray bark and glossy dark-green leaves which are composed of 5-7 coarsely toothed oblong leaflets. It is a striking sight in the spring as it blooms on bare branches with many 6-8" long flower spikes of fragrant cream-colored flowers. These are followed by big pear-shaped fruits which split open when ripe to reveal large shiny brown seeds which were once used as food by the original Californians.

The California Buckeye is completely hardy to cold and will also withstand heat and dry winds. There is a pink flowered form called 'Canyon Pink'. Other related trees commonly called "horse chestnuts" are sometimes grown here, but generally need more winter chill that our San Diego climates offer. **B4**

Private residence, Leucadia

Afrocarpus gracilior
(aff-roe-CAR-pus gruh-SILL-ee-or)
FERN PINE
Podocarpaceae
Eastern Africa

Formerly known as *Podocarpus gracilior* (and still often sold under that name), the Fern Pine is a handsome evergreen tree that grows easily with little care. Native to the mountains of Ethiopia, Kenya, and Uganda, it has recently been reclassified into the new genus *Afrocarpus* on the basis of its fruiting structure, with some botanists considering it a variety of *Afrocarpus falcatus* and others retaining its separate species designation.

The Fern Pine grows at a moderate rate to an eventual 50-60' tall and wide. Young trees are upright, with narrow, 2-4" long dark green leaves, but as trees mature they develop a spreading canopy with a dense foliage of somewhat shorter leaves. Clusters of light green new leaves at the ends of the branches contrast nicely with the darker green older growth. Fern Pines are technically conifers, but instead of woody cones mature female trees produce fleshy "fruits" which contain a single seed if a pollinating male tree is nearby.

The Fern Pine tolerates a variety of adverse conditions, including drought, poor soil, ocean winds, and air pollution, and is cold-hardy to around 15°F. For a sturdy tree, seed-grown plants are preferred. Occasionally, cutting-grown or grafted plants are grown and sold under the name *Podocarpus elongatus*, but these are grown that way so that they stay small and shrubby, to be used for espalier or in containers. **B37,QBG**

1704 Oliver Ave., Pacific Beach

Agathis robusta
(AG-uh-thiss roe-BUS-tuh)
QUEENSLAND KAURI
Araucariaceae
Northeastern Australia

Imposing is the word for the Queensland Kauri, an unusual evergreen Australian conifer that is related to the more familiar Norfolk Island Pine. Never common, its tall straight trunk and thick leathery leaves always attract attention. An important timber tree in its native land, its thick sap is the source of a resin called copal which is used to make varnishes and lacquers—a sap which makes all *Agathis* species extremely resistant to decay and quite long-lived.

Although the Queensland Kauri in nature can grow to huge proportions, this can take some time. The specimen pictured at Quail Botanical Gardens is around 40 years old and 40' tall, and the tallest specimen in California is 100 years old and 100' tall. Even when young, however, the Queensland Kauri is very ornamental, and can grow for years in a container. New growth is particularly striking, with both the color and texture of thick rubber bands; older growth on mature trees is a glossy dark green. This tree is happiest with regular watering and is hardy to at least 25°F.

A related Kauri from northern New Zealand is *Agathis australis*, which is famous there for the huge ancient specimens that dominate the forest north of Auckland—much like our Giant Sequoias do near Yosemite. More open than the Queensland Kauri and with bronze foliage rather than green, a big specimen of the New Zealand Kauri can be seen in Balboa Park across from the Organ Pavilion. **B35,QBG**

Near Lawn House
Quail Botanical
Gardens

3537 Addison St., Point Loma

Agonis flexuosa
(uh-GOE-nis fleks-yoo-OH-suh)
PEPPERMINT TREE
Myrtaceae
Western Australia

The Peppermint Tree is one of the best small evergreen trees for gardens where temperatures stay above 27°F. Growing fairly quickly to 25-35' tall and 15-30' wide, it has a dense foliage of narrow, dark green willow-like leaves to 6" long and graceful, weeping branches. Foliage when crushed smells strongly of peppermint. Small white flowers bloom profusely all along the branches in late spring and early summer, and its dark furrowed bark and eventual stout trunk are also ornamental.

The Peppermint Tree is tolerant of a wide range of garden conditions, and may be grown in a wide variety of soils with much or little water. It tolerates drought and wind even near the beach, and even succeeds admirably as a lawn tree as long as drainage is good. In colder climates, plants will freeze to the ground at around 25°F., but can resprout after temperatures as low as 10°F. to grow as a large shrub.

A related species, *Agonis juniperina*, is called the Juniper Myrtle. Somewhat smaller than the Peppermint Tree, it is also more open and finely textured with its 1/4"-1/2" needle-like foliage but is just as rugged. **B30,QBG**

15

140 Deer Springs Rd., San Marcos

Ailanthus altissima
(ay-LAN-thus al-TISS-ih-muh)

TREE-OF-HEAVEN
Simaroubaceae
China

Fast-growing and very tolerant of any climate and soil conditions, the Tree-of-Heaven is not considered a good garden tree because of its aggressive nature. However, you may see it growing mightily without any care in very old yards or even abandoned sites. This deciduous tree was introduced from China in the 1800's and planted extensively in California's Gold Country, where it gave welcome shade to early settlers without needing irrigation. It soon naturalized into extensive colonies there, as it eventually did over much of the U.S. This tree is so tolerant of adverse conditions that it became legendary as the tree that survived all odds in *A Tree Grows In Brooklyn.* In San Diego County this tree has persisted around abandoned homesteads in coastal, mountain, and desert sites.

The Tree-of-Heaven grows quickly to 30-50' tall, typically with multiple trunks. It has bold, tropical-looking leaves to 3' long that are composed of many 3-5" long leaflets. In summer, the bright red show of color on female trees is actually seed pods, which are good in dried arrangements. Especially under adverse conditions, it has an incredible ability to sucker, and cutting down a main trunk will usually produce many new shoots from the root system. New plants may also sprout from seed. The Tree-of-Heaven is cold-hardy to below 0°F. and survives with no irrigation once established.

715 Valley Dr., Vista

Albizia julibrissin
(al-BIH-zee-uh joo-lih-BRISS-in)

SILK TREE
Fabaceae (Leguminosae)
Iran to Japan

The Silk Tree is a tropical-looking tree that is much hardier than it looks and is popular for its pink powderpuff flowers which cover the tree from late spring to mid-summer. Hardy to at least 10°F., it is a fast grower that makes a spreading canopy often twice as wide as tall. Its fine-textured fern-like foliage is deciduous in winter, revealing a graceful branch structure that is equally ornamental. Unpruned, the Silk Tree grows 25-40' tall, but may be trained to a smaller size and can make a fine patio tree. It looks best with multiple trunks in locations where it has room to spread, and when in bloom is particularly beautiful when viewed from above.

Since they are grown from seed, individual Silk Trees may vary somewhat in the color of their flowers—the most popular ones are a seed strain with darker pink flowers called 'Rosea'. All the Silk Trees do best with high summer heat, which is why you'll see more of them in inland regions than on the coast. Although Silk Tree is somewhat drought-tolerant, it looks and performs better with regular watering. **B4,QBG**

16

Allocasuarina verticillata
(al-loe-kazh-yoo-RYE-nuh ver-tih-sill-AY-tuh)
COAST BEEFWOOD
Casuarinaceae
Southeastern Australia

Formerly known as *Casuarina stricta*, the Coast Beefwood is a graceful evergreen tree that grows easily even in the toughest of conditions. Fast growing to 20-35' tall and wide, it succeeds in wet or dry soils of nearly any type and withstands dry desert heat as well as salty ocean winds.

The Coast Beefwood is grown mainly for its graceful form and rounded crown of dark green weeping foliage, which is actually composed of slender jointed branchlets that have only minute rudimentary leaves. Also handsome is its dark, furrowed bark. Male trees are tipped with golden-brown flower clusters from winter to early spring, and female trees produce interesting clusters of 1" long cone-like fruits.

The common name Beefwood refers to the dark reddish-brown color of this tree's wood, which has been used for cabinetry, and it is also known as She-oak in its native Australia in reference to the oak-like qualities of its wood. It is a very drought-tolerant tree that is useful as either a specimen tree or as a windbreak, and is cold-hardy to 15°F.

Coronado Municipal Golf Course, 1312 Glorietta Blvd., Coronado

Alnus rhombifolia
(ALL-nuss rom-bih-FOE-lee-uh)
WHITE ALDER
Betulaceae
Western North America

This fast growing deciduous shade tree is native near streams and rivers in many parts of San Diego County and succeeds anywhere it receives adequate water. For this reason it is often planted as a lawn tree. It is an upright grower to 50' or more tall, narrow when young but spreading with age. In early spring, greenish-yellow tassel-like flowers hang from the bare branches, followed by toothed dark green 2-4" leaves which drop cleanly in the fall. Small woody cone-like fruits decorate the branches in winter, attracting both birds and flower arrangers. Both trunk and branches are handsome, with a gray color and smooth texture.

The White Alder is quite tolerant of heat and wind as long as it is watered regularly. It is also tolerant of a wide variety of soils, including heavy clay, and is cold-hardy to below 0°F. This tree is a good choice for shading a house in the summer but not in winter, and can help save money on utility bills. Although it doesn't specifically need pruning, a laced specimen can be particularly handsome. White Alder can also be planted as an informal grove for a streamside effect. **QBG**

17398 Avenida Peregrina, Rancho Santa Fe

1257 Hymettus Ave., Leucadia

Buena Creek Gardens, San Marcos

Aloe barberae
(AL-oh   BAR-ber-ee)
TREE ALOE
Asphodelaceae
South Africa

Of the many types of succulent aloes in cultivation, *Aloe barberae* is by far the most tree-like, and can indeed grow to 60' tall in its native South Africa. Here, however, it is a fairly slow-growing plant to an eventual 20-30' with a heavy forking trunk that makes its spread as wide. As a landscape specimen, it is unparalleled for its sculpturesque form, especially as a focal point in a succulent garden. Foliage is evergreen, with branches topped with rosettes of thick 2-3' long dark green succulent leaves. Although it can be shy to bloom, when it does each rosette produces a 1-2' tall spike of rose-pink flowers that are very showy.

The Tree Aloe likes full sun, but will also grow in part shade. It needs good drainage but only moderate to little irrigation. Foliage is tender to frost, and sustained temperatures below 27°F. can cause severe damage. Plants may be started from cuttings of almost any size, and even large plants can be successfully moved. Large specimens are always striking and never fail to attract attention.

Although the Tree Aloe is still known by the name *Aloe bainesii*, it was recently discovered that it was originally described as *Aloe barberae*. And so that is now considered the Tree Aloe's correct botanical name, even though books and nurseries may take a while to get used to this change.   **B26, QBG**

Angophora costata
(an-GAH-for-uh   koss-TAY-ta)
APPLE GUM
Myrtaceae
Eastern Australia

The genus *Angophora* is a small group of evergreen Australian trees that greatly resemble *Eucalyptus* but differ by having small petals at the base of their fluffy flowers. Known in Australia as the Smooth-barked Apple Gum, the tall and graceful *Angophora costata* is famous for its striking smooth trunk and colorful pinkish to brownish-orange bark which peels unevenly in summer to reveal patches of cream, rose, and mauve. The Apple Gum has bright green leaves to 6" long and 1" wide that are coppery-red when young. It blooms abundantly in late spring and early summer with large showy clusters of 1" creamy-white flowers composed of many stamens, followed by 1/2" woody seed pods.

The Apple Gum grows quickly to 30-50', and will tolerate poor soils, some drought, and temperatures as low as 20°F. Especially if grown at the coast in the path of ocean winds, trees may assume a distinctively rugged, gnarled shape of great character; plants grown farther inland out of the wind grow more upright. Both the leaves and bark of Apple Gum are used to produce dyes.   **B14**

18

Annona cherimola
(an-NOE-nuh cheh-rih-MOE-luh)
CHERIMOYA
Annonaceae
Peru and Ecuador

Odd and tropical-looking, the Cherimoya is native to the Andes Mountains and is actually one of the hardier tropical fruits, tolerating temperatures as low as 25°F. Although its delicious fruit is its main attraction, it also has beautiful leaves and fragrant flowers that make it an interesting garden tree. The Cherimoya grows quickly the first few years, then slows to eventually form a dense tree of around 20' by 20'. Its large 5-10" long oval leaves (dull green above and velvety-hairy beneath) are shed for a short time in late spring as the first flowers begin to form, but new leaves are quickly produced. The unusual fleshy brownish-green flowers have a sweet fruity fragrance and continue to form into summer, followed by the curious knobby fruits which may weigh from 1/2 to 2 pounds each by the time they are yellowish-green and ripe in late fall or early winter. The ripe fruit of the Cherimoya has a delicious custard-like texture, with a flavor like a blend of pineapple and banana—it is best eaten fresh and with a spoon to avoid the large black seeds within.

For the best quality fruit, it pays to buy grafted Cherimoya trees of superior varieties. Hand-pollination of the flowers (done with a paintbrush and not difficult) always results in better fruit set and larger fruit. Full sun, good soil, and regular watering and fertilizing are also important for a good crop.   **B14,QBG**

2507 San Clemente Ave., Vista

Araucaria bidwillii
(air-ow-KAIR-ee-uh bid-WILL-ee-eye)
BUNYA PINE
Araucariaceae
Northeastern Australia

Unrelated to the true pines in the genus *Pinus*, the Bunya Pine is an unusual evergreen conifer from Australia that is big in every way. With its wide sweeping branches and pointed leathery leaves, it has a unique prehistoric look—in fact, similar trees have inhabited the Earth for as long as 60 million years. Although young seedlings of the Bunya Pine are sometimes used as house plants, this is a tree that just keeps getting bigger and bigger as it gets older. A number of specimens in San Diego County that are at least 70 years old and over 50' tall are in their gigantic prime; older trees continue to grow taller but appear narrower.

The Bunya Pine makes a fine specimen tree where it has room to grow. Needing only average watering and soil, and little pruning, it is also one of the hardiest of the araucarias, withstanding temperatures as low as 10°F. This tree is famous for its giant cones, which are the size and shape of large pineapples and weigh over 10 pounds each. Forming high up in the tree, these cones are part of a rather primitive but effective gravity-based seed dispersal mechanism: when ripe, the cones simply fall a long way down to the ground (watch out if you're nearby!) and "explode" as they hit, thereby propelling their seeds away from the tree.   **B11,QBG**

9210 Lemon Ave., Mt. Helix

19

Araucaria columnaris
(air-ow-KAIR- ee-uh kah-lum-NAIR-iss)
NEW CALEDONIAN PINE
Araucariaceae
New Caledonia, Isle of Pines, and Loyalty Islands

The genus *Araucaria* includes 18 species of Southern Hemisphere conifers of wide distribution, with representatives native to Brazil, Chile, Australia, and the southwest Pacific Ocean region. Most of the species, however, are native to New Caledonia. The New Caledonian Pine is the most famous of these, having first impressed Captain Cook in 1774 and generations of horticulturists since.

The New Caledonian Pine is a tall, columnar evergreen tree that grows at a moderate rate here, with very old trees reaching up to 100' tall. Its habit and general look is similar to the Norfolk Island Pine (*Araucaria heterophylla*), but it has a denser, more graceful foliage, with pendent branchlets that give a more luxuriant effect. Unlike the Norfolk Island Pine, the New Caledonian Pine has a trunk which often leans at the base and main branches that are more horizontal on older trees. Its bright green foliage is composed of small needle-like leaves that densely clothe its 1/2" thick rope-like branchlets.

The New Caledonian Pine likes regular watering, is most tolerant of coastal conditions, and is cold-hardy to 25°F. Another New Caledonian species which is sometimes grown here is *Araucaria luxurians*, which has characteristics somewhat intermediate between *Araucaria columnaris* and *Araucaria heterophylla*. **B5**

2016 Thiobodo Rd., Vista

1975 Sunset Blvd., Mission Hills

Araucaria heterophylla
(air-ow-KAIR-ee-uh   heh-ter-oh-FILL-uh)
NORFOLK ISLAND PINE
Araucariaceae
Norfolk Island

A small but beautiful island in the southwestern Pacific Ocean is the native home of the evergreen Norfolk Island Pine, which has become the most widely grown species of *Araucaria* in the world. Although it eventually grows to be a large tree, young plants may be grown successfully in containers for years, and have been enjoyed as house plants in many parts of the world for generations. Outdoors in San Diego County, the Norfolk Island Pine makes a beautiful ornamental tree, and especially in our coastal areas there are many large old specimens to be seen.

Sometimes called the Star Pine, The Norfolk Island Pine grows at a moderate rate here, with the oldest specimen trees up to 100' tall. It has a very symmetrical growth habit, with distinctively tiered whorls of main branches and a dense foliage of bright green needle-like leaves along upward-facing branchlets. Like most araucarias, it reaches the peak of its gracefulness as a middle-aged tree, when its tall straight trunk, pyramidal shape, symmetrical branching, and soft foliage look their best. The Norfolk Island Pine is remarkably resistant to strong wind and even salt spray, and so makes an excellent tree for gardens near the ocean. **B5,QBG**

20

Arbutus unedo
(ahr-BYOO-tuss   yoo-NEE-doe)
STRAWBERRY TREE
Ericaceae
Southern Europe, Ireland, and United Kingdom

The Strawberry Tree is evergreen, extremely durable, and easy to grow. Shrubby when young, in time it becomes a beautiful multi-trunked small tree that needs little care. It blooms in fall and winter with attractive clusters of small light pink urn-shaped flowers similar to those of the manzanitas, to which it is related. Appearing with the flowers are unusual-looking 1" round fruits which ripen from yellow to red and are the reason for the tree's common name. Although edible, these fruits are usually not particularly tasty—but they often are popular with birds.

From beach to desert, the Strawberry Tree is most tolerant of almost any garden situation imaginable, and is cold-hardy to around 10°F. Its dense foliage may be left unpruned or opened up by regular pruning to reveal its handsome branch structure. Although several dwarf varieties of Strawberry Tree are grown, the common full-sized form is best for a specimen tree, growing at a moderate rate to 15-25' tall.

Even better as a specimen tree is *Arbutus* 'Marina', a hybrid which is intermediate between the Strawberry Tree and the larger Mediterranean species of *Arbutus*. This is a beautiful and easily grown tree to 30-40' tall with large glossy-green leaves to 5" long, large pendant clusters of rosy-pink flowers, and showy brown peeling bark. It is the only Madrone-like tree which tolerates normal garden conditions.   **B22,QBG**

Near Old Globe Theater, Balboa Park

Archontophoenix cunninghamiana
(ar-kon-toe-FEE-niks   kuh-ning-ham-ee-AN-uh)
KING PALM
Arecaceae (Palmae)
Eastern Australia

The King Palm is one of the most tropical-looking palms commonly grown in San Diego, and is a beautiful landscape plant where temperatures do not go much below 27°F. Native to rainforests in eastern Australia, it tolerates shade as well as sun, and even makes a good container plant indoors or out. Medium green feathery leaves arch 8-10' on mature plants atop a stately gray trunk. The King Palm is also a beautiful flowering tree as well, with intricate hanging flower branches that first bear starry lavender flowers, then bright red seeds.

The King Palm is self-cleaning, which means that the old fronds drop cleanly by themselves so that no pruning is required. It is beautiful planted as a grove in partial shade, which makes for an effective rainforest look. Young plants of King Palm are more sensitive to cold than older ones. If cold-hardiness is an issue, a good choice is the seed strain called "Illawarra", which comes from the coldest area of the plant's natural range. A little more tender are the closely related Alexandra Palm (*Archontophoenix alexandrae*), and its variety *beatricae*, which is called the Step Palm for its showy trunk which narrows in steps from a thick base.   **B22,QBG**

1613 Downs St., Oceanside

21

Auranticarpa rhombifolia
(orr-an-tih-KAR-puh rom-bih-FOE-lee-uh)
DIAMOND-LEAF LAUREL
Pittosporaceae
Eastern Australia

Formerly known as *Pittosporum rhombifolium*, the Diamond-Leaf Laurel is popular for its ornamental foliage, flowers, and fruit. Because of recent botanical studies, it has been reclassified into the new genus *Auranticarpa* along with five other species of Australian trees.

While not related to the true Laurel (in the genus *Laurus*), the Diamond-Leaf Laurel is likewise evergreen and does have interesting diamond-shaped leaves. It is a manageable small to medium-sized tree that grows slowly here to 15-30' tall and 12-20' wide, and is well-suited as a street or lawn tree. The Diamond-Leaf Laurel has an attractive foliage of 3-4" long rich green, glossy leaves that have irregularly toothed margins. It blooms in late spring, with clusters of fragrant, 1/2"-3/4" wide creamy-white flowers. Flowering is conspicuously followed by the production of clusters of 1/4" bright orange fruits that ripen in fall and remain showy on the tree through most of the winter.

The Diamond-Leaf Laurel likes full sun, well-drained soil, and regular watering, and is hardy to 20°F. It does have sticky seeds that when shed can be a problem on a patio or driveway, so proper siting is advised. **B21,B28,QBG**

Balboa Park

Quail Botanical Gardens

Banksia integrifolia
(BANK-see-uh in-teh-grih-FOE-lee-uh)
COAST BANKSIA
Proteaceae
Eastern Australia

In 1770, pioneer English botanist Sir Joseph Banks traveled with Captain Cook and his crew to the remote continent of Australia. On that first visit, he saw plants and flowers so unusual to his western eyes that he could scarcely believe what he was seeing—and the most spectacular flower he saw was named after him. Even now, 235 years later, people still can't quite believe their eyes when they first see a *Banksia*.

Although the most spectacular banksias are shrubs, there are some tree species that are quite showy. The easiest of these to grow here is the Coast Banksia, which is a drought-tolerant evergreen tree to 30-50' tall and 15-25' wide. The Coast Banksia has a dense foliage of 3-6" long leathery green leaves which are silvery beneath. From fall through early spring, it produces showy 4-6" tall upright clusters of greenish-yellow flowers that attract hummingbirds and other nectar-loving birds. These are followed by curious gray woody seed pods that are also very ornamental.

The Coast Banksia grows well in sandy soils near the ocean, but is also quite tolerant of clay soils and inland climates. It will tolerate extreme drought but also does well with regular watering, which allows it to grow faster and larger. Unlike many of its relatives, it is quite hardy to cold and will tolerate temperatures as low as 15°F. **B25,QBG**

22

Bauhinia x *blakeana*
(bauw-HINN-ee-uh   blay-kee-AN-uh)
HONG KONG ORCHID TREE
Fabaceae (Leguminosae)
Canton, China

    Bauhinia is a large genus of plants, all with uniquely twin-lobed leaves—which is why the genus was named after the twin sixteenth-century botanist brothers Bauhin. Of the many showy trees in this group, none is more magnificent in bloom than the Hong Kong Orchid Tree, which is the floral emblem of that province. All plants in cultivation come from one original tree in Canton, China (a sterile hybrid, perhaps of *B. purpurea* and *B. variegata*) and so are available as grafted trees only.

    The Hong Kong Orchid Tree is a 15-25' tall semi-evergreen tree with a rounded, spreading crown and large gray-green leaves to 5" across which tend to drop at bloom time or during a cold winter. Showy 6" wide orchid-shaped flowers are produced from fall to spring, but often again in the summer—these are a beautiful blend of maroon, rosy-purple and rose-pink and are fragrant.

    Although hardy to around 25°F., the Hong Kong Orchid Tree deserves a protected site away from strong wind and frost. It is a bit slow to start as a young tree, but is well worth the wait for a mature specimen. Grow it in either full sun or light shade, with good drainage and regular watering. Some pruning to remove crossing branches may be done in the summer, which will help to shape young trees. **B8, QBG**

3334 Ticonderoga St., Bay Park

Bauhinia forficata
(bauw-HINN-ee-uh   for-fih-KAY-tuh)
BUTTERFLY ORCHID TREE
Fabaceae (Leguminosae)
Peru to Argentina and Brazil

    Probably the hardiest Orchid Tree, this handsome white-flowered species is fast-growing and showy in bloom. Usually deciduous in winter (it may be evergreen in the mildest climates), this tree grows upright to 35' tall, a lush growth of bright green 5" pointed leaves each spring, followed by big 5-7" star-shaped pure white flowers in summer. These lightly fragrant flowers open at night and stay open the following day, followed by a new wave of flowers the next evening. Particularly beautiful in bloom in the moonlight or on a cloudy day, this is a tree that creates a decidedly tropical look even though it is hardy to the low 20's°F.

    Because the Butterfly Orchid Tree blooms on new growth, even colder-winter gardeners might try it, as plants frozen to the ground in winter can quickly resprout from the base to make a blooming shrubby small tree by the next summer. As such, it might well be hardy into the mid-teens°F. Besides the tropical look of its flowers and foliage, its other virtues are a fair amount of drought tolerance, fast growth in full sun or light shade, and acceptance of any type of soil. Seeds are abundantly produced, and may be scattered rather explosively from uncoiling seed pods in the heat of autumn. **B7**

511 Valley Dr., Vista

23

Bauhinia variegata
(bauw-HINN-ee-uh   vair-ih-GAY-tuh)
PINK ORCHID TREE
Fabaceae (Leguminosae)
India and China

The Pink Orchid Tree is the most commonly grown Orchid Tree in San Diego and is an excellent street or lawn tree as well as a good garden tree. It grows fairly quickly to 20-25' tall and wide, and can be trained to have either single or multiple trunks. Although cold temperatures can cause the tree to lose its leaves in winter, in mild winters it usually retains most of its foliage until just before it blooms in spring. Following a mild dry winter, it can be spectacular, with hundreds of 3" orchid-like flowers completely covering a mature tree. Although flower color is somewhat variable, it is usually light pink to purplish-pink with dark pink in the center of each petal. Flowering is followed by a fresh growth of light green foliage composed of roundish two-lobed leaves, and long bean-like seed pods.

The Pink Orchid Tree likes a sunny location, good drainage, and regular watering. Because it loves heat and is also cold-hardy to around 22°F., it succeeds in desert as well as coastal and inland climates. There is also a showy white-flowered form that is usually sold as *Bauhinia variegata* 'Candida'. A related species that is sometimes grown is the Purple Orchid Tree (*Bauhinia purpurea*), which blooms in summer and fall with flowers that are more purple than pink. **B8,QBG**

3334 Ticonderoga St., Bay Park

3324 Cadencia St., Carlsbad

Betula pendula
(BEH-tyoo-luh   PEN-dyoo-luh)
WHITE BIRCH
Betulaceae
Europe and Asia Minor

With its graceful weeping form, handsome bark, and delicate foliage, the White Birch is an irresistible choice for many gardeners—although its nature as a truly temperate tree can make it somewhat short-lived in our mild winter climates. This deciduous tree grows quickly to 30-40' tall and about half as wide, with pendulous outer branches. Its airy foliage of 2-3" diamond-shaped leaves flutters in the slightest breeze, and in colder areas can turn color before dropping in the fall. In winter, the branch structure presents a graceful silhouette which is accentuated by the ornamental golden-brown to white peeling bark and its small cone-like fruits. The White Birch needs generous watering and fertilizing to keep it happy. Since it is susceptible to aphids which drip honeydew, it should not be planted where that drip will be a problem.

A number of different forms of White Birch are grown, including cut-leaved and purple-leaved varieties which can be disappointing in our hot summer sun and so should be tried in part shade only. Other species of birch trees which will grow here include the Red Birch (*Betula nigra*), a tall pyramidal tree with decorative curling cinnamon-brown bark, and the Monarch Birch (*Betula maximowicziana*), a big tree with large 6" leaves, orange-brown bark, and reliable golden fall color. **QBG**

24

Bischofia javanica
(bih-SHOFF-ee-uh juh-VAN-ih-kuh)
JAVA CEDAR
Euphorbiaceae
Indonesia and Malaysia to Polynesia

Unrelated to the true cedars, the Java Cedar is a large forest tree in its native lands, where it is valued for its wood as well as its medicinal properties. Although it is vigorous to the point of being weedy in many tropical areas of the world, it is quite tame in cultivation here, growing at a moderate rate to around 40' tall and 30' wide. The Java Cedar is a handsome evergreen tropical-looking tree which is grown primarily for its rounded crown of dense foliage. Its large glossy dark green leaves are composed of three 5-8" long leathery oval leaflets, each with a tail-like tip. Clusters of tiny greenish flowers are produced in the spring, followed in the fall by clusters of pea-sized brownish fruits which are unpalatable to humans but attractive to birds.

The Java Cedar prefers a rich, well-drained soil and regular watering and will grow in full sun or partial shade. Although it can suffer some frost damage at 30°F., mature trees are cold-hardy to around 27°F. This is a good tree for a tropical effect in frost-free locations, but it unfortunately is susceptible to attack by the Giant Whitefly. It may be grown successfully from cuttings or seed. **B22,QBG**

SE Corner of House of Charm, Balboa Park

Bismarckia nobilis
(biz-MARK-ee-uh NOH-bih-liss)
BISMARCK PALM
Arecaceae (Palmae)
Madagascar

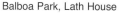

Balboa Park, Lath House

The imposing Bismarck Palm is popular in warm-climate gardens throughout the world for its massive fan-shaped leaves and steely blue-gray color. Although young plants are somewhat slow to establish themselves here, this palm ultimately grows at a moderate rate to 20' tall or more with a 15' spread, a thick gray trunk, and stiff, showy leaves up to 5' across. Young plants of the Bismarck Palm often have reddish-tinged leaves when grown in full sun, with older plants typically developing the bright blue-gray leaf color that this palm is famous for.

The Bismarck Palm prefers a hot, sunny, frost-free location, well-drained soil, and plenty of water and fertilizer during its summer growing season. It resents cold wet soils, and actually likes to be rather dry during our cool winters. Individual plants are either male or female, and both male and female plants are necessary for the production of fertile seed.

The Bismarck Palm is the only species in its genus, which was named by German botanists in 1881 in honor of their famous Chancellor Otto von Bismarck. This was somewhat of a political ploy, since they knew that this would annoy their rival French botanists, who at that time dominated the study of the flora of Madagascar. The French botanists retaliated by trying to reclassify this palm into another genus, but it didn't stick. **B18**

25

Bocconia arborea

(bah-KOE-nee-uh ar-BORE-ee-uh)

TREE POPPY

Papaveraceae

Mexico and Guatemala

The unusual Tree Poppy is in fact the largest member of the poppy family. But it is not what most people would expect from its common name. Growing to 25' tall in its native habitat, this evergreen tree does have leaves that look somewhat like an oversized version of garden poppy leaves, but its flowers are tiny rather than large and are produced in big plume-like clusters.

In Southern California, the Tree Poppy is shrubby when young, but can eventually develop into a small multi-trunked tree to 10-15' tall and 10' wide. It grows in full sun to partial shade, and likes a frost-free location. Impressive for its foliage alone, the Tree Poppy has large, gray-green deeply-cut lobed leaves to 18" long and 12" wide which are downy-gray underneath and usually clustered at the ends of the branches. In late spring or summer, it produces frothy 8" long clusters of small greenish flowers which have no petals.

The Tree Poppy likes regular watering and fertilizing, and is useful for tropical effects. It can die back to the ground in a heavy frost, and so should be considered a shrubby perennial where frosts occur. The sap, leaves, and roots of the Tree Poppy are poisonous, and have been used medicinally.

525 Alameda Blvd., Coronado

Quail Botanical Gardens

Brachychiton acerifolius

(brak-ee-KYE-tun ay-ser-ih-FOE-lee-us)

ILLAWARA FLAME TREE

Sterculiaceae

Eastern Australia

The Illawarra Flame Tree is one of the most spectacular red-flowering trees in the world. It grows fairly quickly to an eventual 40-50' tall with a spread of 25', with a tropical-looking foliage of 6-10" bright green glossy leaves that are deeply lobed on young plants and shallowly lobed to oval on older trees. Although its blooming habits can vary from year to year, it usually blooms from May to July here, when all or part of the tree goes deciduous and is quickly covered with clusters of 1" bright red bell-shaped flowers. These flowers fall cleanly from the tree while still fresh, creating a carpet of red on the ground, and are followed by interesting clusters of 5" boat-shaped seed pods.

In bloom, the bright red flower color of the Illawarra Flame Tree looks especially stunning in combination with the blue flowers of Jacaranda trees, which bloom at the same time of year. Cold-hardy to 25°F., it is usually grown from seed and so may take several years to attain blooming size, but it is well worth the wait. A related tree called the Pink Kurrajong (*Brachychiton* x *acero-populneus*) is actually a hybrid between the Illawarra Flame Tree and the Bottle Tree (*Brachychiton populneus*). It is a small to medium-sized tree with pink flowers that is intermediate between its two parents and is sold as a grafted plant. **B15,QBG**

Brachychiton discolor
(brak-ee-KYE-tun   DISS-kuh-lore)

PINK FLAME TREE
Sterculiaceae
Eastern Australia

With its distinctive bottle-shaped trunk, showy pink flowers, and attractive maple-like leaves, the Pink Flame Tree is a handsome addition to the landscape. Although it is a large tree in its native eastern Australian rainforests, it is usually smaller-growing in cultivation here, growing at a moderate rate to an eventual 40' tall and 30' wide with a characteristic pyramidal shape when young but more spreading in maturity. Its 6" dark green leaves are deeply lobed on young trees, but shallowly lobed on mature specimens. In summer, all or part of the tree can lose its leaves immediately before bloom, when the tree produces showy clusters of 2" bell-shaped rose-pink flowers. Dropping cleanly when fresh, these flowers make a carpet of color on the ground, and are followed later in the year by furry brown boat-shaped seed pods.

The Pink Flame Tree blooms best in warmer inland areas and is cold-hardy to 25°F. It makes an effective and unusual street or lawn tree, prefers good drainage, and is tolerant of either regular watering or some drought. **B25,Q21**

366 San Marcos Blvd., San Marcos

940 Santa Fe Ave., Vista

Brachychiton populneus
(brak-ee-KYE-tun   pah-PUHL-nee-us)

BOTTLE TREE
Sterculiaceae
Queensland and New South Wales, Australia

The Bottle Tree is the cold-hardiest of the commonly grown brachychitons, and is especially popular in our low and intermediate desert areas. Native to dry areas in eastern Australia, it features a heavy, moisture-storing trunk which is broad at the base and tapers toward the top. It grows at a moderate rate to an eventual 50' tall by 30' wide, is hardy to at least 20°F., and is tolerant of a wide variety of temperatures, soils, and watering schedules.

The Bottle Tree is evergreen, with glossy-green 2-3" long leaves which shimmer in the breeze like those of aspens. It blooms in May and June, with clusters of small bell-shaped white flowers that are showy at close range. This is an excellent shade tree for hot-summer areas that is more drought-tolerant than it looks, although it also does well near the coast. Trees planted in deeper soils with adequate water will grow faster and larger than those in tougher sites. **B25,Q22**

27

Desert Garden, Balboa Park

Brachychiton rupestris
(brak-ee-KYE-tun   roo-PESS-tris)
QUEENSLAND BOTTLE TREE
Sterculiaceae
Queensland, Australia

With its fat, bulbous trunk, the Queensland Bottle Tree is an exaggeration in water storage, and a perfect adaptation to life in the dry Australian outback. In cultivation, a mature tree such as the one pictured is a real conversation piece. This is a small tree which grows fairly slowly to about 20' tall and 15' wide, with a stout gray trunk that keeps getting fatter with age and may measure 5-6' in diameter with maturity. Dark green leaves on young trees are deeply lobed with very narrow segments, but on mature trees can be undivided. Foliage is usually evergreen, but may drop completely for a brief time in late spring in a dry site or before flowering. Blooming is unpredictable and usually occurs on older plants only, with the flowers being small yellow bells.

The Queensland Bottle Tree is often grown in containers by collectors, and makes an interesting dwarf specimen with its fat trunk and swollen roots. In the landscape, it is a showy accent plant for a dry garden, and an interesting companion to other desert plants. It prefers good drainage but needs only moderate to little watering, and is cold-hardy to around 25°F. Although it takes a number of years to grow a mature specimen, this is a tree that is definitely worth waiting for. **B26,QBG**

Palomar College, San Marcos

Brahea armata
(brah-HEE-uh   ar-MAY-tuh)
BLUE FAN PALM
Arecaceae (Palmae)
Baja California, Mexico

Slow-growing and choice, the Blue Fan Palm is perhaps the most silvery-leaved palm of all. When young, it makes a pretty container plant, but an older, mature specimen such as the one pictured is remarkable, especially in bloom. Growing to an eventual 35' tall with a stout trunk, the Blue Fan Palm is famous for its crown of silvery-blue fan-shaped leaves which grow to 4' wide and 8' long. Flowering occurs in summer on mature plants and is spectacular, with long feathery white plumes boldly arching some 12-15' toward the ground. After flowering, mature plants produce clusters of 1" brown fruits.

The Blue Fan Palm is remarkably tolerant of heat, wind, drought, and cold. Hardy to 18°F., it thrives in inland and desert climates even in the coldest winters and loves full sun and heat. Individual plants of the Blue Fan Palm are apt to be somewhat variable, with some seedlings being slower and smaller while others are faster and larger. In general, plants with the whitest leaves are dwarf and slow; for the most spectacular landscape specimen, it pays to look for plants that are not only silvery-blue in color but are also vigorous. **B26,QBG**

Brahea edulis
(brah-HEE-uh   ED-yoo-lis)
GUADALUPE PALM
Arecaceae (Palmae)
Guadalupe Island, Mexico

With its stout trunk and bright green fan-shaped leaves, the Guadalupe Palm is a handsome addition to any landscape. Native only to a tiny island off the coast of Baja California, it is endangered in the wild but fairly common in cultivation. The Guadalupe Palm somewhat resembles a Mexican Fan Palm (*Washingtonia robusta*), but is slower growing, more graceful, and not as tall. It is further distinguished by its large tropical-looking leaves which drop cleanly to leave a clean grayish-brown trunk ringed with leaf scars that looks somewhat like elephant hide.

The Guadalupe Palm is easy to grow, and will tolerate most any conditions from beach to desert. Eventually reaching 30' tall by 15' wide, it is also hardy to cold and will tolerate temperatures at least as low as 20°F. A particularly effective way to display it is to plant a grouping of three palms together.   **B16,QBG**

1500 University Ave., City Heights

Brugmansia versicolor
(brug-MAN-see-uh   VER-sih-kuh-lor)
ANGEL'S TRUMPET
Solanaceae
Ecuador

With their huge, powerfully fragrant flowers, the "tree daturas" or angel's trumpets are show-stoppers in any garden. Blooming throughout the year, they are fast and easy to grow anywhere that frosts are not severe. Of the many types of Angel's Trumpets, *Brugmansia versicolor* is the most tree-like, growing upright with multiple stems to 15' tall. It also has the largest flowers of all and more of them at once, with a fully grown plant producing hundreds of pendant trumpets at the same time. Individual flowers on this species are 15" long and hang straight down, with waves of bloom lasting from 2-4 weeks and appearing every couple of months throughout the year. These flowers are powerfully and sweetly scented at night and also early in the morning. Flower color is typically apricot-peach, but pink and white-flowered forms are also grown. Evergreen foliage is composed of large 12" long tropical-looking leaves which may be damaged by frost, although plants can quickly recover from temperatures in the mid-20's°F. The Angel's Trumpet likes regular watering and fertilizing, and may be grown in full sun or partial shade.

The species *Brugmansia versicolor* has given rise to a number of hybrids, including the Double White Angel's Trumpet (*Brugmansia* x *candida*) that is seen in many older gardens. Of all the hybrids, one of the best is 'Charles Grimaldi', which grows quickly to 12' tall and covers itself with large 12" long peach to bright gold trumpets throughout the year.   **B22,QBG**

14098 Boquita Dr., Del Mar

29

Bucida buceras
(BYOO-sih-duh byoo-SAIR-us)
BLACK OLIVE
Combretaceae
Florida, West Indies, and Central America

Unrelated to true olives, the Black Olive is a decorative small evergreen tree with an elegant architectural form. Although not commonly grown in Southern California, it can be an attractive specimen plant, especially in coastal areas where frosts are not severe. Typically multiple-trunked, the Black Olive grows slowly to 15-20' tall and wide here, with 3" long leathery oval leaves and interesting hanging clusters of small greenish-yellow flowers which are followed by small black fruits. Its main feature, however, is its strongly horizontal branching habit, which naturally gives it the tailored look of a large bonsai tree.

The Black Olive is tender to frost, but it is very tolerant of saline soil and salt spray, so it grows well even on the immediate seacoast. It responds well to regular watering and fertilizing, but otherwise needs no special care. A related species, *Bucida spinosa*, is similar but with a smaller, shrubbier habit that has made it a very popular plant with bonsai enthusiasts.

909 Camino del Mar, Del Mar

1850 Lyndon Rd., Mission Hills

Butia capitata
(BYOO-tee-uh kap-ih-TAY-tuh)
PINDO PALM
Arecaceae (Palmae)
Southern Brazil, Uruguay, and Northern Argentina

This handsome palm is not only one of the hardiest palms but also the tastiest, and can be a real focal point in any garden. Fairly slow growing to an eventual 15-20' tall by 10-15' wide, it features 7-10' long feathery gray-green leaves and a stout heavy trunk boldly patterned with the stubs of old leaves. It prefers sun and is tolerant of a wide range of garden conditions, including temperatures as low as 15°F.

The Pindo Palm flowers in summer with long spikes of small flowers which are then followed by large showy clusters of round 1" fruits which may be yellow, orange, or red when ripe. These fruits are usually tasty and may be eaten fresh or made into jelly, which is why this palm is sometimes called the Jelly Palm. Although fruiting characteristics may vary according to individual plants and growing conditions, the look and flavor of Pindo Palm fruits is typically like a loquat. There are some individuals, however, that have reddish-tinged fruits that taste more like strawberries, and others with yellowish fruits that taste like pineapples. For best flavor, fruits should be allowed to ripen fully on the plant and harvested just as they are ready to drop.

The Pindo Palm is quite variable from seed, and a number of varieties of it have been identified and are grown by specialists. Because of its cold-hardiness, it is most useful for a tropical look in areas that get occasional strong frosts. **B3,B23,QBG**

Calliandra surinamensis

(kal-ee-AN-druh sur-ih-nam-EN-sis)

POWDER PUFF TREE

Fabaceae (Leguminosae)
Brazil and Suriname

Of the 200 species of *Calliandra* worldwide, there are several that can be trained to make beautiful small trees in San Diego County gardens. Blooming over a long season, these evergreens are famous for their exotic-looking bright pink or red flowers that are composed of many stamens and look like little powder puffs all along the branches.

Calliandra surinamensis is an open, multi-stemmed small tree to 10-15' tall for full sun or partial shade. Its airy foliage is composed of divided leaves with 8-12 pairs of small leaflets, and it blooms nearly all year with many 3" flowers that are white at the base but boldly tipped in bright rose-pink. This Powder Puff Tree is happy with regular watering but is also moderately drought-resistant, and is cold-hardy to around 25°F.

Another *Calliandra* that is more spectacular in bloom but more tender to cold is the Pink Powder Puff, *Calliandra haematocephala*. This Bolivian native has lush, tropical-looking foliage and big rose-pink flowers from fall to spring (there is also a white-flowered form) and needs regular watering and protection from frost. A third species that is hardier to cold is the Brazilian Flame Bush, *Calliandra tweedii*. This one has very finely textured foliage and has bright scarlet-red flowers from spring through fall. It loves heat and is cold-hardy to 20°F.

2909 Wishbone Way, Encinitas

Callistemon citrinus

(kah-LISS-teh-mon sih-TRY-nus)

LEMON BOTTLEBRUSH

Myrtaceae
Southeastern Australia

This commonly grown bottlebrush is often seen as a large shrub, but may with some early training be easily trained into a 20-25' small tree. So trained, it becomes one of the showiest red-flowering small trees of all. Very tolerant of harsh conditions, the Lemon Bottlebrush is fast growing and vigorous, succeeding even in extremes of heat, cold, and poor soil. Its foliage is dense, comprised of narrow 3" long leaves that are coppery-colored when new and dark green when mature and smell lemony when crushed. Flowering occurs heavily in late winter or early spring, but plants may also be in bloom at any time of the year, with long 6" clusters of many bright red stamens that cover the plant and attract hummingbirds with their nectar.

Because it is variable from seed, the Lemon Bottlebrush is chiefly known through its cutting-grown selections which are superior in both flower and foliage. The bright red flowered cultivars such as 'Improved' and 'Splendens' are the largest growing and perhaps best-suited for training as a tree, but there are also lavender-purple flowered selections grown, such as 'Violaceus' and 'Mauve Mist', and even pink selections such as 'Perth Pink'. The Lemon Bottlebrush prefers full sun and is hardy to around 20°F.

B25

1700 Security Place, San Marcos

Callistemon viminalis
(kah-LISS-teh-mon vi-mih-NAL-is)
WEEPING BOTTLEBRUSH
Myrtaceae
New South Wales and Queensland, Australia

The Weeping Bottlebrush is a fast-growing tree to 20-30' tall that is showy in both foliage and flower. It is the most widely grown of all bottlebrushes and is popular in subtropical and warm-temperate climates throughout the world. Several different forms are grown in California, all of which bear many large clusters of bright red flowers from late spring into summer and often throughout the rest of the year as well. Because of their nectar, these flowers attract hummingbirds and also orioles to the garden.

A commonly cultivated form of the Weeping Bottlebrush is an upright tree to 30' tall by 15' wide, although with some pruning it may be trained as a more round-headed specimen. It has narrow, soft-green leaves to 6" long on gracefully weeping branches, and may be grown from either cuttings or seeds. Because of its upright nature, it may be planted close to tall buildings with good effect. Other cultivars such as 'McCaskillii' are grown, however, that are smaller-growing with much denser foliage and larger, brighter-red flower clusters—these lend themselves well to training as standards in the manner of the Lemon Bottlebrush. All forms of Weeping Bottlebrush are hardy to around 20°F., prefer full sun and good drainage, and are tolerant of drought or regular watering. **B16,QBG**

Vista City Hall, Vista

605 9th Ave., Escondido

Calocedrus decurrens
(kal-oh-SEE-drus dee-KURR-enz)
INCENSE CEDAR
Cupressaceae
Central Oregon to Baja California, Mexico

As a native plant, the Incense Cedar grows naturally on the slopes of our San Diego County mountains, and may be easily spotted along the roadsides on Palomar Mountain and in the Laguna and Cuyumaca Mountains. As a cultivated tree, it is far more adaptable, and grows easily anywhere in the county from seashore to desert with only minimal care. This majestic evergreen conifer forms a dense narrow pyramid of flat sprays of bright green foliage that gives the tree a formal, tailored look. The foliage has a pleasing incense-like fragrance, and on a warm day can perfume the garden. Small reddish-brown cones are produced at the branch tips.

No matter where you live in the county, the Incense Cedar can bring a refreshing touch of the mountains to your garden. It is tolerant of heat and cold, and grows well even in poor soils with only moderate watering. A bit slow at first, it can grow 2' a year once established, to an eventual height of 60' or more with a spread of 10-15'. In fall and winter, its fragrant foliage is most useful for wreaths and many other holiday decorations. **B29,Q29**

Calodendrum capense
(kal-oh-DEN-drum   kuh-PENCE)
CAPE CHESTNUT
Rutaceae
Southern and Eastern Africa

Magnificent is the word for a mature Cape Chestnut in bloom, and it is certainly a tree that once planted will entertain generations to come. Unrelated to the true chestnuts, this African tree is famous in Kenya for a large specimen that forms part of the structure of the Tree Tops Hotel. In Southern California, the Cape Chestnut is a slow-growing evergreen or briefly deciduous tree to 25-40' tall and wide whose dense, gradually spreading crown deserves the space it needs to show off its handsome dark green foliage and showy flowers. Flowering usually occurs in late spring or early summer, when the whole tree is covered with candelabra-like basketball-sized flower clusters composed of many individual 3" rosy-lilac blooms. Although this tree seldom blooms when young, a mature specimen will often rebloom in the fall. Seed pods are produced on mature trees and when ripe split open to reveal shiny black seeds.

The Cape Chestnut is somewhat frost-tender when young, but mature trees will withstand temperatures as low as 15°F. It prefers a deep soil in full sun, and will usually lose most of its leaves for a brief time following cold winter temperatures.   **B30,QBG**

Mission Hills Park, Mission Hills

Carya illinoinensis
(KAIR-ee-uh   ill-ih-noh-in-EN-sis)
PECAN
Juglandaceae
Central and Southern U.S. to Central Mexico

This stately North American native tree is the source of pecan nuts, a delicacy especially prized by those who live within its native range. Although most commercial pecan production is in the southern U.S., the Pecan may be successfully grown in all San Diego County climates, where it is a big deciduous tree to 50' tall or more that needs room to grow but can also be useful as a shade tree in larger gardens. The Pecan has big compound leaves composed of 11 to 17 leaflets each 4-7" long. It is hardy to well below 0°F., and loves a long hot summer for best nut production. Inconspicuous flowers are produced as the tree leafs out in spring, followed by the pecan nuts (which are enclosed in husks) that ripen and drop in the fall.

As a shade tree, the Pecan will tolerate poor soil and some drought, but for best nut production it prefers a deep, rich, well-drained soil with plenty of water and fertilizer, plus a sunny location where it won't get crowded out by other trees. Although most Pecan trees will set a light crop without cross-pollination, you'll get much better production by planting two different grafted varieties (consult your local nursery for the best varieties for your area). Even young Pecan trees have a very large tap root, which is why they are usually planted from bare-root stock during their winter dormancy.   **B4**

1275 Foothill Dr., Vista

1970 Edgehill Rd., Vista

2074 Pleasant Heights Dr., Vista

Caryota obtusa 'King Kong'
(kair-ee-OH-tuh ob-TOO-suh)
KING KONG FISHTAIL PALM
Arecaceae (Palmae)
Thailand

Many palm collectors have searched for cold-hardy forms of Fishtail Palms over the years—a noble endeavor, since this group contains some of the most majestic palms in the world. The King Kong Fishtail Palm is the crowning achievement of this search, and is perhaps the most astounding palm now grown in San Diego County. Only recently introduced into cultivation here, it was at first known simply as the "Thai Mountain Giant", then as *Caryota gigas*, but now is considered a form of *Caryota obtusa*.

The King Kong Fishtail Palm is indeed a giant in all respects. In its native habitat it grows to 100' tall, with leaves up to 30' long. Although its ultimate dimensions will probably be smaller in cultivation here, young plants are already reaching impressive proportions, with 10-15' long leaves composed of many large fishtail-shaped leaflets, and may be expected to reach an eventual 60' tall. Cultural requirements seem to favor lots of water and a mild climate with no frost, although it has survived 27°F. Young plants prefer partial shade, but older plants are fine in full sun. **QBG**

Caryota urens (high mountain form)
(kair-ee-OH-tuh YER-enz)
HARDY FISHTAIL PALM
Arecaceae (Palmae)
India and Myanmar

At one time thought to be too tropical for Southern California, this impressive species became popular here a generation ago when seeds of cold-hardy individuals which grew at the highest elevations in its range began to be grown. Trees grown from this high-mountain seed have tolerated our cool winter temperatures successfully, and have even survived temperatures in the low 20's°F. Though tolerant of cold, the Hardy Fishtail Palm retains all of the exotic appearance of its tropical kin, and is a stunning addition to the landscape. This is a tall, fairly fast-growing palm with a handsome light gray trunk and large 10-12' long arching leaves composed of many bright green fishtail-shaped leaflets.

The Hardy Fishtail Palm grows to its mature height of 40-50' in about 15-20 years (plants near the coast tend to grow faster than those farther inland), then flowers and fruits for up to ten more years. As is the case with all single-trunked caryotas, the plant dies after fruiting is complete.

The Hardy Fishtail Palm is best in partial shade when very young (when it is tender to frost), but adapts easily to full sun as a 15-gallon plant. It likes regular watering and fertilizing for best growth, and is especially impressive for its tropical-looking silhouette against the sky. **B23,QBG**

Casimiroa edulis
(kaz-ih-mir-OH-uh   ED-yoo-lis)
WHITE SAPOTE
Rutaceae
Mexico

The White Sapote is a beautiful subtropical tree that also bears delicious fruit. Its culture is similar to that of an avocado tree, but it is hardier to cold and is easily grown anywhere that lemons succeed. A mature White Sapote tree is prolific, producing hundreds of 3-4" round fruits that have a unique custard-like texture and a tropical flavor, like a blend of bananas and peaches.

The foliage of White Sapote is composed of palmately-divided leaves with 3-5" leaflets each that are reddish when new and dark green when mature. Normally evergreen, these leaves may partially drop in either very cold or very hot weather. Clusters of tiny green flowers are heavily produced in spring, followed by green fruits which mature to a pale yellow color from late spring to late fall, depending on climate and variety. Fruit should be picked and eaten fresh when fully ripe and ready to drop from the tree (some varieties ripen well off the tree, while others do not).

In California, a number of grafted varieties of White Sapote are grown, some with much larger fruits than others. This tree does best with regular watering and fertilizing, but because of its heavy crop of fruit should be planted in a site where excess fruit drop is not a problem.   **QBG**

1402 Montgomery Dr., Vista

Cassia leptophylla
(KASS-ee-uh   lep-toe-FILL-uh)
GOLD MEDALLION TREE
Fabaceae (Leguminosae)
Southeastern Brazil

Less than 40 years after it was first introduced into cultivation by the Arboretum of Los Angeles County, the Gold Medallion Tree has become a real success story as an increasingly common public landscape tree. Despite its tropical appearance (it's related to the Golden Shower and Rainbow Shower trees that are popular in Hawaii but don't grow well here), it has proven remarkably hardy to extremes of cold and heat and is a reliable bloomer in many San Diego climates.

The Gold Medallion Tree is a fast-growing evergreen tree (it may lose some leaves in a frost) that grows to 20-30' tall and wide, with dark brown furrowed bark. It has a dense foliage of dark green compound leaves, with each leaf composed of 9-14 elliptic leaflets. The tree blooms in summer, with showy basketball-sized flower clusters each composed of 30-50 fragrant bright yellow 3" flowers. These are followed by foot-long dark brown seed pods.

The Gold Medallion Tree is often trained to a single trunk and used as a street tree, but is also effective as a lawn tree or as a background tree in the garden. Best in full sun and well-drained soil, it is hardy to at least 25°F. It is easy to grow and brings a beautiful tropical look to the landscape.   **B20,QBG**

605 A Avenue, Coronado

35

Casuarina cunninghamiana
(kazh-yoor-EYE-nuh kuh-ning-ham-ee-AN-uh)
HORSETAIL TREE
Casuarinaceae
Eastern Australia

Sometimes called the "Australian Pine" (there are no true pines native to Australia), this evergreen tree resembles a pine because of its foliage, which is pine needle-like but is actually composed of thin gray-green branchlets (these do have rudimentary leaves, but they are tiny and inconspicuous). This foliage is jointed somewhat like horsetail plants (*Equisetum*), which is why it is also called the Horsetail Tree. Its common name in Australia is River Oak, and although it is not related to the true oaks (*Quercus*), it does have strong, oak-like wood with similar uses.

The Horsetail Tree is one of the toughest, most drought-tolerant trees of all, succeeding equally well at the beach or in the desert—and can even take wet soil. Valuable for providing shade in difficult situations, it grows quickly to an eventual 50-70' tall and 30' wide. Its finely-textured foliage and open branching structure give it a delicate look in the landscape, but it is completely tolerant of poor soil, wind, heat, salinity, and temperatures down to 15°F. Although its tiny flowers are not showy, the small, round 1/2" cone-like seed pods which appear along the branches are interesting, and dried branches may be used for ornament. **B25**

1445 Broadway, El Cajon

860 W. 9th, Escondido

Catalpa bignonioides
(kuh-TAL-puh big-noe-nee-OY-deez)
CATALPA
Bignoniaceae
Southeastern United States

The Catalpa is a large-leaved deciduous tree that is familiar to many who have lived in the southeastern area of the United States where it is either native or naturalized. It is tolerant of a wide range of soils, is completely adaptable to any extremes of heat and cold, and grows well in any San Diego County climate.

A bold, tropical-looking tree, the Catalpa has a dense foliage of 5-8" bright green heart-shaped leaves that have an odor when crushed. It blooms in summer with large showy upright clusters of 2" trumpet-shaped white flowers marked in the center with yellow stripes and light brown spots. These are followed by long narrow hanging seed pods sometimes called "Indian Beans." In the fall, the leaves of the Catalpa turn bright yellow before dropping.

The Catalpa likes full sun and regular watering, but will grow in almost any soil. It is most useful for bringing a tropical look to the landscape even in the coldest of climates, as is the Northern Catalpa (*Catalpa speciosa*), a related tree native to the central United States. This tree is similar to the Catalpa but larger in size, with larger leaves that have no odor and fewer flowers per cluster **B12**

Cedrus atlantica
(SEE-druss at-LAN-tih-kuh)
ATLAS CEDAR
Pinaceae
Northern Africa

Although many plants throughout the world are called "cedars," the evergreen conifers in the genus *Cedrus* are the only true cedars. Because of their adaptability to many California climates, they are among the most widely grown conifers in our state. The true cedars are somewhat similar to fir trees (*Abies*), but they are much more heat-resistant, drought-resistant, and require less winter chill—and so are particularly useful in San Diego County.

The Atlas Cedar is a big tree with age, but it takes quite a while to get that big. In youth, it is open and angular, but becomes more dense as it reaches its ultimate size of 60' tall by 30' wide. Foliage is composed of 1" long needles that are bluish-green in the typical species form. Female cones are rounded to 3" long, and as with all true cedars, male cones produce large amounts of yellow pollen in season. Trees are quite drought-tolerant once established, and are hardy to at least 0°F.

Several selections of the Atlas Cedar are grown, including 'Glauca' with silvery-blue foliage, 'Pendula' with a strongly weeping habit, and 'Glauca Pendula' with both silver foliage and weeping habit. These are often grown in large containers and pruned and trained in a decorative manner. **B6**

6th Ave. & Quince St., San Diego

1561 Thomas Ave.
Pacific Beach

941 Tiger Tail Ln., Vista

Cedrus deodara
(SEE-druss dee-oh-DAR-uh)
DEODAR CEDAR
Pinaceae
Himalayas

Although this majestic evergreen conifer is native to the Himalayas, it is well-adapted to life in San Diego County. Fairly fast growing to an eventual size of 80' tall and 40' wide at the base, the Deodar Cedar has a characteristic tall pyramidal shape and symmetrical branches which gracefully sweep down and then up at the tips. Softer in appearance than the Atlas Cedar, its foliage is a beautiful bluish gray-green with needles to 2" long. Female cones are rounded, to 5" long.

Because of its rather formal appearance (especially when young), the Deodar Cedar is sometimes sold as a living Christmas tree, and is a good choice for planting in a front lawn where it may be decorated with lights during the holidays. Unlike many other symmetrical conifers, the Deodar Cedar is easy to grow here and tolerates extremes of heat, cold, and drought. Good drainage and regular watering will, however, produce the most attractive specimen. For an extremely formal look, Deodar Cedar may even be sheared like the Pacific Beach tree pictured. **B12,QBG**

1016 Valley Parkway, Escandido

1641 Montgomery Dr., Vista

Ceiba insignis
(SEE-buh in-SIG-niss)
WHITE FLOSS-SILK TREE
Bombacaceae
Peru

With their thorny trunks and exotic-looking flowers, the Floss-Silk Trees are among the most distinctive ornamental trees for the landscape. They are closely related to the tropical Kapok Tree (*Ceiba pentandra*), and like the Kapok Tree, their large seed pods contain a silky white cotton that is used for stuffing pillows and cushions.

Formerly known as *Chorisia insignis*, the White Floss-Silk Tree is notable for its characteristic fat, thorny trunk and branches, plus its showy display of large 5" hibiscus-like white to pale yellow flowers when the leaves drop in fall and winter. A mature tree in bloom can be an arresting sight—with thorns, flowers, and even seed pods fully displayed on bare branches. In spring and summer the tree is also handsome, covered with a lush foliage of bright green palmately-divided leaves.

Because it is usually grown from seed, the White Floss-Silk Tree is somewhat variable in its form. Mature trees are typically short and stout to around 30' tall and wide, although some may grow taller and be more open in structure. Although it is fast-growing when young, this is a tree that needs several years to reach blooming size and just gets better with age. It loves heat, and although very young plants are somewhat tender to frost, mature trees are hardy to the low 20s°F. **B10, QBG**

Ceiba speciosa
(SEE-buh spee-see-OH-suh)
PINK FLOSS-SILK TREE
Bombacaceae
Brazil and Argentina

Formerly known as *Chorisia speciosa*, the Pink Floss-Silk Tree is an attention-getter at all seasons because of its thick, heavy trunk studded with large gray thorns. But it is spectacular in the fall (or as early as midsummer in hot-summer areas) when it comes alive with a profusion of exotic-looking 5-6" pink hibiscus-like flowers.

Fast growing when young, the Pink Floss-Silk Tree slows conveniently after a few years, eventually reaching 30-60' tall. It appreciates good drainage and regular watering, although mature trees are quite drought-tolerant. Very young trees are somewhat sensitive to frost, but established trees will tolerate temperatures as low as 24°F. Trees usually shed some or all of their palmately-divided leaves just before bloom, and can also be deciduous during a cold winter.

Both seedlings and grafted varieties of the Pink Floss-Silk Tree are sold. Most of the grafted varieties such as 'Majestic Beauty' have smooth, thornless trunks and deep pink flowers. Although they bloom when young, grafted trees tend to be slower-growing and smaller-growing than seedlings, with a spreading, sometimes asymmetrical crown. Seedling trees grow tall and straight with thorny trunks, but need to be established for several years to bloom. **B10, QBG**

Ceratonia siliqua
(sehr-uh-TOE-nee-uh sih-LEE-kwuh)
CAROB TREE
Fabaceae (Leguminosae)
Eastern Mediterranan Sea Region

1361 Reed Ave., Pacific Beach

Thought by some to have originated in Arabia, the Carob Tree has been cultivated in the Middle East for centuries for its seed pods, which are rich in sugar and made into a variety of animal and human foods including carob powder, which is sold as a chocolate substitute. In San Diego County, this tree is also grown as an ornamental, and is notable for its dense evergreen foliage and drought tolerance. Often multistemmed, the Carob Tree is a thick, bushy tree that grows at a moderate rate to an eventual 30-40' tall and wide. Foliage is a glossy dark green, with compound leaves composed of 4-10 round leaflets each around 2" long. Small red flowers are followed by the conspicuous dark brown leathery seed pods.

Although mature Carob Trees are hardy to 18°F., very young trees will benefit from protection from hard frosts. Good drainage and regular deep watering is preferred for best seed pod production, but trees will also grow in tougher and drier spots and tolerate quite a bit of neglect. If you grow the Carob Tree for seed pod production, it is advisable to plant a cutting-grown or grafted variety with the best fruiting characteristics. **B13,QBG**

Cercis canadensis
(SIR-siss kan-uh-DEN-siss)
EASTERN REDBUD
Fabaceae (Leguminosae)
Southeastern Canada, Eastern U.S., and N.E. Mexico

403 Poinsettia Ave., San Marcos

Valuable for their showy spring flower displays, redbuds are hardy deciduous trees and shrubs which are enjoyed in gardens throughout the United States. The Eastern Redbud is the largest, fastest-growing, and most tree-like of this group, and also the most adaptable in all San Diego County climates. Although it is hardy to well below 0°F., the Eastern Redbud is also a good bloomer in coastal gardens that lack winter chill.

The Eastern Redbud is a round-headed tree that grows to 25-35' tall and wide. In early spring it comes alive as all of the bare branches become covered with clusters of 1/2" magenta-pink flowers. After flowering, the tree leafs out with heart-shaped 4-6" rich green leaves which partially conceal 2-3" long flattened seed pods. With some chill, the leaves will turn yellow or even reddish before they drop in the fall.

The best flowering on an Eastern Redbud occurs after a cool winter, but it doesn't need frost to bloom well. It makes an attractive specimen or understory tree, and will grow in full sun or partial shade. Regular watering is preferred, but it will tolerate some drought. White, light pink, and even double-flowered varieties are grown, and there is also a highly recommended purple-leaved variety called 'Forest Pansy' which has pink flowers and dark maroon leaves that are very showy. **B39**

39

Japanese Friendship Garden, Balboa Park

Quail Botanical Gardens

Chionanthus retusus
(kye-oh-NAN-thuss reh-TOO-suss)
CHINESE FRINGE TREE
Oleaceae
Taiwan

A mature Chinese Fringe Tree in full bloom is a magnificent sight, with the entire tree covered with 4" clusters of lightly fragrant frilly white flowers in late spring. This small deciduous tree is also an attractive tree when not in bloom, providing bright yellow leaf color in the fall and interesting brown and golden bark, and a graceful branching structure that is showy all winter. Although it may be successfully grown anywhere in San Diego County, the Chinese Fringe Tree blooms best with some winter chill and summer heat and so is a good choice for inland areas. Whether it is grown as a multi-trunked specimen or trained to a single trunk, it grows to only 20' tall, which makes it ideal for small gardens.

A related plant that is also called Fringe Tree is *Chionanthus virginicus*, which is native to the southeastern United States. It has somewhat larger clusters of greenish-white flowers that appear a few weeks later than that of its Chinese cousin and is usually more shrubby in habit. Some forms of this species flower well even in coastal gardens without much winter chill. **B34**

Chiranthodendron pentadactylon
(keer-an-thoe-DEN-dron pen-tuh-DAK-tih-lon)
HANDFLOWER TREE
Sterculiaceae
Mexico and Guatemala

Although the botanical name of this tree is somewhat of a tongue-twister, it simply means "five-fingered handflower tree," in reference to its bright red flowers which are among the most unusual flowers in the world. Each waxy flower is a 3" wide cup-shaped calyx that comes complete with a miniature claw-like "hand" which is composed of five red stamens lined with bright yellow pollen. These flowers contain copious nectar which attracts mockingbirds and orioles. As birds drink from the cup, their heads are brushed with pollen, thereby effecting pollination as they go from flower to flower. After flowering, large boat-shaped seed pods are produced which contain small black seeds.

Also called Devil's Hand and Monkey Hand Tree in its native Mexico and Guatemala, the Handflower Tree was well-known to the ancient Aztecs as a sacred tree in their culture with medicinal uses for the flowers, leaves, and bark. It is a fast-growing evergreen tree to 40' tall with large sycamore-like leaves. Flowering occurs in spring and early summer, when a mature tree is covered with hundreds of flowers. Best in full sun with regular watering, the Handflower Tree is cold-hardy to around 22°F. **B14,QBG**

x *Chitalpa tashkentensis*
(chih-TAL-puh tash-ken-TEN-sis)
CHITALPA
Bignoniaceae
Horticultural Hybrid

First created in Tashkent, Uzbekistan in the 1970's, this unlikely hybrid of the Common Catalpa (*Catalpa bignonioides*) and the Desert Willow (*Chilopsis linearis*) has proven to be an excellent flowering tree in all San Diego County climates from seashore to mountains to desert. The Chitalpa (the name is a combination of the generic names of its two parents) is a fast-growing deciduous tree to 20-30' tall and wide that blooms from late spring to fall with large showy clusters of 2" frilly trumpet-shaped flowers displayed against 5" long by 1" wide bright green leaves. The flowers are sterile, so no seed pods are produced. Chitalpa is easy to grow in a wide range of soils and garden conditions, is unfazed by extremes of heat and cold, and is even drought-tolerant once established.

Two selections of Chitalpa are grown. 'Morning Cloud' is a vigorous, upright grower with white flowers that have dark lavender-pink veins in the throat. 'Pink Dawn' has pink flowers with darker veins in the throat and is somewhat smaller and slower growing. Both varieties benefit from some early training to develop an attractive branching structure, and bloom best in full sun with regular watering. **B15**

2900 Park Blvd., Balboa Park

Cinnamomum camphora
(sin-uh-MOE-mum kam-FOR-uh)
CAMPHOR TREE
Lauraceae
China, Taiwan, and Japan

Grown primarily for its foliage instead of its flowers, the Camphor Tree is one of the most beautiful and dependable evergreen trees for the landscape. Although it grows fairly slowly, it eventually becomes a 40-50' spreading tree of strong character and excellent structure. The Camphor Tree is the source of camphor oil, and has a dense foliage of aromatic 3-5" long leaves that smell like camphor when crushed. New foliage in early spring is pink, red, or bronze, and matures to a shiny yellow-green which contrasts dramatically with the dark color of the tree's bark. Inconspicuous but fragrant yellow flowers are produced in late spring which are followed by small black berries.

The Camphor Tree prefers well-drained soil, needs only moderate watering, and is hardy to around 15°F. Although mature trees have a heavy, aggressive root system, it is widely planted as a street tree in Southern California with beautiful results. **B28,QBG**

221 W. 8th Ave., Escondido

41

4428 Olive Hill Rd., Fallbrook

554 Arden Dr., Encinitas

Citrus x *aurantium*
(Sweet Orange Group)

(SIH-truss   or-AN-tee-um)

SWEET ORANGE
Rutaceae
Horticultural Hybrids

Although cities and suburbs have now replaced most of the once-widespread orange groves of Southern California, the Sweet Orange is still one of our signature plants. With its shiny evergreen foliage, intensely fragrant flowers, and bright orange fruits, this well-known small tree is as ornamental as it is useful—and a delight in any garden.

It is said that a century ago eager real estate salespeople would impale fresh oranges onto the dagger-sharp leaves of our native yucca plants in order to lure unsuspecting Easterners into buying land with "orange trees" growing on it. Although that trick doesn't work so well anymore, newcomers to Southern California still are attracted to property with real orange trees, and in their absence will often plant oranges as a first order of business.

There are of course many varieties of citrus grown, most all of which make attractive small evergreen trees where severe freezes seldom occur. The Sweet Orange, however, has the unique ornamental feature of its large round bright orange fruits providing showy color in the middle of winter, just when the rest of the country is snowbound. Long prized as a juice orange, the variety 'Valencia' is the champion for holding its fruits a long time, with some trees seeming to always have ripe fruit. Add to that the intense fragrance of orange blossoms on a warm spring night, and you have the stuff that snowy-climate gardeners' dreams are made of.   **QBG**

Cocculus laurifolius
(KOK-yoo-luss   lor-ih-FOE-lee-us)

HIMALAYAN LAUREL
Menispermaceae
Southern Japan to Himalayas

The Himalayan Laurel is a large evergreen shrub that can be very effective in the landscape when trained as a small multi-trunked tree. So trained, it grows at a moderate rate to 25' tall with an umbrella-shaped crown. This is a tree grown primarily for its foliage and structure, with its clusters of small yellow flowers being secondary. Long arching branches make for a picturesque branching structure, especially when pruned to emphasize them. Attractive dark green foliage is composed of shiny, leathery leaves to 6" long with three prominent veins running the length of each leaf.

The Himalayan Laurel grows in sun or partial shade and appreciates a rich, loamy soil and regular watering. It is long-lived and cold-hardy to the low 20's°F. Since it is a bit slow-growing when very young, it is a good idea to start with a fairly good-sized specimen when planting in the landscape, especially if it is to be a centerpiece tree.   **B24**

Cordyline australis
(KOR-dih-line aw-STRAL-iss)
NEW ZEALAND CABBAGE TREE
Dracaenaceae
New Zealand

Looking like a more tropical version of a yucca tree (to which it is related), the New Zealand Cabbage Tree gets its common name because the fleshy heart of its foliage has in lean times been used as a vegetable in its native land (as is the case with other "cabbage trees" from other parts of the world). In youth, it is a single-trunked fountain of 2-5" wide 3-foot-long leaves, but with maturity it becomes a multi-trunked tree of great character to 20-30' tall and 6-12' wide. In late spring and summer, it blooms with large branched clusters of 1/4" creamy-white fragrant flowers. Although it looks tropical, the New Zealand Cabbage Tree is hardy to 15°F., making it useful for tropical effects even in frosty climates.

The New Zealand Cabbage Tree is evergreen, likes full sun, and needs only moderate watering. Although it is fairly slow-growing, it will grow faster with regular watering in soils deep enough to accommodate its naturally thick tap root. The typical form of the New Zealand Cabbage Tree has green leaves, but a number of colorful-foliaged forms are also grown. These include 'Atropurpurea' with bronzy-red leaves, 'Pink Stripe' with bronze leaves with pink margins, 'Red Star' with purplish-red leaves, 'Sundance' with green leaves with a pink midrib, and 'Albertii' with leaves striped green, cream, and pink. All are sometimes sold as *Dracaena*.   **B21,QBG**

Casa del Prado Theater, Balboa Park

Cornus florida 'Cloud Nine'
(KORR-nuss FLOOR-ih-duh)
FLOWERING DOGWOOD
Cornaceae
Eastern United States

In temperate climates throughout the world, the many varieties of Flowering Dogwood are popular for their lavish springtime displays of colorful floral bracts. In Southern California, however, our hot, dry summers and lack of winter chill severely limit their performance, which is why they are seldom grown here except in our mountain communities. There is one variety of Flowering Dogwood, however, that does better than all the rest in our warm-winter climates, and it is well-worth a try for those that are homesick for these trees.

'Cloud Nine' is an unusual variety of Flowering Dogwood not only in that it blooms well without winter chill but also seems to bloom well in very cold climates. It is a relatively dwarf variety, shrubby at first but eventually growing to 10' tall and wide. 'Cloud Nine' blooms heavily even when it is a young plant, with large 2-4" white to greenish-white floral bracts in spring before the new leaves emerge. Like other flowering dogwoods, it is deciduous in winter and has an elegant horizontal branching structure when mature.

The 'Cloud Nine' Flowering Dogwood likes regular watering and fertilizing and protection from hot, dry winds. It will grow in full sun or partial shade, and is fully cold-hardy to below 0°F.

1337 Peach Ave., El Cajon

Spreckels Park, Coronado

Marston House, 3525 7th Ave., San Diego

Corymbia calophylla
(korr-IMM-bee-uh   kal-oh-FILL-uh)
MARRI
Myrtaceae
Southwestern Australia

No group of plants is more emblematic of Australia than the eucalypts, and in fact all but two of the over 700 species of eucalypts are native there. In California, over 200 species of eucalypts have been tried in cultivation, with a number of these now commonly grown and a few widespread.

A recent revision of the genus *Eucalyptus* has seen some of the eucalypts reclassified into the new genus *Corymbia*, based in part on the structure of their flower clusters. These include the Marri, the Lemon-Scented Gum, and the Red-Flowering Gum described in this book. Nurseries may be slow to assimilate this name change, however, and so you may still see them sold as *Eucalyptus* and also listed that way in older books.

The Marri is a stout evergreen tree to 40' tall, with thick branches, rough gray to dark brown bark, and a dense spreading crown. Its leathery, dark green leaves are up to 7" long and 2-4" wide. Flowering occurs in summer, often heavily, with large clusters of white, cream, or light pink flowers, depending on the individual tree. After flowering, it produces clusters of large woody seed capsules which may be used in crafts. The Marri is tolerant of poor soil and drought, and is hardy to 20°F.

Corymbia citriodora
(korr-IMM-bee-uh   sih-tree-oh-DOOR-uh)
LEMON-SCENTED GUM
Myrtaceae
Queensland, Australia

With its striking white trunk and graceful silhouette, the Lemon-Scented Gum is a prominent element in the San Diego landscape. This is a big, tall tree that grows quickly to 45-75' tall and about half as wide, with some very old trees even taller. The Lemon-Scented Gum gets its name from the pleasant lemony scent of its foliage, which is evergreen and composed of dark green leaves to 7" long and 1" wide. Like many eucalypts, its outer bark is seasonally shed—in this case revealing the smooth creamy-white trunk so characteristic of this species. In the fall, 3/4" white flowers appear in clusters at the end of pendulous young branches. The Lemon-Scented Gum is less cold-hardy than many eucalypts, but mature trees will tolerate temperatures in the mid-20's°F.

Although the Lemon-Scented Gum has been reclassified as a *Corymbia*, it is still often sold as a *Eucalyptus*, and still listed that way in older books. Because of its tall, narrow growth habit, the Lemon-Scented Gum has found a home in many public landscapes and is often planted near tall buildings. Unfortunately, there is a recently-introduced pest called the Spotted Gum Lerp Psyllid that attacks this tree—hopefully, biological controls will be forthcoming.   **B1,QBG**

44

Corymbia ficifolia
(korr-IMM-bee-uh fiss-ih-FOE-lee-uh)
RED-FLOWERING GUM
Myrtaceae
Western Australia

The Red-Flowering Gum is rare in the wild, growing only in small scattered stands in the far southwestern corner of Western Australia. But because of its extremely showy flowers, it is one of the most popular eucalypts in cultivation worldwide. The Red-Flowering Gum grows to 20-45' tall and wide, with a thick trunk, rough dark brown bark, and a dense crown of evergreen foliage composed of 5" by 2" leathery, glossy dark green oval leaves. Flowering can occur at any season, but is heaviest in the summer, when an entire tree can be covered in dense foot-long clusters of 1-2" wide brightly-colored flowers which are usually bright red but in some individual trees may be white, cream, pink, salmon or orange.

The Red-Flowering Gum is drought-tolerant and grows best in coastal locations with good drainage. It dislikes heavy frost, but mature trees will tolerate temperatures in the low 20's°F. Because grafting and cuttings are difficult, only seedling material is usually offered in nurseries, with unpredictable bloom color—so it is best to choose a tree in bloom to get the color you want. Although the Red-Flowering Gum has been reclassified as a *Corymbia*, it is still often sold as a *Eucalyptus*, and still listed that way in older books.   **B42,QBG**

135 Marcheta St., Encinitas

Cupaniopsis anacardioides
(kew-pan-ee-OP-sis an-uh-car-dee-OY-deez)
CARROT WOOD
Sapindaceae
Eastern Australia

The Carrot Wood is a popular tree for commercial plantings because of its shiny evergreen foliage and its tolerance of extreme conditions. Usually trained to a single trunk, it grows at a slow to moderate rate, eventually to 30' tall with an equal spread. The Carrot Wood has glossy green compound leaves which are divided into 6-10 leathery 4" long leaflets. Most trees sold are grown from seed, and so the form on individual trees varies somewhat, but the best seedlings have a dense, rounded crown of dark green foliage. Older trees bloom with clusters of small white flowers followed by yellow-orange fruits that look like garbanzo beans.

Although it looks tropical, the Carrot Wood is remarkably tolerant of a variety of harsh conditions, including heat, drought, wind, poor soil, and salt spray. It is cold-hardy to around 23°F. Its only notable "fault" is some fruit-drop on older trees, yet many trees produce few fruits. Because the Carrot Wood is often used as a landscape tree in parking lots and along streets, increased development and marketing of superior grafted selections with dense foliage and less fruit production would seem to be a good idea.   **B13,QBG**

878 Beryl St., Pacific Beach

Behind the Aerospace Museum, Balboa Park

Cupressus cashmeriana
(kew-PRESS-us cash-meer-ee-AN-uh)
KASHMIR CYPRESS
Cupressaceae
Bhutan

With its tall, narrow form and weeping blue-gray foliage, the evergreen Kashmir Cypress is considered by many to be the most beautiful cypress of all. A native of the Himalayan Mountains, it grows at a moderate to fast rate to 25-40' tall and 15-20' wide in full sun to partial shade, and needs regular watering and protection from hot, dry winds. The foliage of the Kashmir Cypress is strongly pendulous, which is a water-shedding adaptation shared by many conifers that come from rainy climates. Although a specimen Kashmir Cypress can be impressive when standing alone, this tree also looks good when combined with other trees in the garden, where it can evoke the image of mountain forests.

The Kashmir Cypress has been known in cultivation for years, but it was only fairly recently that a wild population was found in Bhutan. Its botanical name is sometimes listed as *Cupressus himalaica*, although its original name *Cupressus cashmeriana* is still favored by many botanists. Most, if not all, of the Kashmir Cypress trees in cultivation locally appear to be the variety *darjeelingensis*, which is distinguished by its more silvery foliage color. **B32,QBG**

849 Coast Blvd., La Jolla

Cupressus macrocarpa
(kew-PRESS-us mak-roe-CAR-puh)
MONTEREY CYPRESS
Cupressaceae
Monterey Peninsula, California

Native only to a small coastal area of Monterey County, the picturesque Monterey Cypress has been planted in beach towns throughout California for generations, so there are many old specimens to be found outside of its native range. In San Diego County, many of the grandest specimens of this evergreen conifer have succumbed to old age over the past 20 years, yet there are still many large trees of a slightly younger vintage to be seen.

Shrubby and pyramidal when young, the Monterey Cypress spreads as wide as high as it grows to 40-50' tall, ultimately with its characteristic horizontally tiered silhouette. Though unmistakably beautiful, this is a tree recommended only for immediate coastal conditions, since it depends on cool coastal winds for a healthy life. Although it is hardy to cold, it is disease-prone away from the coast, often falling victim to a canker fungus for which there is no cure.

A hybrid of Monterey Cypress that is perhaps too often tried here as a quick tall screen is the Leyland Cypress (x *Cupressocyparis leylandii*). Though fast-growing, this evergreen can become a disappointment after several years because it is very susceptible to canker fungus. **B5**

46

Cupressus sempervirens
(kew-PRESS-us sem-per-VEER-enz)
ITALIAN CYPRESS
Cupressaceae
Southern Europe and Western Asia

The Italian Cypress is a classic Mediterranean landscape plant, seldom seen here in its species form but maybe too well known for its cutting-grown columnar forms. This evergreen conifer is popular for its dense foliage and tolerance of adverse conditions. Seedling trees of Italian Cypress are dark green and pyramidal, growing ultimately to 40' or more with a spread of around 15' at the base. The columnar forms, however, are almost unbelievably fastigiate, with even the tallest, oldest spires no more than 5-7' wide at the base. The most common columnar forms are 'Stricta' with dark green foliage, and 'Glauca' with blue-green foliage.

Though useful for bringing a formal look to the garden, the columnar Italian Cypress can be and has been over-used in many landscapes. Although it is often planted in multiples to create a very tall, narrow hedge, such plantings frequently end up looking like prison bars when the plants are placed far enough apart that they never quite meet.

Italian Cypress is easy to grow in full sun and easily tolerates extremes of heat and cold, poor soil, and drought—in fact, the columnar forms tend to get floppy with too much fertilizer and water. It is best to let plants grow slowly, since very fast growth will make them top-heavy, leading to disastrous results. **B32,QBG**

140 E. 5th St., Escondido

1050 Valley Rd., Vista

Cyathea cooperi
(sye-AYTH-ee-uh KOO-per-eye)
AUSTRALIAN TREE FERN
Cyatheaceae
Australia

The Australian Tree Fern is the easiest and fastest-growing tree fern for San Diego County gardens, especially in its extra-vigorous form called 'Brentwood'. Although other species of tree ferns may be grown here, none are as tolerant of low humidity, alkaline conditions, and cold temperatures as this one. Nevertheless, it is a very tropical-looking "tree," and a most effective choice for a "tropical rainforest" look. The Australian Tree Fern grows in full sun or partial shade on the coast, but needs partial shade inland. It thrives in mild conditions, but will survive both frost and heat with only cosmetic damage. As a fern, it appreciates regular watering, especially overhead watering.

The Australian Tree Fern grows to an eventual 20' tall and 12' wide, with a crown of bright green finely divided fronds. The trunk on the typical species form grows about a foot a year in optimal conditions, but the variety 'Brentwood' is especially fast-growing and can double that rate of growth. The Australian Tree Fern looks especially beautiful planted in groups as an understory planting beneath taller trees. It is sometimes sold under the now-outdated names *Alsophila australis*, *Alsophila cooperi*, and *Sphaeropteris cooperi*. **B18,QBG**

2900 Nichols St., Point Loma

47

1361 Vereda Barranca, Vista

West side of Presidio Park, San Diego

Diospyros kaki
(dye-oh-SPY-rohs   KAH-key)
ORIENTAL PERSIMMON
Ebenaceae
Eastern Asia

The Oriental Persimmon is one of the most ornamental of all edible fruiting trees, providing startling color in the fall and early winter when its brilliant orange fruits are displayed on bare branches. These fruits are deliciously sweet and custard-like, to be eaten fresh or used for baking, and are a wonderful addition to fall and winter holiday festivities.

Growing to an eventual 30' tall and wide, the Oriental Persimmon has a beautiful furrowed gray bark and a dense foliage of 6-7" long leathery oval leaves. Small pale yellow flowers appear in the spring, followed by the roundish fruit which develops over the summer and turns bright red-orange in the fall as the leaves drop.

Two types of Oriental Persimmon are grown, both of which improve in flavor when allowed to fully ripen off the tree. Astringent types such as 'Hachiya' (pictured) and 'Tamopan' have 4" acorn-shaped fruit that should be picked when fully colored but still hard, and allowed to ripen to softness off the tree. Non-astringent types such as 'Fuyu' and 'Gosho' ('Giant Fuyu') have baseball-sized tomato-shaped fruits that are still hard when ripe and may be eaten directly from the tree, but with better flavor when allowed to soften slightly off the tree.   **QBG**

Dombeya cacuminum
(DOM-bee-yuh   kak-yoo-MINE-um)
STRAWBERRY SNOWBALL TREE
Sterculiaceae
Madagascar

Introduced by the Huntington Botanical Gardens in the 1970's, the tropical-looking Strawberry Snowball Tree is spectacular in mid-winter when it is covered with football-sized hanging clusters of bright magenta-pink flowers that look like upside-down hydrangea blooms. Equally spectacular are its thick slate-gray trunk and dense bright green foliage of 6-9" fan-shaped leaves. This is a fast-growing, broadly columnar evergreen tree to 40' tall that is easy to grow where frosts are not severe. Unlike other dombeyas, its flowers fall cleanly from the tree when fresh, creating a carpet of 2" bell-shaped pink flowers beneath the tree just in time for Valentine's Day.

The Strawberry Snowball Tree grows in full sun or partial shade, likes regular watering, and prefers a sheltered spot away from strong wind. Although its foliage may be damaged in a frost, it is tolerant of temperatures as low as 27°F. Flowering occurs from February into early April. Individual trees need to attain some size and age before they bloom, but typically reach blooming size about five years after planting and produce more and more flowers the older they get.   **B30,QBG**

48

Dombeya x *cayeuxii*
(DOM-bee-yuh kye-YOOKS-ee-eye)
PINK SNOWBALL TREE
Sterculiaceae
Horticultural Hybrid

The Pink Snowball Tree is a tropical-looking evergreen that is showy in both foliage and flower. Shrubby and multi-trunked, it grows quickly to 10-15' tall with a wider spread and a very dense dark green foliage of large, fuzzy broadly lobed leaves each up to a foot across. In fall and winter it is sensational, with many large bright pink flower clusters hanging from the branches. These softball-sized flower clusters are perfectly round and are composed of many honey-scented pink flowers.

The Pink Snowball Tree is a hybrid between *Dombeya wallichii* from Madagascar and *Dombeya burgessiae* from southern and eastern Africa. It grows in full sun or part shade and needs regular watering and protection from strong wind. Although frost may damage its foliage, it recovers quickly from temperatures as low as 27°F.

A number of other evergreen snowball trees are grown, many of which are shrubby but may be trained as small multi-trunked trees. *Dombeya burgessiae* is a variable species to 15-20' tall with pink or white flowers from fall to spring, depending on the variety grown. *Dombeya calantha* grows 15-20' tall, blooming with pink flowers in fall and winter. *Dombeya tiliacea* grows to 25' tall and blooms in late summer and fall with fragrant clusters of white to pale pink flowers.   **B30**

3048 Jefferson St., Carlsbad

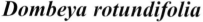

Dombeya rotundifolia
(DOM-bee-yuh roe-tun-dih-FOE-lee-uh)
SOUTH AFRICAN WILD PEAR
Sterculiaceae
Southern Africa

Although it is not related to the true pear (*Pyrus communis*), the South African Wild Pear does resemble a true pear in full bloom—and in its native southern Africa, it is considered a harbinger of spring. Unlike most of the other dombeyas in cultivation, this is a winter-deciduous tree which flowers on bare branches before the new leaves appear, making it very showy in bloom.

The South African Wild Pear grows quickly to around 15' tall here, with a gray-green foliage of 4-6" long roundish leaves. It blooms in late winter or early spring, typically with many clusters of sweetly fragrant 3/4" white flowers, although there are also pink-flowered forms that are grown. These flowers turn light brown as they fade and persist on the tree until the small fruit capsules ripen, then the flowers act as wind-driven wings to help distribute the seed.

Growing easily in full sun or partial shade, the South African Wild Pear is fairly drought-tolerant, but it also appreciates regular watering. It is heat-tolerant and also cold-tolerant to at least 25°F. In its native Africa, it is used medicinally for various purposes, including a love potion which is made from the flowers. In the past, it has also been grown and listed as *Dombeya spectabilis*.   **B26**

Desert Garden, Balboa Park

999 Adella Lane, Coronado

Dracaena draco
(druh-SEE-nuh   DRAY-koe)
DRAGON TREE
Dracaenaceae
Canary Islands

With its stout trunk and majestic silhouette, the Dragon Tree is one of the most unusual trees in the world. This slow-growing succulent tree is emblematic of its native Canary Islands and is famous for several gigantic old specimens still living there, although much larger and older ones once existed (one tree in 1868 measured 70' tall and 40' in girth and was alleged to have been 6000 years old). The red sap of the Dragon Tree is the source of "dragon's blood," which is a resin long-used in the making of varnishes. This tree is also emblematic of our own Quail Botanical Gardens in Encinitas, where an impressive group of specimens grows among other Canary Islands native plants.

As a young seedling, the Dragon Tree is often grown in containers, where it can live for many years. In the landscape, it takes a generation or more to produce a sizeable specimen, and even the largest, oldest plants in cultivation here rarely top 20' tall. Old plants produce clusters of greenish-white flowers followed by bright orange fruits. The Dragon Tree prefers well-drained soil and full sun, does not need much water, and is hardy to around 22°F.   **B26,QBG**

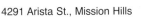

4291 Arista St., Mission Hills

Duranta erecta
(dur-AN-tuh   ee-REK-tuh)
SKY FLOWER
Verbenaceae
Tropical America.

The Sky Flower is a fairly fast-growing evergreen shrub that may be easily trained as a small tree. Especially as a multi-trunked specimen, it makes a beautiful addition to the landscape. The Sky Flower is valued for its pretty blue flowers which are produced in clusters nearly all year, attractive golden berries which are displayed in summer and fall, and dense foliage of 2" glossy-green leaves displayed on broadly arching branches. It grows easily in most soils in full sun or partial shade, needs only average watering, and is cold-hardy to around 20°F.

Individual flowers of the Sky Flower are small at 1/2", but come in large clusters and are fragrant as well. Besides humans, they attract both hummingbirds and butterflies. Both light blue and dark blue-flowered selections are grown, as well as the white-flowered 'Alba'. There is also a compact gold-leaved cultivar called 'Gold Tip'.

Other durantas grown include the hybrids and selections of the Brazilian species *Duranta stenostachya*, which have larger leaves and flower clusters, are more tender to frost, and also may be trained into small trees. These include the dark blue-flowered 'Sarasota' and the purple-flowered 'Sweet Memory', both of which are heavy bloomers with very sweetly scented flowers, plus several colorful-leaf selections such as the white-variegated 'Silver Lace' and the gold-variegated 'Gold Edge'.   **B12,QBG**

Dypsis decaryi
(DIP-siss   dee-KAIR-ee-eye)
TRIANGLE PALM
Arecaceae (Palmae)
Madagascar

Formerly known as *Neodypsis decaryi*, the Triangle Palm is one of the most dramatic palms for San Diego landscapes. Because of its unique architectural form, it makes a striking focal point wherever it is grown. The Triangle Palm is a feather palm with gray-green, upswept fronds that are arranged in a triangular pattern on the trunk, hence its common name. The leaf bases are boldly furred with black hair, contrasting with the clean gray trunk and furthering the dramatic effect. Though slow-growing, the Triangle Palm eventually grows to around 20' tall and 10-12' wide with fronds to 6-8' long and a trunk diameter of 12". It looks beautiful in all stages of life, however, and particularly as a young plant makes an attractive container specimen.

Like most subtropical palms, the Triangle Palm likes heat and grows fastest when the weather is warm. It grows fine in partial shade and along the coast, but is also conveniently tolerant of full sun and low humidity, making it adaptable to inland gardens if frosts are not severe. It needs only average watering and is cold-hardy to around 27°F. The Triangle Palm is especially dramatic when lit with spotlights at night.   **B23,QBG**

7975 Saint Louis Terrace, La Jolla

Ensete ventricosum
(en-SEH-tay   ven-trih-KOE-sum)
ABYSSINIAN BANANA
Musaceae
Ethiopia

The Abyssinian Banana is an excellent choice for creating an immediate tropical effect in the landscape. Plant a 5-gallon sized nursery plant now, and you'll have a big 15' tall by 10' wide specimen in as little as two years. Famous for its thick trunk and massive crown of bright green 10-15' leaves, this African native may not be exceptionally long-lived, but it makes up for it with its impressive form and growth rate.

Although the Abyssinian Banana does produce fruit, its bananas are small and not particularly edible. But even its fruiting habits are grand. Five to ten years after planting, it produces a huge bloom stalk from its crown of foliage, which develops over the next year into a 2-foot wide cylinder of bronzy-red bracts which hangs nearly to the ground and is full of 2" roundish fruits with large seeds. After fruiting is complete, the entire plant dies to the ground, but the seeds sprout easily and may be used to replace the plant.

The Abyssinian Banana is easy to grow in full sun or partial shade with regular watering, and looks best when protected from strong winds. Although frosts may damage the leaves, plants will recover quickly from temperatures as low as 22°F. It makes a good container plant as well, and will be much smaller and usually much longer-lived when its roots are confined. A showy red-leaved form called 'Maurelii' has dark red leaf stalks and reddish-tinged leaves, making it a fine centerpiece plant.   **B18,QBG**

Quail Botanical Gardens

51

Southwestern College, Chula Vista

Eriobotrya deflexa
(air-ee-oh-BAH-tree-uh   dee-FLEKS-uh)
BRONZE LOQUAT
Rosaceae
Taiwan

The Bronze Loquat is a popular small evergreen tree that is tougher than it looks. Its lush foliage makes it look tender, but it is actually one of the cold-hardiest tropical-looking evergreen trees of all, making it useful in all climate zones of San Diego County from desert to mountain to seacoast.

The most popular feature of the Bronze Loquat is its dense, showy foliage, which is composed of 5-10" long and 2" wide shiny leaves. These leaves emerge a bright coppery-red color and hold that color a long time before turning dark green. In spring, the Bronze Loquat is also showy in bloom, with clusters of creamy-white flowers that look like garlands on the tree.

The Bronze Loquat appreciates a well-drained soil in full sun to partial shade and is easy to grow. Because of its shrubby growth habit, it is sometimes grown as a large shrub or even as an espalier on a fence or trellis, and it also grows well in large containers. With just a little early training, it makes a handsome single or multi-trunked tree to 15-20' tall. The Bronze Loquat needs only moderate watering and is cold hardy to around 10°F.   **B16,B21,QBG**

4240 Arguello St., San Diego

Eriobotrya japonica
(air-ee-oh-BAH-tree-uh   juh-PAH-nih-kuh)
LOQUAT
Rosaceae
China and Japan

Valuable for its foliage, flowers, and fruit, the Loquat is an excellent small tree for the landscape. At all seasons, its bold foliage gives the garden a tropical look, even though it is cold-hardy to 10°F. In late fall or winter, it blooms with clusters of white flowers that are deliciously fragrant. In late winter and spring, it bears a big crop of tasty 1-2" orange to yellow fruits.

The Loquat's foliage is distinctive: big leathery corrugated leaves to 12" long and 5" wide that are dark green above and wooly beneath. Growth is shrubby and fairly fast to 15-30' tall and wide in full sun, somewhat narrower in partial shade. Many trees sold are seedlings, which all have nice foliage but usually inferior-tasting fruit—so if it's fruit you're after you should plant only grafted varieties. 'Champagne' has large yellow fruit with a white flesh that is juicy and tart, and does best in warm areas. 'Gold Nugget' bears a heavy crop of large sweet apricot-colored fruit, and does best near the coast. 'MacBeth' has exceptionally large fruit. All Loquat fruits contain one or more large, glossy dark brown seeds which are not edible. Trees grown primarily for fruit should be protected from excessive freezing when the trees are in flower and fruit.   **B1,QBG**

52

Erythrina × *bidwillii*
(air-ith-RYE-nuh bid-WILL-ee-eye)
BIDWILL'S CORAL TREE
Fabaceae (Leguminosae)
Horticultural Hybrid

The genus *Erythrina* is named from the Greek word *erythros*, which means red, and in fact this popular group does include many of the finest red-flowering trees in the world. Collectively called "coral trees," they are native to subtropical regions throughout the world and are among the most beautiful and ornamental flowering trees for Southern California landscapes. Different types of coral trees flower at different times of the year, providing bright color for many months—and as a bonus, the nectar-rich flowers attract and feed birds such as hummingbirds and orioles.

One of the most brilliant of all coral trees in bloom is Bidwill's Coral Tree (*Erythrina* × *bidwillii*). This hybrid between the South American Cockspur Coral Tree (*Erythrina crista-galli*) and the shrubby North American Cherokee Bean (*Erythrina herbacea*) is shrubby when young, but may with age be trained into a small tree to 15' tall and wide. It is deciduous in the winter, but blooms continuously from late spring to late fall with showy 2' long flower spikes of 2" long brilliant dark red flowers. Its foliage is bright green with thorny stems.

Bidwill's Coral Tree likes full sun and regular watering. Old flowering stems should be cut back after bloom, and it may be pruned hard in late winter. This is one of the cold-hardiest coral trees of all, tolerating temperatures down to 20°F. without damage, and it can also resprout from the base after much lower temperatures.

Buena Creek Gardens, San Marcos

Erythrina caffra
(air-ith-RYE-nuh KAFF-ruh)
SOUTH AFRICAN CORAL TREE
Fabaceae (Leguminosae)
South Africa

The South African Coral Tree is the most common and also the largest species of coral tree in cultivation in Southern California. This briefly-deciduous tree grows quickly to 40' tall and up to 60' wide and makes a beautiful specimen tree when it is given plenty of room and allowed to spread naturally. All too often, however, it is planted in locations where it doesn't have enough room to grow, with the unfortunate result being constant severe pruning and misshapen trees.

The South African Coral Tree blooms in winter to early spring with big, showy clusters of red-orange flowers (there is also a rare yellow-flowered variety). After flowering, it produces a lush foliage composed of compound leaves with light green 4" pointed oval leaflets. This is a drought-tolerant tree that is not recommended for areas where it gets too much water. Even though it is sometimes planted in lawns, its overly-exuberant growth there usually means weak wood, too much pruning, and poor flowering. **B8,QBG**

2051 Palomar Airport Rd., Carlsbad

Park Blvd., Balboa Park

Erythrina coralloides
(air-ith-RYE-nuh kor-ul-OY-deez)
NAKED CORAL TREE
Fabaceae (Leguminosae)
Mexico and Arizona

Perhaps the most colorful and also one of the hardiest coral trees, the deciduous Naked Coral Tree is so-named because it blooms on bare branches in the spring. In April and May it is sensational with its large cone-shaped clusters of fiery red flowers at the tips of its many thorny, twisting branches. After flowering, a dense foliage of 8-10" tropical-looking leaves creates shade all summer before turning yellow and dropping in the fall.

The Naked Coral Tree grows fairly quickly to around 25' tall and wide, but can easily be kept smaller by pruning. Its thick trunk and heavy branches are of great character, especially with some early training to help it develop a good branching structure. It likes full sun, is tolerant of most soils, and needs only moderate watering. It is quite hardy to cold, surviving temperatures as low as 20°F., and is also tolerant of desert heat. A rose-pink flowering form is also sometimes grown. **B26,QBG**

4120 Ingalls St., Mission Hills

Erythrina crista-galli
(air-ith-RYE-nuh kriss-tuh-GAL-ee)
COCKSPUR CORAL TREE
Fabaceae (Leguminosae)
Uruguay, S. Brazil, Paraguay, and N. Argentina

The unusual Cockspur Coral Tree has been grown for well over a century in California for its bright spring to fall flower color, usually bright scarlet-red but sometimes wine red or even a warm pink on certain plants. Unlike most coral trees, its flowers bloom on long flowering stems which should be cut back after the flowers are gone. Individual flowers are bird-shaped and up to 2" long, with new flowering stems produced in up to three waves of bloom during the warmer months. This is a deciduous tree that is decidedly shrubby when young, only gradually developing a tree-like form (early training will help here) as it eventually reaches its mature size of 15-20' in height and width. As the tree matures, it develops a characteristic dark rough bark.

The Cockspur Coral Tree is one of the hardiest coral trees of all, and also one of the most adaptable to a variety of climate zones from temperate to tropical. Although it's likely to remain shrubby in cold-winter areas, it is fully hardy to at least 14°F. because of its ability to resprout from its base and bloom the following year on new wood. It is tolerant of most any type of soil and may be grown with regular or very little watering. **B16,QBG**

Erythrina falcata
(air-ith-RYE-nuh   fal-KAY-tuh)
EVERGREEN CORAL TREE
Fabaceae (Leguminosae)
Brazil, Peru, Paraguay, Argentina, and Bolivia

The majestic Evergreen Coral Tree is different from other coral trees because of its tall upright habit and evergreen foliage. It grows quickly to 40-50' tall and makes a beautiful specimen tree. A mature tree in spring or early summer can be spectacular, with long dense hanging clusters of bright red sickle-shaped flowers displayed prominently against its lush bright-green foliage. When grown from seed (as it often is), this is a tree that needs to be in the ground for 10-15 years before it begins to bloom well. Although this flower show is well worth the wait, less-patient gardeners should choose a cutting-grown specimen which will bloom right away.

The Evergreen Coral Tree may shed some leaves during blooming season or in very cold or dry weather, but it is seldom completely leafless and is a beautiful tree for its foliage alone. It likes full sun and regular watering and is cold-hardy to 25°F. It has been suggested that it blooms best here after a dry winter.

B2

6th & Upas, Balboa Park

Erythrina humeana
(air-ith-RYE-nuh   hyoo-mee-AN-uh)
NATAL CORAL TREE
Fabaceae (Leguminosae)
South Africa and Mozambique

The Natal Coral Tree is one of the best choices for a small garden tree with showy flowers. Tidier than other coral trees, it presents a tailored yet tropical look, with the added bonus of attracting birds to the garden. The Natal Coral Tree grows at a moderate rate to about 25' high and wide, and looks best when allowed to develop multiple trunks. It has a dense, glossy dark green foliage of bold triangular leaflets to 7" long, usually deciduous in the winter but in the mildest sites nearly evergreen. Flowering occurs in summer, when the entire tree is covered with bold spikes of 2" long bright orange-red flowers displayed above the foliage, providing a brilliant show that can last well into the fall. These flowers are full of nectar, which hummingbirds and orioles find irresistible.

Although this tree is deciduous with frost, mature specimens are cold-hardy to at least 25°F. The Natal Coral Tree blooms profusely even as a young plant, and since it blooms in the summer on new growth, any frost damage will not hinder its flowering. This tree appreciates full sun and good drainage, and needs only average watering.

A dwarf selection of Natal Coral Tree, *E. humeana* 'Raja', is a shrubby small tree to 10-12' tall and wide. It has smaller leaves and blooms later, from September to December, with darker red flowers. This form should be grown from cuttings to remain true, as seedlings tend to vary toward the typical species form.

B15,QBG

4400 N. Oceanside Dr., Oceanside

Quail Botanical Gardens

Quail Botanical Gardens

Erythrina lysistemon
(air-ith-RYE-nuh   lye-SIS-teh-mun)

TRANSVAAL CORAL TREE
Fabaceae (Leguminosae)
Southeastern Africa

The Transvaal Coral Tree is big, bold, and showy. In late winter and early spring it produces a colorful bloom of reflexed flower clusters to 8" long which look like bright red skyrockets at the ends of the bare branches. This is a fast-growing tree to 40' tall and wide with lush, dark green foliage composed of divided leaves with tapering leaflets to 7" long. It has a heavy brownish-gray trunk and branches that are studded with black thorns. Like the closely related South African Coral Tree (*Erythrina caffra*), it has a graceful, spreading growth habit and makes a beautiful large specimen tree.

The Transvaal Coral Tree prefers full sun and good drainage, and does not like cold wet soil. It is cold-hardy to around 25°F., although a late frost can damage developing flowers. The Transvaal Coral Tree is somewhat variable from seed, and there are forms with smaller leaflets that typically have a wider-spreading growth habit than the larger-leaved forms. Although they are not common, there are also forms with pink, orange, and cream-colored flowers. Flowering time can be variable as well, with some trees blooming intermittently from fall to spring (perhaps in response to weather). A warm, dry winter will often encourage trees to bloom heavily, with spectacular results.   **B14,QBG**

Erythrina speciosa
(air-ith-RYE-nuh spee-see-OH-suh)

BRAZILIAN CORAL TREE
Fabaceae (Leguminosae)
Southern Brazil

With its extra-large leaves and thorny trunks and branches, the Brazilian Coral Tree looks like an odd gigantic rose bush. Growing quickly to 15-18' tall and 10-15' wide in full sun or partial shade, this winter-deciduous small tree typically has multiple trunks and is definitely one of the thorniest coral trees of all.

The Brazilian Coral Tree is spectacular in bloom in late winter or early spring, when foot-tall candelabras of 3" long bright red flowers erupt from the ends of its bare branches. In some years and in some locations, it can also bloom later in the spring after it has leafed out. Its large, tropical-looking leaves are impressive, and are composed of three 5-8" wide heart-shaped leaflets that themselves even have thorns on their lower surfaces.

The Brazilian Coral Tree prefers regular watering, but will grow in drier sites as well. It grows best where frosts are not severe, and will suffer damage below 27°F. Besides the typical red-flowered form, there are also pink-flowered and white-flowered forms grown, both of which were received from the Sao Paulo Botanical Garden in Brazil.   **QBG**

Erythrina x *sykesii*
(air-ith-RYE-nuh SYKES-ee-eye)
HYBRID CORAL TREE
Fabaceae (Leguminosae)
Horticultural Hybrid

Known only in cultivation, the Hybrid Coral Tree is a fast-growing and showy tree that may just be the best coral tree of all. Reputedly originating in Australia, it is thought to be a hybrid of *Erythrina lysistemon*, perhaps with *Erythrina coralloides*. It is a handsome tree to 25-40' tall and 20-30' wide, with smooth bark and a lush bright green foliage of large 7" tropical-looking leaves that in most years drop cleanly when the tree comes into bloom. The Hybrid Coral Tree typically blooms in mid-winter, although depending on the year and microclimate, flowering may occur any time between November and March. In full bloom it is spectacular, with the tree covered with large clusters of 2" bright orange-red flowers for several weeks or more before the foliage returns.

Because the Hybrid Coral Tree does not set seed, it is always grown from cuttings and so will flower even as a young plant. It is easily grown anywhere where frosts are not severe, but even if frost damage does occur, it will recover quickly from temperatures as low as 25°F. It likes full sun but needs only moderate watering and will grow even in dry sites. Its size may be controlled by pruning, but it will also stay smaller and more compact if it is not overwatered. **B25**

Heritage Park, Old Town, San Diego

Eucalyptus camaldulensis
(yoo-kuh-LIP-tus kuh-mal-dyoo-LEN-sis)
RED GUM
Myrtaceae
Australia

A century ago, the Australian Red Gum held great promise for San Diego County as a pest-free timber tree that would grow quickly and produce high-quality lumber without the need for irrigation even in our very dry climate. Many thousands of seedlings were planted as landowners eagerly anticipated the huge profits that awaited them. But as the first trees were harvested, there was great disappointment—for the wood of the Red Gum proved of poor quality, not even usable for railroad ties! As it turned out, in the absence of its native pests the Red Gum grew much faster in our climate than it did in Australia, and once harvested the wood twisted and cracked as it dried. Perhaps a better species might have been tried, but by then no one wanted to.

A century later, these great Red Gum forests still persist, and great communities such as Rancho Santa Fe have grown up around them—but there is more disappointment. In recent times, two major insect pests (first the Eucalyptus Longhorn Beetle in 1984 and then the Red Gum Lerp Psyllid in 1998) have been inadvertently imported from Australia and have caused much damage and even death to many Red Gum trees. The defoliating lerp psyllid in particular is a grave threat, but it is hoped that recently introduced biological control insects will eventually provide a solution. **B38,QBG**

5527 Beaumont Ave., La Jolla

5835 Bellevue Ave., La Jolla

Old Town, San Diego

Eucalyptus cinerea
(yoo-kuh-LIP-tus   sin-ER-ee-uh)
SILVER DOLLAR TREE
Myrtaceae
New South Wales and Victoria, Australia

The Silver Dollar Tree grows up to 50' tall and 40' wide, with bright silvery-gray foliage that really stands out in the landscape. This is a densely foliaged evergreen tree that prefers well-drained soils and is very drought-tolerant as well as cold-hardy, withstanding temperatures down to 15°F.

An interesting feature of nearly all eucalypts is their variety of leaf shapes on the same tree. Young trees and even new shoots from the trunks of older trees produce juvenile leaves, which are often rounder and sometimes more silvery than the adult leaves which are produced on older growth as the tree matures. In many eucalypts, adult foliage is rather quickly produced, but in others juvenile foliage persists for many years.

The Silver Dollar Tree is especially prized for its juvenile foliage, which consists of pairs of round silvery leaves that clasp the branchlets, and is even cultivated as a cut-foliage crop by regularly cutting back the plants to force new juvenile growth. On older Silver Dollar Trees left to grow naturally, mature leaves are longer and pointed, but in this species even the adult leaves are silvery and sometimes even mixed with juvenile leaves at the ends of the branches.   **QBG**

Eucalyptus cladocalyx
(yoo-kuh-LIP-tus   klad-oh-KAY-liks)
SUGAR GUM
Myrtaceae
South Australia

The many old specimens of Sugar Gum in coastal San Diego County are testimony to the ruggedness of this imposing tree, for many of them have lived a good part of their lives without irrigation. This is a big evergreen tree, growing to 45-75' tall, with a beautiful silhouette against the sky of puffy clouds of foliage separated by open spaces. It has a dominant and handsome mottled trunk, with tan-colored bark peeling to reveal creamy patches in ever-changing patterns. Its 3-5" long leaves are dark green above and paler below and are crowded at the end of its distinctively reddish branchlets. Summer flowers are creamy-white and fairly small, but are freely produced.

Although it is too large for a small garden, the Sugar Gum makes a handsome skyline tree where space is not an issue. The biggest Sugar Gums in San Diego County are among our most massive trees, including impressive specimens in Old Town, at Quail Botanical Gardens, and a spectacular street planting along Grand Avenue in downtown Carlsbad. The Sugar Gum has the ability to succeed in spite of poor soil and extreme drought and is cold-hardy down to 24°F. In its native range, there are both tall-growing and dwarf forms of this species; the dwarf form is sometimes sold as the variety 'Nana'.   **B1,QBG**

Eucalyptus conferruminata
(yoo-kuh-LIP-tus   kon-fair-oo-min-AY-tuh)

BUSHY YATE
Myrtaceae
Western Australia

The Bushy Yate is a coastal species in its native Western Australia, and is a particularly good choice for a small multi-stemmed tree at the seashore or in coastal gardens. It is fast-growing, quickly making a dense, flat-topped windbreak or specimen tree to 12-25' tall and 15-25' wide, and is very tolerant of drought and poor soil. In spring and summer, the Bushy Yate blooms with rather spectacular 4" puffy green flower clusters composed of many individual flowers opening together from a fused cluster of odd horn-shaped buds. These clusters persist on the branches as large woody seed capsules with horn-like projections. The foliage of the Bushy Yate is evergreen, with some of the light green 2" leaves turning red in the fall, and established plants are cold-hardy to 25°F.

The Bushy Yate was formerly included in the species *Eucalyptus lehmannii*, and it is often still sold under that name. However, a recent reclassification has made it a separate species, with *Eucalyptus conferruminata* the correct name.   **B4**

5821 Sweetwater Road, San Diego

Eucalyptus deglupta
(yoo-kuh-LIP-tus   dee-GLUP-tuh)

RAINBOW GUM
Myrtaceae
Indonesia, Philippines, and New Guinea

The majestic Rainbow Gum is one of only two species of *Eucalyptus* that are not native to Australia. Instead, its native habitat is the tropical rainforests of the Philippines, Indonesia, and New Guinea. Unlike most eucalypts, it needs regular watering and is somewhat cold-tender, but it nevertheless has proven adaptable to many San Diego landscape situations where frosts are not severe. The Rainbow Gum gets its common name from its spectacular trunk, which is tall, straight and massive, with showy peeling bark in an ever-changing color show of green, yellow, orange, red, purple, and brown. Its evergreen foliage is unusual for a eucalypt, being composed of large tropical-looking compound leaves with bright green 6" oval leaflets, and it blooms lightly with clusters of small creamy-white flowers in summer.

The Rainbow Gum is a fast-growing tree, probably to an eventual 60' or more tall and half as wide here, and is best when protected from strong winds. Although it is frost-tender when young, established trees will tolerate temperatures as low as 26°F. Because of its upright growth habit and tall, colorful trunk, it can be most effective when planted near tall buildings. A colorful specimen in the author's garden is a proud reminder of his Filipino heritage.   **B37**

Sports Arena, San Diego

Eucalyptus erythrocorys
(yoo-kuh-LIP-tus air-ith-roe-KOR-iss)
RED-CAP GUM
Myrtaceae
Western Australia

The colorful Red-Cap Gum gets both its common and botanical names because of its striking bright red bud caps, which are unique among eucalypts. These contrast beautifully with its bright yellow flowers which are produced in big, showy clusters. A native of the west coast of Australia, the Red-Cap Gum is a small evergreen tree that grows quickly with multiple trunks to 12-25' tall and 10-20' wide in full sun. It has smooth gray or light yellow-brown bark which sheds to reveal bright white trunks. Its mature leaves are thick and bright green, and are 5-10" long and 1-2" wide. Although some flowering may occur at any season, the Red-Cap Gum is showiest in winter, when it blooms heavily with its large clusters of 2" bright yellow flowers.

The Red-Cap Gum is best in sun, appreciates good drainage, and is cold-hardy to 25°F. It is drought-tolerant but will take regular watering as long as drainage is good. It benefits from regular pruning, and may be made more dense by heading back the main stems. Because it grows from an underground crown called a lignotuber, mature plants may be renewed by cutting all the way to the ground, after which they will resprout from the base. **B25**

18966 Avenida La Valencia, Poway

5800 El Camino Del Norte, San Diego

Eucalyptus globulus
(yoo-kuh-LIP-tus GLOB-yoo-lus)
BLUE GUM
Myrtaceae
Victoria and Tasmania, Australia

The Blue Gum is so familiar as the most widely planted eucalypt in California that many people think of it as a native tree. In fact, the cold-hardiness and vigor of this predominantly Tasmanian native have enabled it to adapt so well to many areas of California that it has naturalized in parts of our state. Although it is too large, too greedy, and too messy to be considered for most landscapes these days, there are many who live with established trees and either cherish or curse their grandeur.

Dominant in every way, the Blue Gum is a big tree to 75' or more here, shorter in drought and attaining its largest proportions in deep soil with ample moisture. Its trunk is massive and thick, with copious amounts of peeling bark. Evergreen foliage of long 6-10" sickle-shaped leaves is highly aromatic, and is used in commerce to make eucalyptus oil. The Blue Gum flowers in winter and spring with cream-colored flowers and distinctive whitish bud caps. It grows very quickly, and is cold-hardy to 18° F., but aggressive surface roots and leaf litter make it a difficult tree to garden under. There is a dwarf form of the Blue Gum which is sold as the variety 'Compacta'. It grows to around 30' tall, with a shrubby growth habit when young and a more tree-like form as it matures. **B4,QBG**

Eucalyptus leucoxylon

(yoo-kuh-LIP-tus   loo-KOKS-ih-lon)

WHITE IRONBARK

Myrtaceae

Southeastern Australia

The White Ironbark is an extremely variable species, with a number of forms and varieties suitable for use in the landscape. Although the typical species can be a fairly large tree, there are other, smaller forms that make colorful garden and street trees of very manageable size. All forms are very tolerant of adverse conditions from seashore to desert, including heat, wind, drought, poor soil, and cold temperatures down to 18°F.

The most common type of White Ironbark in cultivation here is the subspecies *leucoxylon*, which is a fast-growing evergreen tree to 40-70' tall and half as wide. Although different seedlings vary in size and habit, it is usually an upright, open tree with pendulous branches and distinctive brownish bark which sheds to reveal white new bark. Foliage is composed of 3-6" gray-green sickle-shaped leaves, and the tree flowers in winter and spring with clusters of 1" flowers that are typically white or cream, but sometimes pink in certain seedlings.

Another type of White Ironbark that is dependably more compact and colorful is the subspecies *megalocarpa* (often sold as *macrocarpa* 'Rosea'), which grows quickly to 25' tall with big, showy clusters of bright magenta-pink flowers in spring and summer. A third type is the subspecies *petiolaris*, which grows quickly into a small multi-trunked tree to15-25' tall (pictured at right) and blooms profusely over a long season from fall to spring with showy clusters of bright rose-pink, or sometimes cream-colored flowers. **B10**

3070 Skyline Dr., Oceanside

Van Zanten Park, El Cajon

Eucalyptus nicholii

(yoo-kuh-LIP-tus   nik-KOE-lee-eye)

WILLOW-LEAFED PEPPERMINT

Myrtaceae

New South Wales and Queensland, Australia

The Willow-Leafed Peppermint is an attractive evergreen tree which is useful in both private and commercial landscapes. It grows quickly to 35-50' tall and 15-35' wide, with a dense, willowy foliage of narrow 3-5" long bluish-green leaves that smell like peppermint when crushed. Its strong trunk is also ornamental, with its rich reddish-brown furrowed bark. Although the individual white flowers are small, they make a pretty effect in late summer as they bloom.

The Willow-Leafed Peppermint likes good drainage, is drought-tolerant, and should not be overwatered. It is quite cold-hardy, tolerating temperatures down to 15°F. As a garden or a street tree, its graceful form is dependably attractive, and its water-saving advantages should not be overlooked. **QBG**

61

Eucalyptus polyanthemos

(yoo-kuh-LIP-tus   pah-lee-ANTH-em-ose)

SILVER DOLLAR GUM

Myrtaceae

New South Wales and Victoria, Australia

The attractive Silver Dollar Gum is a popular landscape tree because of its graceful form and pretty foliage. It is also a dependable tree, even in very shallow soils. This is an evergreen tree that grows quickly to 40-50' tall and about half as wide, with a dense foliage of 2-3" gray-green leaves which are round on young trees (like silver dollars) but more pointed on mature specimens. Its strong trunk and branches have an irregular pattern of growth that makes for an interesting structure, and they are covered in grayish bark which sheds to reveal patterns of gray, cream, and pink. Flowering occurs in winter and spring, when the entire tree is covered with puffy clouds of many small creamy-white flowers.

The Silver Dollar Gum is a vigorous tree that is cold-hardy to 15°F., grows well in any type of soil, and is very tolerant of drought. If it gets too much water, it often grows so vigorously that it needs regular pruning to keep it from becoming top-heavy (when pruning, trees should always be thinned but never "cut back"). This is one of the best eucalypts for shallow, rocky soils, and it is especially effective when planted as a small grove. The foliage of young trees is often used for indoor decoration. **B15,QBG**

4603 Sports Arena Blvd., San Diego

Behind Hall of Champions, Balboa Park

Eucalyptus sideroxylon

(yoo-kuh-LIP-tus   sye-der-OKS-ih-lon)

RED IRONBARK

Myrtaceae

Eastern Australia

Although most eucalypts are known for their ornamental bark, the Red Ironbark is one that really merits a double-take because of its strongly furrowed, nearly black trunk and lower branches. The unusual look of this tree is even more striking because of its willow-like blue-green foliage that contrasts so strongly with its dark bark and also its showy pink to red flowers. This is a handsome and durable evergreen tree that is most tolerant of harsh conditions, including considerable drought.

The Red Ironbark grows upright at first, then spreading to an eventual size of 30-60' tall and 20-40' wide. Young trees can be quite dense, although older ones are usually more open, with weeping blue-green foliage composed of narrow leaves to 6" long and 1/2" wide on pendulous branches. The Red Ironbark blooms abundantly in winter and spring, although some bloom may occur at any season. Individual flowers are 1/2" to 3/4" wide and are produced in hanging clusters.

Despite its common name, flowers of the Red Ironbark may be white, cream, pink, or red, depending on the individual tree, with the most popular type being rose-pink to red flowering trees that are usually sold as the variety 'Rosea'. **B30,QBG**

Eucalyptus torquata
(yoo-kuh-LIP-tus   tor-KWAH-tuh)
CORAL GUM
Myrtaceae
Western Australia

Because of its manageable size and long bloom season, the Coral Gum is an excellent choice for the smaller garden. It also has the advantage of blooming well as a young plant, and is easily grown even as a container specimen. This is an evergreen tree which grows fairly quickly to 15-25' tall and wide, but it may be easily trained to a smaller size. It has a graceful foliage of willowy gray-green leaves set along reddish branchlets which often droop with the weight of its showy flower clusters. Flowering occurs off and on throughout the year, with reddish lantern-shaped flower buds opening to fluffy coral-pink flowers which make good cut-flowers.

The Coral Gum is drought-tolerant, and succeeds in a variety of soils. Although very young plants are somewhat sensitive to frost, mature trees are cold-hardy to at least 20°F. This is a tree recommended for many climates and exposures, including desert areas. Although it occurs naturally in just a small part of Western Australi[...]ular in cultivation worldwide as a garden plant.   **B3**

SW side Plaza Camino Real, Carlsbad

4566 Santa Cruz Ave., Point Loma

Euphorbia c[...]
(yoo-FOR-bee-uh   ko[...]
CARIBBEA[...]
Euphorbiaceae
Mexico to Vene[...]

With some 2[...] [...]orbia is quite possibly th[...] [...]t diverse genera of flower[...] [...] includes nearly every kir[...] [...] succulents to trees and shr[...] [...]—all united in the similarities o[...] [...]te milky sap. One of the more unusual tre[...] [...]he Caribbean Copper Plant, which is shrubby when [...] [...] may easily be trained into a multi-stemmed small tree to 10-15' tall in frost-free gardens. This is a cold-sensitive plant that is often evergreen near the coast but is deciduous in winter when grown inland, and won't take temperatures much below 26°F. The most common form of the Caribbean Copper Plant in cultivation is the variety 'Atropurpurea', which is distinguished by its bright burgundy-red foliage comprised of 4" long by 3" wide oval leaves that usually appear in threes. This foliage is remarkable for the consistency of its coloration throughout the warm season, especially in full sun. Although its creamy-white summertime flowers are tiny, they appear in clusters at the end of the branches and are pretty against the red foliage.

As with all euphorbias, care must be taken when pruning the Caribbean Copper Plant, for its white milky sap can cause skin allergies and should never be allowed to get in your eyes. **B26,QBG**

Euphorbia ingens
(yoo-FOR-bee-uh ING-enz)
CANDELABRA TREE
Euphorbiaceae
South Africa to Kenya

The Candelabra Tree is one of the strangest trees in the world. Often mistaken for a cactus, it is actually a giant cactus-like euphorbia that attains massive proportions in its native South Africa, and in fact its specific name means "huge." Although it is somewhat smaller in cultivation here, this is a plant that is conspicuous and always dramatic when used in the landscape. Shrubby at first, the Candelabra Tree grows somewhat slowly to an eventual 20' tall, with thick, four-winged cactus-like branches. At the tips of these branches are tiny spines and small round reddish flowers that appear in late fall or winter, but true leaves are seldom produced.

The Candelabra Tree grows easily from even large cuttings, which may be rooted either in pots or in the ground. It needs sun and good drainage, and looks good when planted with other succulents. It is very drought-tolerant but is cold-tender and can be damaged in a frost. Its growth habit is dense when given some supplemental watering, but it can be sparse and tall in more challenging sites, with variation in individual plants perhaps due to different cutting-grown forms being in cultivation. An unusual twisted, weeping form of the Candelabra Tree (*Euphorbia ingens* 'Pendula') which is always grown from cuttings matures into a rather fantastic shape because of its spiraling stems. **B26,QBG**

633 Mar Vista, Vista

944 Cornish Drive, Encinitas

Euphorbia tirucalli
(yoo-FOR-bee-uh teer-uh-KAL-ee)
PENCIL TREE
Euphorbiaceae
Southern and Eastern Africa

Another odd succulent tree from Africa is the Pencil Tree, which is again very cactus-like but of course not a cactus at all. Shrubby at first, this unusual evergreen plant can grow to an eventual 15-25' tall and wide with a noticeable rough trunk—a remarkable sight if you've never seen a mature specimen before. The Pencil Tree is distinguished by its dense "foliage" of bright-green pencil-sized branchlets, which are not spiny. It blooms in spring with small, inconspicuous yellow flowers, and its tiny true leaves are only present for a short time on actively growing branch tips in the summer.

The Pencil Tree likes full sun and good drainage. It is very drought-tolerant and even does well at the beach, but does not tolerate much frost. A cutting-grown selection called 'Sticks On Fire' is popular for its very colorful stems, which vary from pale pink to bright salmon-pink when young, aging to cream, orange, and chartreuse-green. One very important word of caution about all forms of the Pencil Tree is that the white milky sap of this species is extremely toxic to the skin and especially the eyes. Even a small amount of sap can cause severe burning and loss of vision if medical attention is not quickly obtained. **B26,QBG**

Ficus auriculata

(*FYE-kuss oh-rik-yoo-LAY-tuh*)

ROXBURGH FIG

Moraceae
Himalayas

The genus *Ficus* is a big group of over 750 species of mostly trees and large shrubs that are native to the tropics and subtropics worldwide, all with a milky sap and a most unique flowering habit. Have you ever seen a *Ficus* tree in flower? Well, yes you have—for what looks like a berry or a fleshy fruit is actually an inside-out flowering structure with many tiny true flowers and fruitlets inside (the tiny true seeds which follow are also inside, but not produced here by many species in the absence of their specialized native insect pollinators). We call these flowering structures "figs"—and although only one species (*Ficus carica*) is commonly cultivated for its edible figs by humans, many species of *Ficus* produce figs which are food for birds and other animals.

Formerly known as *Ficus roxburghii*, the Roxburgh Fig is a spectacular shrubby tree to 25' tall and wide that is at its best in protected sites with no frost. In either sun or partial shade, its main feature is its dense foliage of big, bold heart-shaped leaves a foot or more across which emerge a bright mahogany-red and mature to deep green. Figs are large, to 3" in diameter, and are produced in unusual clusters along the heavy trunk and branches. Although it can be essentially evergreen, the Roxburgh Fig may drop some or even all of its leaves for a brief time in late spring. **B18,QBG**

1440 Sunrise Drive, Vista

Ficus benjamina

(*FYE-kuss ben-juh-MYE-nuh*)

WEEPING FIG

Moraceae
Tropical Asia

Familiar to many as a house plant, the Weeping Fig is also a graceful evergreen landscape tree in our climate if it is grown in a site that is protected from frost and strong wind. Although it grows to a larger size in the tropics, its typical maximum height in our climate is around 25-30', and it can easily be kept smaller with occasional pruning. It is happy in sun or part shade, and will even grow well in full shade, which is why it is often used as a small tree for shady entryways.

The Weeping Fig has an attractive foliage of leathery glossy-green leaves to 5" long which densely clothe its drooping branchlets. It is usually seen as a multiple-trunked, upright-growing tree, sometimes with braided trunks, and can live for many years as a potted specimen. Though not always produced, figs are a reddish-tan and 1/2" in diameter. The most commonly grown form of Weeping Fig is the variety 'Exotica', with wavy-edged leaves with long twisted tips. A number of fancy-foliaged varieties are also grown, but these are mainly useful as smaller container plants. One unusual tree type that is sometimes seen here is the variety *nuda*, which is more robust and spreading, with an interesting buttressed trunk, larger, non-weeping foliage, and larger orange figs. **B38,QBG**

7711 Ivanhoe, La Jolla

Ficus carica
(FYE-kuss KAIR-ih-kuh)
EDIBLE FIG
Moraceae
Western Asia and Mediterranean Sea Region

The Edible Fig is one of the oldest of cultivated fruits, having been first brought into cultivation in western Asia at least 5000 years ago. Very popular in the Middle East and throughout the Mediterranean region, it is perfectly suited to nearly all San Diego County climates and quite easy to grow. The Edible Fig is a multi-trunked deciduous tree to 15-30' tall and as wide, although it is frequently kept smaller by pruning to make fruit harvesting easier. Its large figs are sweet and delicious, with most of the home-garden varieties bearing crops in both early summer and also in the fall. The Edible Fig is also a fine ornamental tree, with large tropical-looking lobed leaves and a picturesque branching structure.

There are many excellent varieties of Edible Fig for the home-garden, with figs ranging in color from white to red to purple when ripe, depending on variety. Coastal gardeners should choose varieties that don't need much winter chill or summer heat; gardeners farther inland can also choose varieties that need more heat and cold. The Edible Fig loves sun and regular watering and is fully hardy to 10-15°F., but can even survive colder temperatures and grow successfully as a shrub. It needs little maintenance, although you may need to protect ripening figs from birds and fig beetles.   **QBG**

1940 Nevada St., Oceanside

NW side of park, SeaWorld, San Diego

Ficus dammaropsis
(FYE-kuss dam-uh-ROP-sis)
DINNER PLATE FIG
Moraceae
New Guinea

The rare and magnificent Dinner Plate Fig has one of the largest undivided leaves of any tree in the world, and it is certainly worth the price of admission to SeaWorld to see the large traffic-stopping specimen there. Its huge, leathery, corrugated leaves are up to 3' long by 2' wide, like giant dark green dinner plates. Its figs are also spectacular—curious light green grapefruit-sized structures with overlapping scales that reputedly are boiled and eaten as a vegetable in its native New Guinea. The Dinner Plate Fig is evergreen and multi-trunked, maturing at around 25' tall and 35' wide in the warmest frost-free coastal climates, where it will grow in full sun but is best in part shade. Away from the coast, it is best in part shade and must be protected from frost.

Formerly known as *Dammaropsis kingiana*, the Dinner Plate Fig does not produce viable seed here and is difficult from cuttings, and so is rare in the nursery trade. It deserves to be more widely grown, perhaps from tissue culture. In the garden, it prefers high humidity, regular watering and fertilizing, and protection from strong winds. Give it a special spot in the garden, and of course plenty of room to grow.   **QBG**

Ficus elastica
(FYE-kuss ee-LASS-tih-kuh)
RUBBER TREE
Moraceae
India and Malaysia

In the mid-nineteenth century, the Rubber Tree was tapped for an early form of commercial rubber in its native India. Later, it became well known as an indoor plant in colder climates, appreciated for its ability to withstand low light and dry air. In San Diego gardens, it is easily grown as an outdoor tree in frost-free sites, where its bold shiny foliage gives a tropical look to the landscape. Typically multi-stemmed, the Rubber Tree is evergreen, with a dense spreading foliage of large 8-12" leathery leaves that unfold from rosy-red leaf sheaths. Small 1/2" figs are produced on older plants. Although it grows large in the tropics, the Rubber Tree seldom exceeds 25' here, and is often seen as a smaller specimen in shady entryways. It is fine in either sun or shade along the coast, but needs at least partial shade to look its best inland.

The most common form of the Rubber Tree in cultivation is the variety 'Decora', which has very glossy dark green leaves that are bronzy when young. There are also variegated forms with leaves patterned in light green, yellow, and creamy-white, forms with reddish new growth, and even a black-leaved variety. All are best without frost and make fine container plants. When planted in the ground, however, aggressive roots on very old plants can be a problem. **B35,QBG**

637 Arden Road, Encinitas

Ficus lutea
(FYE-kuss   LOO-tee-uh)
ZULU FIG
Moraceae
Tropical Africa

Once known as *Ficus nekbudu* (among other names), the Zulu Fig has most recently been combined with some of its relatives into a single species for which the name *Ficus lutea* takes priority. Although it grows larger in the tropics, in our climate it takes the form of a spreading tree to around 25' tall and 35' wide at maturity, with a dense canopy of large 6-12" glossy leathery leaves. Its heavy gray trunk and branches are quite ornamental, as are its colorful 3/4" orange to red figs which are crowded along the branch tips.

The Zulu Fig prefers a frost-free coastal climate in full sun or partial shade and is evergreen by nature, although the tree may lose some or all of its leaves in a frost. It makes a beautiful multi-trunked specimen, but is often seen trained to a single trunk. As with all figs, it prefers a deep, well-drained soil and responds well to regular watering and fertilizing. **B14,QBG**

Mission Hills Park, Mission Hills

Ficus lyrata
(FYE-kuss lye-RAY-tuh)
FIDDLE-LEAF FIG
Moraceae
Tropical Africa

The bold, dramatic leaves of the Fiddle-Leaf Fig are familiar to many who grow it as a house plant. Growing up to 15" long and 10" wide, these prominently veined, dark green leathery leaves are shaped somewhat like the body of a violin, and give the tree its common name. The Fiddle-Leaf Fig is native to tropical rainforests in central and western Africa, and so grows much larger in a tropical climate than it does in San Diego. But it is surprisingly adaptable outdoors here in frost-free or frost-protected sites, where it grows as an upright small evergreen tree to around 20' tall with a dense canopy of foliage. On older trees, 1" long green figs are produced, usually somewhat hidden under the leaves.

The Fiddle-Leaf Fig grows well in either full sun or shade on the coast, but its foliage looks better with at least partial shade inland. It will tolerate cold but does not like direct frost, and grows best with regular watering and fertilizing. For a dense branching structure, head back the main stems while the plant is still young.   **B35**

2253 Juan St., Mission Hills

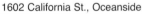
1602 California St., Oceanside

Ficus macrophylla
(FYE-kuss mak-roe-FILL-uh)
MORETON BAY FIG
Moraceae
Northeastern Australia

Impressive for its size alone, the Moreton Bay Fig is a remarkable evergreen tree with large buttressing roots and thick heavy trunks that support an enormous spreading canopy of foliage. Unlike many other tropical Figs, it in time gets just as big in Southern California as it does in its native land, with the largest cultivated specimens as much as 100', 150', and covering over 1/4 acre after 100 years of growth. In San Diego County, the Moreton Bay Fig is represented by a number of mature trees that are the most massive cultivated trees in the area. All have heavy gray trunks and branches, large dark green glossy leaves to 10" long and 4" wide, 1" figs that are purple spotted with white, and the large gray snake-like surface roots that are so characteristic of this species.

Although very young plants may be somewhat frost-tender, the Moreton Bay Fig quickly attains both size and hardiness, tolerating temperatures as low as 24°F. Needless to say, it requires lots of room to grow, and because of its overpowering size and root system is not the best choice for a small garden.   **B16,QBG**

Ficus microcarpa
(*FYE-kuss mike-roe-CAR-puh*)
INDIAN LAUREL FIG
Moraceae
Southern China and Japan to Northeastern Australia
and Japan to Northeastern Australia

The Indian Laurel Fig is a variable species in the wild, with a big native range that extends all the way from China to Australia. The most common form of it in San Diego County is a large but popular street tree formerly known as *Ficus retusa* var. *nitida* and still sometimes sold under that name. This evergreen tree grows quickly to an eventual 40' high with a wider, broadly spreading crown, although heavy pruning is practiced on most street trees that keeps them smaller (sometimes ridiculously so). Dark green foliage is very dense and crowded, with individual leaves 2-4" long and pointed. It also has a characteristic smooth light gray trunk and branches and bears many 3/8" round figs which are purple-black when ripe.

Another form of the Indian Laurel Fig is an equally dense evergreen tree with rounder leaves and weeping branchlets that was formerly known as *Ficus retusa*. Unlike the pointed-leaf form, this one sometimes produces aerial roots here (a great many Figs, including the tropical Banyan Tree, are famous for their aerial roots in the tropics but do not produce them much here in our dry climate).

Both forms of the Indian Laurel Fig are fairly hardy to cold, and can easily tolerate temperatures in the mid-20's°F. They are big trees that are useful for casting shade, but they have very strong, heavy roots that can cause damage to sidewalks and foundations. **B22,B33,QBG**

SE corner Automotive Museum, Balboa Park

4201 Mt. Casas Drive, Clairemont

Ficus religiosa
(*FYE-kuss reh-lih-jee-OH-suh*)
SACRED FIG
Moraceae
India to Southeast Asia

Native to the mountains of southeast Asia and the Himalayan foothills, the Sacred Fig is revered by Buddhists and Hindus (who call it Bo and Peepul) as the tree that Buddha sat under when he attained enlightenment. A cutting-grown plant of that original tree was planted in Anuradhapura, Sri Lanka in 288 B.C., and is the oldest living cultivated tree known.

Apart from its religious significance, the most distinctive feature of the Sacred Fig is its graceful foliage of heart-shaped 5-9" long leaves, which have a long tail-like point called a "drip tip" that helps shed water in its rainy native climate. These leathery, glossy green, prominently veined leaves drop in late spring or early summer, but are quickly replaced with a fresh crop of new leaves. Although the Sacred Fig grows quite large in the tropics, in our climate it is slower and smaller, to an eventual 30-40' tall. Its round figs are 1/2" across and dark purple when ripe.

The Sacred Fig makes a handsome multi-trunked tree in full sun or partial shade. It is somewhat frost-tender when young, but older trees are hardy to 25°F. **B19,QBG**

69

Spreckels Park, Coronado

1860 Diamond St., Pacific Beach

Ficus rubiginosa
(FYE-kuss   roo-bih-jin-OH-suh)
RUSTYLEAF FIG
Moraceae
Eastern Australia

Native to Queensland and New South Wales, Australia, the Rustyleaf Fig is a variable species with several different forms in cultivation here. All are densely foliaged evergreen trees 20-50' tall and 30-50' wide that sometimes develop aerial roots. Leaves are dark glossy green above and sometimes rust-colored underneath, typically to 4-5" long. Figs are round, 1/2" across, and are produced in pairs at the ends of the branches. Often heavily produced, they start out a yellowish-green and mature to a reddish-purple before they drop. Unlike most other cultivated species here, the ripe figs contain tiny fertile seeds, and trees grown from these seeds will exhibit a certain amount of diversity.

The Rustyleaf Fig grows quickly and easily, often with picturesque multiple trunks and always with attractive foliage. It prefers good drainage and is hardy to the mid-20's°F. Selected forms with green leaves are available, and a creamy-white and green variegated-leaf form is also grown. A small-leaved form that is sometimes sold as *Ficus microphylla* is particularly widespread in San Diego County and was supposedly introduced to horticulture here. It is a very densely foliaged, compact evergreen tree with dark green 3-4" oval leaves that takes well to pruning and has been used as a street tree. Heavy fruit drop and aggressive roots, however, make it a poor choice near paved areas.   **B13,QBG**

Fraxinus uhdei
(FRAK-sin-us YOO-dee-eye)
EVERGREEN ASH
Oleaceae
Mexico and Central America

For many years, the Evergreen Ash was a popular street and shade tree in Southern California because of its fast growth and easy care. In recent times, however, it has fallen into disfavor in many communities because of its aggressive roots and problems (now mostly solved) with an introduced pest called ash whitefly. Particularly if you choose a selected variety, it is still a valuable shade tree for desert areas and difficult sites, but it is not as popular as it once was.

The Evergreen Ash grows quickly (to 25-30' tall in 10 years) to an eventual 40-60' tall. Upright and narrow when young, it takes on a spreading form as it gets older. Its large leaves are divided into 5-9 dark green glossy leaflets, each about 4" long. In the mildest climates, these leaves remain on the tree throughout the winter, but in colder areas the tree is usually leafless for a short time. Flowers are tiny, followed in the late summer and fall by single-seeded winged fruits. The Evergreen Ash is somewhat drought-tolerant but does best with regular watering, and is cold-hardy to 15°F. Selected varieties are better choices than seedling trees because they have more attractive foliage and growth habits.   **QBG**

70

Geijera parviflora
(gye-JER-uh   par-vih-FLOOR-uh)

AUSTRALIAN WILLOW
Rutaceae
Eastern Australia

The Australian Willow is a graceful evergreen tree that is tougher than it looks. Its narrow, drooping 3-6" long leaves give a willow-like effect, but the tree is much more drought-tolerant and tidy than a true willow (to which it is not related). Growing at a moderate rate to 20-30' tall and 20' wide, the Australian Willow is mainly valued as a foliage tree, although it does produce loose clusters of small creamy-white flowers from spring to fall. Its foliage is olive-green and fine-textured, forming a dense, rounded crown atop a smooth light gray trunk that becomes roughened and reddish-brown with age.

The Australian Willow prefers a well-drained soil, but is tolerant of either regular watering or some drought. It needs little pruning, has deep, non-invasive roots, and is a good patio or street tree that is not messy. It is also quite cold-hardy, tolerating temperatures down to at least 20°F.   **B25,QBG**

550 C Ave., Coronado

Ginkgo biloba
(GINK-goe   bye-LOE-buh)

MAIDENHAIR TREE
Gingkoaceae
Eastern China

Now native to just two small areas in China, the Maidenhair Tree is the sole survivor of an ancient group of plants that grew worldwide in prehistoric times. It is virtually identical to trees that lived 200 million years ago, and botanically very different from any other living plant on Earth. Slow-growing and long-lived, it has been cultivated for thousands of years in China, where there are specimens on temple grounds that are over 1000 years old. In California, it is a popular street and garden tree that is valued for its graceful structure and beautiful foliage as well as its toughness.

The Maidenhair Tree grows slowly to 35-50' tall and 20-30' wide, although very old specimens can be larger. It has an angular branching structure when it is young, but becomes more dense as it gets older. Its broad, 1-4" leaves are leathery, light green and fan-shaped, like the shape of maidenhair fern leaflets. This foliage can be spectacular in the fall when it turns bright gold before dropping cleanly, leaving the tree leafless during the winter.

The Maidenhair Tree is very hardy to cold, and will tolerate temperatures below 0°F. It is also remarkably tolerant of heat and smog. It appreciates a deep, well-drained soil, but needs little pruning. Only grafted trees of selected male varieties should be planted to assure the best form, fall color, and lack of fruit production. Seedlings may turn out to be female trees, which when mature produce a heavy crop of nauseatingly stinky fruits which contain edible and pharmaceutically useful seeds.   **B29,Q85**

211 Front St., San Diego

71

South of Alcazar Gardens, Balboa Park

1975 Calle Sinaloa, Vista

Gleditsia triacanthos
(gleh-DITT-see-uh try-uh-KAN-thoce)
HONEY LOCUST
Fabaceae (Leguminosae)
Eastern United States

In its native habitat, the deciduous Honey Locust is a large thorny tree with an abundance of messy seed pods that limit its effectiveness as a garden tree. But over the years, a number of more compact, thornless and seedless selections of this species have been made that have become some of the most popular shade trees throughout the U.S.A. These modern varieties of Honey Locust are fast-growing and completely tolerant of heat and cold, and are particularly useful for creating quick shade in our inland regions that get some winter chill.

Honey Locust selections such as 'Moraine' and 'Shademaster' grow quickly to 35-40' tall and 20-30' wide in full sun with regular watering. Their bright green foliage is composed of fern-like leaves to 10" long that are composed of many 1" long oval leaflets. Although the Honey Locust leafs out fairly late in the spring, it is useful for providing just the right level of filtered shade in the summer that allows for other plants and lawn grasses to grow happily underneath. In the fall, its foliage turns yellow before dropping.

The Honey Locust is fully cold-hardy to below 0°F., and loves summer heat as well as winter cold. Although it is not recommended for the immediate coast, it will grow well in all other San Diego climates. **B22**

Grevillea robusta
(greh-VILL-ee-uh roe-BUS-tuh)
SILK OAK
Proteaceae
Eastern Australia

Completely unrelated to true oaks, the Silk Oak is the largest member of a primarily Australian genus that includes many showy ornamentals for California gardens. It is a tall, fast-growing tree to 50-60' that is pyramidal and upright when young but somewhat broader with age. The Silk Oak has an unusual foliage of deeply divided leaves 6-12" long and up to 6" wide that are dark green above and silvery-gray and silky underneath. Some or all of this foliage may be shed in the spring, when the tree is often spectacularly covered with large 4-6" long golden-orange flower clusters composed of many stamens, held horizontally all along the branches like giant toothbrushes.

The Silk Oak is tolerant of heat, drought, and cold, with young plants hardy to 24°F. and older trees hardy to 16°F. It can succeed even in poor, hard soils if not overwatered, but will also take regular watering as long as drainage is good. Though showy in bloom, the Silk Oak is a big tree that sheds plenty of leaves and can be too messy for some gardeners. In addition, it does have brittle wood that can be damaged in high winds. **QBG**

Harpephyllum caffrum
(har-peh-FILL-um KAFF-rum)
SOUTH AFRICAN WILD PLUM
Anacardiaceae
South Africa

Unrelated to true plums, the South African Wild Plum is a medium-sized evergreen tree from South Africa that is in the same plant family as mango and cashew. It grows fairly quickly to 30' tall and as wide, with a broad dense crown of foliage that casts dense shade underneath it. Its foliage is composed of dark green glossy divided leaves with 2-4" narrow leaflets, with new growth a bright coppery-red. Flowering occurs in August, with clusters of inconspicuous cream to yellow-green flowers, which are followed on some trees by red fruits. These fruits are about the size of an olive, edible but slightly acidic to the taste, and may be used for making jelly.

South African Wild Plum trees are either male or female, and so you must have a female tree to produce fruits, which it will do only if a male tree is nearby to pollinate it. Most people, however, grow the South African Wild Plum simply because it is a fairly well-behaved evergreen tree. Some early training is recommended, as young trees can otherwise tend to be rather awkward in shape, but a well-trained older tree has good character.

The South African Wild Plum is tolerant of most soils and watering schedules. It is hardy to the mid-20's°F., but may suffer some leaf damage with frost. Propagation is by seed, which sprouts readily. **B5,QBG**

578 Ford Ave., Solana Beach

Harpullia pendula
(har-POO-lee-uh PEN-dyoo-luh)
TULIPWOOD
Sapindaceae
Northeastern Australia

The Tulipwood is an elegant evergreen tree that is a member of the same plant family that includes such tropical fruits as litchi and rambutan. Although its fruits are not edible, they are showy and provide color nearly all year long. It grows at a moderate rate to 30' tall here, with young trees fairly upright and narrow and older trees rounded and spreading. It can grow in either full sun or partial shade, and prefers a rich, well-drained soil with regular watering. Its glossy foliage is dense and bright green, with individual compound leaves composed of up to 8 leaflets. Small greenish-yellow flowers are produced in pendant clusters, followed by showy clusters of bright orange seed pods which contain black seeds.

Best in a protected spot, the Tulipwood will tolerate light frost but can be damaged in temperatures below 26°F. It looks best when protected from strong wind. A related species, *Harpullia arborea*, is similar, differing mainly in the size and number of leaflets on its leaves. **B30,QBG**

East side of Federal Bldg., Balboa Park

73

Quail Botanical Gardens

Heteromeles arbutifolia
(heh-terr-AH-meh-leez ahr-byoo-tih-FOE-lee-uh)
CALIFORNIA HOLLY
Rosaceae
California and N. Baja California, Mexico

Although it is unrelated to the true hollies in the genus *Ilex*, our native California Holly is similar in that it produces large clusters of bright red berries that are useful for holiday decorations. Commonly found growing wild in the foothills of Southern California, it is famous as the "holly" that gave Hollywood its name.

The evergreen California Holly is popular and long-lived in cultivation, and makes a good garden plant as long as it is not overwatered in the summer. It is often grown as a large shrub, but may easily be trained as a small multi-trunked tree to 15' tall and wide. The California Holly has a dense foliage of 2-3" long glossy dark green leathery leaves that have toothed margins. It blooms in June and July, with large showy clusters of 1/2" white flowers which are followed in the fall by the equally large clusters of bright red berries.

Also known as Toyon, the California Holly is drought-tolerant and also cold-hardy to 10°F. It is a good wildlife tree, as its berries attract birds. There are selections grown that have yellow berries, and there is also a handsome variety that is native to the California Channel Islands that has very large red berries. **B39,QBG**

2605 Carlsbad Blvd., Carlsbad

Hibiscus rosa-sinensis
(hye-BISS-kuss roe-zuh-sih-NEN-sis)
TROPICAL HIBISCUS
Malvaceae
Horticultural Hybrids

The popular flowering shrubs that we know in cultivation as *Hibiscus rosa-sinensis* are all horticultural hybrids, some of which have been grown since ancient times. After many generations of hybridizing, there are now hundreds of Tropical Hibiscus hybrids grown all over the world, with flowers in an incredible variety of colors and sizes.

Although most of the largest-flowered "show" hybrids are shrubs, there are many taller varieties of Tropical Hibiscus that may be trained as small multi-trunked evergreen trees to 10-15' tall and wide. Large-flowered (5-7" wide) varieties that are best for training as trees include vigorous hybrids such as 'White Wings' (single white), 'Agnes Gault' (single pink, pictured), 'Brilliant' (single red), and 'Kona' (double pink). In addition, there are several smaller-flowered hybrids grown with smaller leaves, tall upright habits, and 3" flowers in white, pink, and red.

The Tropical Hibiscus prefers full sun and well-drained soil, but needs protection from frost. Especially near the coast, plants can bloom throughout the year when watered and fertilized regularly. A troublesome pest called Giant Whitefly can be a real problem here, particularly on plants growing in partial or full shade. Plants that grow in full sun and are fertilized well are generally more resistant to this pest. **B14,QBG**

74

Howea forsteriana
(HOW-ee-uh for-ster-ee-AN-uh)
KENTIA PALM
Arecaceae (Palmae)
Lord Howe Island, Australia

Although it is native to just one tiny South Pacific island, the Kentia Palm is one of the most commonly grown palms in the world. Also called the Paradise Palm, its graceful fronds and tremendous ability to withstand neglect as a potted specimen have made it the most popular palm for indoor decoration since its introduction in the 1850's. Where frosts are not severe, it is a first-class garden and landscape palm that provides a truly tropical look even in less-than-tropical climates.

The Kentia Palm will eventually grow to 30' tall and 10-15' wide here, but because it is a slow grower it stays much smaller than that for many years. It has an elegant foliage of long spreading fronds with drooping dark green leaflets somewhat suggestive of the tropical Coconut Palm (which doesn't grow well here). Mature plants often have showy hanging clusters of 1" orange or red fruit. The Kentia Palm looks good either planted singly or in groups, and since it grows well in either partial or full shade, it is often used as an understory plant beneath tall trees or in shady entryways. Older plants can tolerate full sun, especially along the coast, but do not like hot dry winds. Although foliage can be damaged by frost, mature plants will recover from temperatures as low as 26°F.   **B21,QBG**

6206 Camino de la Costa, La Jolla

Hymenosporum flavum
(hye-men-uh-SPORE-um FLAY-vum)
SWEETSHADE
Pittosporaceae
Eastern Australia

288 Rancheros Dr., San Marcos

Native to the coastal rainforests of Queensland and New South Wales, the Sweetshade is a popular evergreen tree because of its narrow, upright growth habit and sweetly fragrant flowers. With regular watering, it grows at a moderate rate to 25-40' tall, with an open, tiered branching structure and glossy dark green leaves 3-6" long and 1-2" wide. The Sweetshade flowers in spring and early summer, with terminal clusters of 1-2" wide flowers that are cream colored when they open and age to a golden-yellow. To most people, these flowers have a pronounced sweet fragrance of orange-blossom honey, although there are some who notice no fragrance at all.

The Sweetshade prefers a rich, well-drained soil and regular watering. It flowers best in a warm spot away from coastal wind, and will grow in full sun or partial shade. It is fairly cold-tolerant, with mature trees tolerating temperatures as low as 20°F. Because of its narrow, upright habit, the Sweetshade can be particularly useful in confined areas or near tall buildings, and also looks good when planted in groups. Early training by heading back branches is recommended to produce a stronger branching structure and more compact growth.   **B7,QBG**

75

2178 Emerald St., Pacific Beach

Inga affinis
(ING-uh   uh-FIH-nis)
ICE CREAM BEAN
Fabaceae (Leguminosae)
Brazil, Argentina, and Bolivia

The genus *Inga* is a large one, with some 350 species native to tropical and subtropical America. Included here are a number of trees that are grown for the sweet white pulp which surrounds the seeds in their bean-like fruits. This pulp not only looks somewhat like ice cream but also is sometimes used to flavor it, and so both the trees and their fruits are called Ice Cream Bean. Although most types of Ice Cream Bean are too tropical to grow well in the San Diego area, *Inga affinis* is one species that may be successfully grown here in gardens where frosts are not severe.

Our Ice Cream Bean is an evergreen tree to about 25' tall and wide with a fairly dense foliage of large bright green pinnately divided leaves, each with 4-6 pairs of leaflets. It flowers during the warmer months, with clusters of 2" puffy white flowers composed of many stamens. These flowers are followed by rather curious 6" fruits, which are shaped liked large ribbed bean pods and like other parts of the tree are somewhat velvety. When the fruits are ripe, the mildly sweet white pulp inside may be eaten fresh or used for flavoring. The Ice Cream Bean prefers a protected spot with good drainage, regular watering, and does not like frost.   **QBG**

2599 Ridge Rd., Oceanside

Jacaranda mimosifolia
(jak-uh-RON-duh   mih-moe-sih-FOE-lee-uh)
JACARANDA
Bignoniaceae
Western Argentina

Although blue-flowered trees in general are rare in cultivation here, the popular Jacaranda makes up for that almost single-handedly in late spring and early summer, when our streets and gardens come alive with bright clouds of lavender-blue.

Growing fairly quickly to an ultimate height of around 40' with a nearly equal spread, the Jacaranda has a graceful branching structure and a delicate fern-like foliage of 12-24" long divided leaves with many tiny leaflets. This foliage usually drops in mid to late winter in preparation for the large clusters of 2" tubular lavender-blue flowers which typically cover the tree in May and June, but can appear as early as March in some years and last well into summer in others. The flowers are followed by 2" round, flat seed capsules which contain papery seeds.

The Jacaranda is quite tolerant of drought once it is established, but also does fine with regular watering. Although young plants can be tender to frost, mature trees are hardy to around 23°F. Flowering is best in warmer areas away from immediate ocean influence, and in some years trees may rebloom in the fall. A white-flowered selection called 'Alba' is grown as a grafted plant—it has a longer bloom period but fewer flowers at a time and is more tender to cold.   **B8,QBG**

76

Jubaea chilensis
(joo-BEE-uh chi-LEN-sis)

CHILEAN WINE PALM
Arecaceae (Palmae)
Chile

Slow-growing but impressive when mature, the Chilean Wine Palm has the most massive trunk of any palm in the world. Although it takes many years to develop a large specimen, old plants may be as much as 50-60' tall with a distinctive and imposing gray trunk 3-5' in diameter. Individual leaves on mature plants are pinnate and 10-12' long, forming a crown of foliage 20-25' across. On older plants, flower clusters appear among the leaves, and fruits which resemble miniature coconuts may be produced.

The Chilean Wine Palm is unusually hardy to cold, and will tolerate temperatures at least as low as 20°F. even when young. It is also drought-tolerant. This is a palm that requires patience in cultivation because its seed is difficult to germinate and young plants typically take at least 10 years before they begin to develop a trunk, but the prospect of a mature specimen is well worth the wait.

In its native Chile, the Chilean Wine Palm has become rare in the wild because mature plants have been cut down for their sugary sap, which is distilled to make a delicacy known as palm honey, and also used to make palm wine. Wild plants are now protected, however, and reforestation projects are underway.　**B23,QBG**

998 W. Mission Bay Drive, San Diego

Juniperus chinensis 'Torulosa'
(joo-NIH-per-us chi-NEN-sis tor-yoo-LOE-suh)

HOLLYWOOD JUNIPER
Cupressaceae
Horticultural Selection

The junipers are a large and diverse group of cold-hardy evergreens that range in size from low ground covers to medium-sized trees. Valued for their drought resistance and tolerance of adverse conditions, they are known in cultivation primarily through their many horticultural selections. Of the tree-like junipers grown in the San Diego area, certainly the most common is the selection known in California as the Hollywood Juniper.

Although it is often grown as a foundation plant or as a tall hedge, a single specimen of the Hollywood Juniper when mature can take the shape of a multiple-trunked tree to 20-25' tall of interesting character and form. Selected for its twisted, spiraling growth habit and irregular branching structure, the Hollywood Juniper is also valued for its dense dark green foliage and thick trunks with rough brown bark. It is most tolerant of poor soil, drought, heat, and wind, and will take cold to well below 0°F. When trained as a tree, it should not be heavily pruned but instead allowed to develop its own naturally informal shape. The Hollywood Juniper is also known by the name *Juniperus chinensis* 'Kaizuka'.　**B29,QBG**

77

1224 Virginia Way, La Jolla

2026 Lincoln St., Oceanside

North of the Aerospace
Museum, Balboa Park

Juniperus scopulorum
'Tolleson's Blue Weeping'
(joo-NIH-per-us skop-yoo-LOR-um)
WEEPING JUNIPER
Cupressaceae
Horticultural Selection

The Weeping Juniper is one of the many horticultural selections of the Rocky Mountain Juniper, which is native from British Columbia south to Arizona and Texas. It is a small evergreen tree to 20' tall and 15' wide that is grown for its strongly weeping habit and graceful branching structure. It has a fairly dense blue-green foliage and is easy to grow, but should be given adequate water and good, well-drained soil to look its best.

The Weeping Juniper actually comes in two forms, both of which are grown from either cuttings or as grafted plants. 'Tolleson's Blue Weeping' (also known as 'Repandens') has blue-green foliage and 'Tolleson's Green Weeping' has dark green foliage, but are both similar in growth habit and culture. They are both very hardy to cold, tolerating temperatures well below 0°F. They can be slow-growing, especially when young, but for those who want a small tree this can be an advantage. Little pruning is necessary except for basic shaping (they can both be easily trained to almost any size) and both forms make fine container plants as well.

Kigelia africana
(kih-GEHL-ee-uh af-ri-KAN-uh)
SAUSAGE TREE
Bignoniaceae
Tropical Africa

The unusual Sausage Tree gets its common name from its odd woody (inedible) fruits which hang from the tree and look like sausages. But just about everything is unusual about this strange African tree. In cultivation here, the Sausage Tree grows fairly slowly to 20-25' tall, upright at first and then spreading with age. In the absence of frost its foliage is evergreen, consisting of pinnate leaves to 20" long composed of stiff leathery leaflets each 3-8" long and 2-3" wide.

The Sausage Tree blooms on old wood, with the heaviest bloom on older trees in the summer months. The odd 4" funnel-shaped maroon flowers appear in hanging clusters and are scented at night like rotten plums, which attract bat pollinators in their native habitat. Flowers on mature trees are typically followed by 10-12" long hanging fruit here, but if you take the time to pollinate the flowers yourself you can get spectacular "sausages" up to 2' long and up to 6" in diameter.

When established, the Sausage Tree is cold-hardy to around 25°F., but in general it does not like frost. It prefers full sun, well-drained soil, and regular watering, and is sometimes sold under the synonymous name *Kigelia pinnata*. Uncommon in nurseries, it is definitely a curiosity worth looking for.   **B32,QBG**

Koelreuteria bipinnata
(kole-roo-TEER-ee-uh bye-pih-NAY-tuh)

CHINESE FLAME TREE
Sapindaceae
Southwestern China

160 Los Vallecitos Blvd., San Marcos

The Chinese Flame Tree is an easy and fast-growing patio, lawn, or street tree that combines showy color over a long season with excellent cold-hardiness. This small to medium-sized deciduous tree grows to 20-40' tall and wide with a dense, rounded, flat-topped crown and long divided leaves which are composed of many 2-3" long bright green leaflets. In mid to late summer, the tree produces large showy clusters of tiny bright yellow flowers, which are quickly followed by 2" papery lantern-shaped seed pods that turn brilliant shades of salmon, orange, and red and cover the tree. Foliage often turns bright gold before dropping in the fall, and the tree is hardy to 18°F.

Closely resembling the Chinese Flame Tree is *Koelreuteria elegans*, a native of Taiwan which is also known as Flamegold. It has a more rounded crown of glossier foliage and is somewhat more cold-tender, with bright yellow flowers in late summer and salmon-orange seed pods in the fall. A third species is the Goldenrain Tree, *Koelreuteria paniculata*, from China, Korea, and Japan. Although its seed pods are not quite as showy, it is extremely hardy to cold (to below 0°F.) and is a useful small shade tree even in the most difficult climates. **B8,QBG**

Lagerstroemia indica
(lah-gur-STREE-mee-uh IN-dih-kuh)

CRAPE MYRTLE
Lythraceae
China

Van Zanten Park, El Cajon

With its small size, tidy shape, and bright summer flower color, the Crape Myrtle has long been a popular garden, patio, and street tree in our hot inland climates—but it traditionally has been disappointing in areas with ocean influence because of its susceptibility to powdery mildew. In recent years, however, many fine mildew-resistant selections have been introduced, with a number of newer hybrids between the Chinese species *Lagerstroemia indica* and the Japanese species *Lagerstroemia fauriei* that are particularly adaptable in a wide range of climate zones.

Trained as a tree, the Crape Myrtle grows from 15-25' tall with a dense, rounded crown. It gets its common name from the crepe paper-like texture of its frilly 1-2" flowers, which are produced in big 6-12" long showy clusters in the summer and early fall. Depending on the variety grown, flower color varies from white through many startlingly brilliant shades of pink, red, and purple. Dark green foliage of 1-2" oval leaves is deciduous, usually providing bright yellow, orange, or red leaf color in the fall before the leaves drop. The bark of the Crape Myrtle is also exceptionally showy, with colorful patterns of gray, tan, and pink, and plants are very hardy to cold. **B28,QBG**

7231 Monte Vista, La Jolla

1600 Pacific Highway, San Diego

Lagunaria patersonii
(lah-goo-NAIR-ee-uh   pat-er-SOE-nee-eye)
PRIMROSE TREE
Malvaceae
Norfolk Island, Lord Howe Island, and Eastern
Australia

The Primrose Tree is a fairly fast-growing evergreen tree to 30-50' tall and 25-30' wide, with young trees narrow and upright and older ones spreading with age. It is densely covered with 2" long leathery oval leaves that are olive-green above and gray underneath. From late spring to late summer, it produces an abundance of 2" wide funnel-shaped flowers which resemble tiny hibiscus blooms—depending on the individual tree, these may be light pink, rose pink or even reddish-purple with a center column of golden-yellow anthers.

The Primrose Tree also produces 1-2" brown seed pods, which are popular with flower arrangers but unfortunately contain short stiff fibers that can irritate the skin and eyes. Use caution when handling these seed pods, which give the tree its other common name, the Cow Itch Tree. The Primrose Tree prefers full sun and tolerates a wide range of soils and growing conditions, including high heat and even the salty wind of the immediate seacoast. Foliage may be damaged at 25°F., but mature trees are hardy to 20°F. Two cutting-grown selections with superior flower color are 'Princess Rose' with dark rose-pink flowers and 'Royal Purple' with reddish-purple flowers.   **B5,QBG**

Laurus nobilis
(LOR-us   NO-bih-lis)
BAY LAUREL
Lauraceae
Mediterranean Sea Region

Also called Sweet Bay and Grecian Laurel, the Bay Laurel is the source of bay leaves used in cooking and also the tree whose leaves were used by the ancient Greeks to make the "crown of laurel" which honored notable human achievement. Such modern-day terms as "poet laureate," "baccalaureat," and even "resting on your laurels" have come about as a result of the significance of this plant. In the landscape, the Bay Laurel is often clipped as a shrub, but can easily be trained as a small tree.

The Bay Laurel grows slowly to an eventual maximum of 20-30' tall and 15-20' wide, but may easily be kept smaller with occasional pruning. Its dense, rounded crown of foliage is composed of 2-4" long dark green leathery oval leaves that are pleasantly fragrant and are even used in aromatherapy. Clusters of small light-yellow spring flowers are followed by dark purple or black 1/2-1" fruits. The Bay Laurel tolerates a wide range of soils as long as drainage is good, and is hardy to at least 20°F. Its dense foliage takes well to topiary pruning if desired. An improved selection called 'Saratoga' has broader leaves, a more erect growth habit, and is more resistant to an insect pest called laurel psyllid.   **QBG**

Leptospermum laevigatum
(lep-toe-SPUR-mum   lee-vih-GAY-tum)

AUSTRALIAN TEA TREE
Myrtaceae
Southeastern Australia and Tasmania

With its muscular, twisting trunks and delicate foliage, the Australian Tea Tree is one of the most picturesque small trees for the landscape. Native to coastal areas of Australia, it is particularly suited to seashore gardens, where its naturally windswept form fits in so well. It also is a strong grower inland, however, and is tolerant of frost, drought, and alkaline soil.

Although it can be planted as a hedge or windbreak, the Australian Tea Tree should be grown as a single specimen to develop its characteristic form. It grows to 10-20' tall and wide, with older specimens often becoming wider than tall. Its evergreen foliage is composed of gray-green oval leaves to 1" long, and it blooms in spring with many 1/2" white flowers. For best effect, its gnarled grayish trunks and branches should be allowed to spread and develop on their own without severe pruning.

Dwarf forms of the Australian Tea Tree are sold, but these typically grow only as shrubs, as do the various forms of the New Zealand Tea Tree (*Leptospermum scoparium*).   **B3,QBG**

1224 Santa Barbara St., Point Loma

Leptospermum petersonii
(lep-toe-SPUR-mum   pee-ter-SOE-nee-eye)

LEMON-SCENTED TEA TREE
Myrtaceae
Eastern Australia

The Lemon-Scented Tea Tree is a graceful, willowy evergreen that can be most effective when trained as a small weeping tree. Growing to just 10-15' tall, it is useful even in smaller gardens where space is at a premium, and as a bonus it has a pleasant lemony scent to its leaves.

The Lemon-Scented Tea Tree has a weeping, see-through foliage of 1" long, narrow dark green leaves. New leaves and branchlets are an attractive reddish-bronze, and as trees mature, they develop handsome trunks with a flaking grayish-brown bark. Flowering occurs in summer, with many 1/2" white flowers dotting the tree.

The Lemon-Scented Tea Tree is very drought-tolerant, but it also accepts regular watering as long as drainage is good, and can even be grown in a large container as a patio tree. It is very adaptable to the immediate seashore as well as sites farther inland which do not get heavy frost, and is cold-hardy to around 27°F. The leaves and stems of the Lemon-Scented Tea Tree are used in making scented soaps, candles, perfumes, and the dried leaves are used in potpourri. Fresh leaves may be used as a tea substitute, or try adding a few fresh leaves to a pot of brewing tea for a pleasant lemony flavor.   **B25**

Buena Creek Gardens, San Marcos

Mission Hills Park, Mission Hills

Ligustrum lucidum
(lih-GUSS-trum   LOO-sih-dum)
GLOSSY PRIVET
Oleaceae
China and Korea

The evergreen Glossy Privet makes a dense, round-headed small tree that is tolerant of nearly any soil and climate, and so is frequently used as a street tree in tough situations. It grows to 20-30' tall and is usually trained as a single-trunked specimen that may be maintained at almost any size by pruning. Its 4-6" pointed leathery leaves are dark green and glossy. In late spring and early summer, the tree blooms with large feathery clusters of small white flowers with a rather odd scent that many people find disagreeable. These are followed by clusters of small blue-black fruits which are attractive to birds.

The Glossy Privet is tolerant of heat and wind, is cold-hardy to 0°F., and will grow in any type of soil—but it has some drawbacks that are worth noting. Although it can be showy in bloom, its flowers have an unpleasant scent, and many people are allergic to them. Because the heavy crop of fruits produced by a mature tree can be messy and can stain cars and pavement, it is not the best choice for a street or patio tree. In addition, birds tend to distribute its seeds quite effectively, so new plants can readily volunteer around the garden.   **QBG**

18966 Cloudcroft Dr., Poway

Liquidambar styraciflua
(lih-kwid-AM-ber   sty-ruh-SIH-floo-uh)
SWEET GUM
Hamamelidaceae
Eastern U.S., Mexico, and Central America

Because of the absence of very cold temperatures here, coastal San Diego landscapes in particular are not famous for the spectacular color of autumn leaves that most of the country enjoys. There are, however, a number of ornamental trees that do provide showy autumn leaf color in our climate, and the Sweet Gum is one of the most popular of these.

The Sweet Gum grows at a moderate rate to an eventual 60' tall here, with a characteristic pyramidal growth habit. Its 3-7" wide-lobed, maple-like leaves are dark green in spring and summer, turning yellow, orange, red, or purple in the fall before they drop. In winter, a handsome structure of bare branches is accentuated by spiky 1-2" seed pods. The Sweet Gum is native to wet soils and does well in lawns, but it also can be quite drought tolerant. It grows in almost any type of soil and is cold-hardy to below 0°F. Its roots are shallow and aggressive, however, and may in time be a problem near paved areas.

Since seedling Sweet Gum trees are variable and unpredictable, only grafted plants of select varieties of the Sweet Gum should be planted for the best fall show. Different selections have different leaf colors, which allow you to choose the colors you want. All Sweet Gum trees have even better autumn leaf color in inland areas that have colder nighttime temperatures.   **B3,QBG**

Liriodendron tulipifera
(leer-ee-oh-DEN-drun too-lih-PIH-fer-uh)
TULIP TREE
Magnoliaceae
Eastern United States

The majestic Tulip Tree is one of the most beautiful of our country's native trees, and one of the best deciduous trees for Southern California. It grows to 50-80' tall and about half as wide here, with a straight, columnar trunk and a tall, pyramidal crown. The Tulip Tree has a lush foliage of 5" wide bright green maple-like leaves with a unique lyre shape that turn bright yellow in the fall before dropping. In late spring and early summer, mature trees produce unusual 2" tulip-shaped flowers that are greenish-yellow with orange markings at the base—very pretty close-up but not conspicuous on the tree from a distance because they are somewhat hidden in the foliage.

The Tulip Tree grows fairly quickly, likes full sun and regular watering, and is cold-hardy to below 0°F. It does best in a deep, rich, well-drained soil and makes an excellent shade tree in a lawn as long as it is given plenty of room to grow. It has a shallow root system that can make it difficult to garden under. Two selected varieties that are somewhat smaller than the typical species are 'Aureomarginatum', with yellow-edged leaves, and the narrowly columnar 'Arnold', both of which are sold as grafted plants and so will bloom even when young.   **B12**

6059 Cornerstone Court, Sorrento Valley

NW side of park, SeaWorld, San Diego

Livistona australis
(lih-vih-STOE-nuh aw-STRAL-is)
AUSTRALIAN FAN PALM
Arecaceae (Palmae)
Eastern Australia

The Old World fan palms in the genus *Livistona* include a number of excellent species for Southern California gardens. One of the best of these is the Australian Fan Palm (*Livistona australis*). Sometimes called Cabbage Palm, the Australian Fan Palm somewhat resembles our common *Washingtonia* palms but is smaller, slower-growing, and has a more graceful, weeping habit. Tolerant of both heat and cold, it is particularly useful for providing a tropical look in frosty inland areas. The Australian Fan Palm grows slowly to an eventual 40-50' tall, with a dense crown of 3-5' wide glossy green fan-shaped leaves with drooping leaf tips. Planted singly or in groups, it makes an elegant display in the landscape, and may even be grown as a container specimen. It grows well in full sun or partial shade, and is cold-hardy to 22°F.

A related palm with even showier foliage is the Chinese Fan Palm (*Livistona chinensis*) from Taiwan and Japan. Best in part shade or filtered light, it grows slowly to 30' tall with a broad crown of 3-6' wide bright shiny green fan-shaped leaves with dramatically weeping leaf tips. The Chinese Fan Palm likes regular watering, and although quite tropical-looking is cold-hardy to 22° F.   **B23,QBG**

Livistona decipiens

(lih-vih-STOE-nuh dee-SIH-pee-ens)

RIBBON FAN PALM
Arecaceae (Palmae)
Queensland, Australia

The Ribbon Fan Palm is distinctive for its strongly weeping foliage. It is a vigorous, easy-to-grow palm which looks tropical but is cold-hardy enough to succeed in inland gardens. Although it is sometimes confused with the more-common Australian Fan Palm (*Livistona australis*), it is distinguished by its lighter foliage color, more finely-divided leaves, and strongly drooping leaf tips.

The Ribbon Fan Palm grows at a moderate to fast rate to an eventual 40-50' tall, with a rounded crown of 3-5' wide yellowish-green fan-shaped leaves that are divided nearly to the base into many long, narrow hanging segments. It has a ringed brownish trunk up to 1' in diameter that becomes smooth and light gray as the old leaf bases are shed. Flowering occurs in spring, with bright clusters of small yellow flowers in the center of the foliage crown which are followed by small glossy black fruits.

Growing easily in full sun or partial shade, the Ribbon Fan Palm will tolerate full sun even when young. It is fairly drought-tolerant but likes regular watering and fertilizing to look its best. It is tolerant of dry inland heat as well as coastal conditions, and is cold-hardy to 22°F.　　**B23**

1781 Sunrise Dr., Vista

2865 Jefferson St., Carlsbad

Lophostemon confertus

(loh-foe-STEE-mun kun-FUR-tus)

BRISBANE BOX
Myrtaceae
Eastern Australia

Formerly known as *Tristania conferta*, the Brisbane Box has become a popular landscape tree because of its consistently good-looking foliage, fairly fast growth, and tolerance of a wide variety of soils. Although it is a large tree in the wild, in cultivation here it grows to just 30-45' tall and 25' wide, with a manageable growth habit that is narrow and upright on young trees and more spreading on older ones. The dense evergreen foliage of the Brisbane Box is composed of 4-6" long dark green leathery oval leaves, and it also has an ornamental trunk and branches with madrone-like reddish-brown bark that peels to reveal lighter-colored bark beneath. In summer, 3/4" fringed cream-colored flowers appear in clusters, followed by woody seed capsules which resemble those of eucalyptus (to which this tree is related).

The Brisbane Box makes a good street or lawn tree that tolerates a variety of garden conditions. It grows in full sun or partial shade, and appreciates regular watering. It is successful in almost any soil, and is cold-hardy to the mid-20's°F. A showy variegated-leaf form of the Brisbane Box ('Variegata') with leaves boldly marked with bright yellow is also grown, but care must be taken to remove any non-variegated growth as the tree grows to prevent it from reverting to all-green foliage. **B22,QBG**

Lyonothamnus floribundus
ssp. *asplenifolius*
*(lye-ahn-oh-THAM-nus   flohr-ih-BUN-dus
ass-plee-nih-FOE-lee-us)*

FERNLEAF CATALINA IRONWOOD
Rosaceae
California Channel Islands

Native to just four islands off the coast of Southern California, the unusual Catalina Ironwood is represented by two subspecies: the undivided-leaved *floribundus*, which is native to Santa Catalina Island, and the divided-leaved *asplenifolius*, which is native to Santa Rosa, San Clemente, and Santa Cruz islands.

The Fernleaf Catalina Ironwood is a slender evergreen tree that grows at a moderate to fast rate to 20-35' tall and 15' wide. It is distinguished by its fern-like foliage of dark green pinnate leaves that are composed of deeply cut leaflets to 4" long, and also by its shredding reddish-brown bark that peels off in long thin strips. In late spring and early summer, large showy clusters of small white flowers are produced that later turn brown and persist on the tree.

The Fernleaf Catalina Ironwood likes full sun and good drainage, and should not be overwatered in the summer. It tolerates cold down to 23°F. and is especially effective when several plants are planted to make a small grove.   **B18,QBG**

1781 Sunrise Dr., Vista

Macadamia integrifolia
(mak-uh-DAY-mee-uh   in-teg-rih-FOE-lee-uh)

MACADAMIA
Proteaceae
Eastern Australia

Macadamia nuts are a well-known delicacy to many, and are commercially produced in abundance in Hawaii. But Australia is their original home, and they are also successfully grown in Southern California where frosts are not severe. There are actually three types of Macadamia trees grown for their nuts: the Smooth-Shell Macadamia (*M. integrifolia*), the Rough-Shell Macadamia (*M. tetraphylla*), and the hybrids between these two species. All are 25-35' tall evergreen trees with a dense foliage of leathery dark green leaves to 5-12" long. In winter and spring, they produce long hanging cylindrical clusters of white to pale pink flowers, which are followed by 1" round green leathery pods. These pods ripen and split open the following fall and winter to reveal the hard-shelled brown Macadamia nuts, which must be opened with a strong nutcracker to obtain the edible portion inside.

For the best crop of Macadamia nuts, it is best to plant only grafted trees of superior selections such as the hybrid 'Beaumont', which is one of the best varieties for Southern California. Planting more than one variety often increases yields. Macadamia trees prefer a rich, well-drained soil in full sun with regular watering, and are cold-hardy to around 25°F.   **B42,QBG**

1781 Sunrise Dr., Vista

2408 1st. Ave., San Diego

SeaWorld, San Diego

Magnolia grandiflora
(mag-NOE-lee-uh   gran-dih-FLOOR-uh)
SOUTHERN MAGNOLIA
Magnoliaceae
Southeastern United States

The genus *Magnolia* is a big group of over 100 species of trees and shrubs, many of which are cultivated worldwide for their large and often colorful cup-shaped flowers. The most popular magnolia in California is the Southern Magnolia, which is a robust evergreen tree that is native to, and practically emblematic of, the southeastern United States.

The Southern Magnolia is a heavy-set tree that grows to from 20-50' tall here, depending on which of the many varieties of it you grow. It has a rounded crown and a dense foliage of 4-8" long glossy, leathery oval leaves that are dark green above and rusty-colored underneath. From late spring to fall, it produces large, very fragrant 6-12" wide white flowers that are followed by unusual cone-shaped seed pods.

The Southern Magnolia appreciates a rich, well-drained soil with regular watering and fertilizing, and is cold-hardy to around 0°F. It casts dense shade when it gets big and is difficult to garden under because of its surface roots and litter, but is nevertheless loved by many. Although seedling trees are sometimes sold, they may take many years to bloom and are generally inferior to the select grafted varieties available which bloom right away. Two of the most popular and vigorous varieties here are 'Majestic Beauty' and 'Samuel Sommer', both of which grow to 30-40' tall and have very large flowers and leaves. **B3,QBG**

Magnolia grandiflora 'Little Gem'
(mag-NOE-lee-uh   gran-dih-FLOOR-uh)
LITTLE GEM MAGNOLIA
Magnoliaceae
Horticultural Selection

Many gardeners these days have small gardens where a big tree just won't fit. Because of this, there is a significant need for smaller trees—and horticulturists are always looking for smaller-growing varieties of the most popular trees. A good example of this is a dwarf form of the Southern Magnolia called 'Little Gem', which makes a nice evergreen lawn tree even where space is limited.

Unlike most varieties of the Southern Magnolia, 'Little Gem' grows slowly to just 20-25' tall and 10-15' wide. With both leaves and flowers just half the size of most Southern Magnolias, it is a true miniature, and may even be grown in a large pot on a patio. Flowers on 'Little Gem' are 5-6" wide, and its 4" long leaves are glossy dark green above and rust-colored underneath. Culture and blooming habit are the same as other Southern Magnolias, and because it is grown as a grafted plant, it blooms well even as a young tree.

Other smaller-growing grafted Southern Magnolia varieties with full-sized leaves and flowers include 'St. Mary', which grows to around 20' tall with a heavy production of 8-10" wide flowers, and 'Victoria', which grows to 20' tall and is exceptionally hardy to cold. **B13**

86

Magnolia x *soulangiana*
(mag-NOE-lee-uh soo-lan-gee-AN-uh)
SAUCER MAGNOLIA
Magnoliaceae
Horticultural Hybrids

Although there are many kinds of deciduous magnolias that may be grown in Southern California, they often perform poorly because of our hot, dry air, warm winters, and alkaline soil and irrigation water. When well-sited, however, the Saucer Magnolia can be a spectacular small tree even here. Often called Tulip Tree because of the resemblance of its flowers to oversized tulip flowers, the Saucer Magnolia is actually a group of hybrids involving the Chinese species *M. denudata* and *M. liliiflora*.

Although it may be grown as a large shrub, the Saucer Magnolia can be easily trained into a multi-stemmed tree, usually to around 15' tall and wide here. In late winter and early spring, it is spectacular in bloom, when its bare branches are covered with large fragrant cup-shaped flowers. Depending on the variety grown, flowers may be white, pink, or purplish red and from 5-10" wide. Summer foliage is medium green, with soft, pointed oval leaves to 5-9" long that may suffer from leaf burn in hot, dry conditions.

946 Heather Dr., Vista

The Saucer Magnolia needs a rich, well-drained slightly acid soil with plenty of organic matter and regular watering and fertilizing. It will grow in full sun or partial shade and is cold-hardy to 0°F., but needs protection from hot, dry winds. There are many showy varieties available, so choose plants in bloom to get the color and flower form you want. **B29**

3689 Texas St., North Park

Mangifera indica
(mang-IH-fur-uh IN-dih-kuh)
MANGO
Anacardiaceae
Tropical Asia

Known as the "king of fruits," the Mango is grown in tropical climates throughout the world, where it is a large tree that produces heavily. It also can be grown in the mildest climates of Southern California, however, even though our Mango trees never get as big as they do in the tropics. There are many varieties of Mango, and it pays to grow only the best grafted varieties that are recommended for our local climate if you want the best-tasting fruit.

In cultivation here, the Mango is a small evergreen tree that grows fairly slowly to 15-25' tall and wide in warm, frost-free locations. In cooler sites or with any frost, it is likely to remain shrubby and may not get as large. The Mango has 8-16" long glossy leaves that are coppery red when young and age to dark green. Long clusters of small yellow to reddish flowers are produced from spring into summer that are followed by large oval fruits, with trees tending to bear more heavily in alternate years. Mango fruits are ready to harvest 4-5 months after bloom, and taste best if they are allowed to fully ripen on the tree. Trees appreciate full sun, good drainage, and regular watering and fertilizing, and do not like frost or cool winds. **B14,QBG**

1800 Torrey Pines Rd., La Jolla

Markhamia lutea
(mark-HAM-ee-uh LOO-tee-uh)
AFRICAN TRUMPET TREE
Bignoniaceae
Tropical Africa

The tropical-looking African Trumpet Tree is a wonderful addition to Southern California gardens and landscapes where frosts are not severe. Fast-growing and slender when young, it slows conveniently as it matures to an upright tree of 20-30' tall and about half as wide. It has a handsome glossy-green foliage of pinnately divided leaves to 20" long that are composed of pointed oval leaflets to 8" long and 2" wide. In summer and fall, it blooms with showy terminal clusters of 2" trumpet-shaped flowers that are bright yellow with red markings in the throats. After flowering, the tree produces clusters of twisting seed pods up to 20" long which split open to shed papery seeds.

The African Trumpet Tree grows best in rich, well-drained soil in either full sun or partial shade, with regular watering and fertilizing. It loves heat and humidity and blooms best when protected from cool, foggy winds. Although it is basically evergreen, it may lose its leaves in a frost; mature trees, however, will recover from temperatures as low as 26°F.

Because of its narrow habit, the African Trumpet Tree is gaining favor as a street tree in frost-free areas. It is often sold under the name *Markhamia hildebrandtii*, and there is also a related tree that has been grown as *Markhamia platycalyx*, but both are now included within the species *Markhamia lutea*.   **B30,QBG**

Seaport Village, San Diego

Melaleuca armillaris
(meh-luh-LOO-kuh ahr-mih-LAIR-iss)
WEEPING MELALEUCA
Myrtaceae
Southeastern Australia

The genus *Melaleuca* contains over 200 species of evergreen shrubs and trees, nearly all of which are native to Australia. They are closely related to the "bottlebrushes" in the genus *Callistemon*, and like them have showy clusters of flowers that are composed of many stamens. Melaleucas are in general very rugged plants that are easy to grow and tolerant of a variety of garden conditions, including the immediate seacoast.

The Weeping Melaleuca is a particularly tough and adaptable species that may either be grown as a shrub or trained as a tree. It grows quickly to 15-25' tall and wide, but may be kept smaller with occasional pruning. It naturally develops a spreading, picturesque branching structure which is accentuated by its gracefully drooping branches, evergreen foliage composed of 1" light green needle-like leaves, and an ornamental grayish bark which peels off in strips near the base of the trunk. From spring through fall, it produces 1-3" long fluffy white flower clusters. The Weeping Melaleuca likes full sun, is tolerant of most soils and watering schedules, and is hardy to around 18°F. It is particularly useful in areas that get strong ocean winds.   **B43**

Melaleuca linariifolia
(meh-luh-LOO-kuh lih-nair-ee-ih-FOE-lee-uh)
SNOW IN SUMMER
Myrtaceae
Eastern Australia

The fanciful common name for this Australian tree might seem a bit farfetched, but when it blooms in May and June it really does look like the tree is covered with newly fallen snow. Even out of bloom, however, the Snow In Summer is an attractive evergreen tree with graceful foliage and handsome form, plus the bonus of ornamental white papery bark.

Upright and willowy when young, the Snow In Summer grows fairly quickly into a round-headed small tree 20-30' tall and 20-25' wide. It has a dense foliage of narrow 1" long bright green to bluish-green leaves and a strong trunk with thick white spongy bark that peels off in papery sheets. In late spring and early summer it erupts into showy bloom with fluffy spikes of small white flowers that cover the tree.

The Snow In Summer is tolerant of drought, heat, poor soil, salty air, and cold temperatures into the low 20's°F. It also grows well with regular watering, and may be used as a lawn or street tree, with young trees requiring staking until their trunks thicken up. The narrow leaves and distinctive bark of this tree give it its other common name, Flaxleaf Paperbark. **B14,QBG**

418 Buena Creek Rd., San Marcos

Melaleuca nesophila
(meh-luh-LOO-kuh neh-SAH-fill-uh)
PINK MELALEUCA
Myrtaceae
Western Australia

The Pink Melaleuca is the most familiar of the many showy Western Australian melaleucas that may be grown either as small trees or large shrubs. If left unpruned, it grows quickly to an eventual 15-20' tall and wide with gnarled, picturesque trunks and an informal shape. Its evergreen foliage is composed of light green to gray-green leathery oval leaves to 1" long, and it has a thick papery cream-colored bark. The Pink Melaleuca blooms heaviest in spring and early summer, with some bloom occurring throughout the year. Its colorful 1" round flower clusters are produced at the ends of the branches, opening bright pink and fading to white with yellow tips.

The Pink Melaleuca is very drought-tolerant, but will also grow well with regular watering. It is tolerant of poor soils, desert heat, ocean wind, and salt spray, and is cold-hardy to around 25°F. Occasional pruning will control it at nearly any size, but it looks best when allowed to grow naturally. Other melaleucas of similar culture that can be trained as small trees include the lilac-flowered *Melaleuca decussata*, the red-flowered *Melaleuca elliptica*, the cream-flowered *Melaleuca ericifolia*, and the gray-leaved *Melaleuca incana*. **B13,QBG**

2045 Pacific St., Oceanside

Melaleuca quinquenervia
(meh-luh-LOO-kuh   kwin-kweh-NUR-vee-uh)
PAPERBARK TREE
Myrtaceae
E. Australia, New Guinea, and New Caledonia

Because of its ability to tolerate swampy and saline soils, the evergreen Paperbark Tree is widely cultivated in tropical and subtropical climates throughout the world. Although it has become a much-maligned weedy pest in some areas such as southern Florida, it is not troublesome here in California, where it is a popular landscape tree.

Although it can be larger in the tropics, the Paperbark Tree grows to 20-40' tall and 15-25' wide here, with an upright growth habit that is well-suited for use in narrow parking strips and alongside tall buildings. Its prominent trunk has a distinctive thick, spongy, light brown to whitish bark which peels off in sheets. Aromatic foliage is composed of stiff 2-4" long narrow, oval, gray-green leaves that are covered with silky hairs when young and turn purple in a light frost. In summer and fall, trees produce 2-3" long clusters of fragrant creamy-white flowers along the branchlets, giving a bottlebrush-like appearance.

The Paperbark Tree prefers light soils and regular watering but is also very tolerant of poor soil, drought, and wind, including seashore conditions. It is cold-hardy to around 25°F. It has been confused with and is sometimes sold as *Melaleuca leucadendra*, a related but larger species.   **QBG**

111 Alder St., Coronado

Organ Pavilion, Balboa Park

Melaleuca styphelioides
(meh-luh-LOO-kuh   stye-fell-ee-OY-deez)
PRICKLY PAPERBARK
Myrtaceae
Eastern Australia

The Prickly Paperbark is an attractive evergreen tree that tolerates a wide range of adverse conditions. Native to coastal swamps in eastern Australia, it is long-lived in cultivation and makes a good lawn tree that is tolerant of nearly any kind of soil. It is also successfully used as a street tree, and is quite tolerant of smog.

The Prickly Paperbark grows at a moderate to fast rate to 20-40' tall and 10-20' wide, with an upright, fairly narrow habit and gracefully weeping branchlets. It has a thick, spongy gray to brown bark that peels off in papery layers, and dense, dark green foliage composed of 1/2" prickly leaves that are sometimes twisted. Flowering is showy in spring and early summer, with many 1-2" long fluffy clusters of creamy white flowers at the ends of the branchlets.

The Prickly Paperbark grows well in both inland and coastal areas, including the immediate seacoast, and is cold-hardy to around 22°F. It likes full sun, and although it will tolerate some drought, it does best with regular watering and actually prefers heavy, wet soil.   **B13,QBG**

90

Melia azedarach
(MEE-lee-uh a-ZEH-duh-rak)
CHINABERRY
Meliaceae
India and China to Australia

The rugged Chinaberry is grown throughout the world for its medicinal properties, timber, and bead-like fruits as well as for its flowers and foliage. This is a fast-growing, tremendously durable deciduous tree that has the ability to thrive and reproduce itself without any help at all, so much so that many of the trees you'll see in San Diego County have likely been planted by birds, not people.

The Chinaberry grows from 25-50' tall and wide, with a rich green summer foliage of 1-3' long divided leaves composed of many 1-2" long toothed leaflets. It blooms in spring with clusters of fragrant 3/4" pale lilac flowers, which are followed by clusters of hard berry-like yellow fruits about 1/2" wide that are poisonous to us but not to birds. Following a sudden cold snap, its bright golden-yellow fall leaf color can be especially showy, and the tree is further ornamented by the fruit clusters that remain on the tree after the leaves fall.

Although it is too coarse for many gardens and can self-sow profusely, the Chinaberry withstands great extremes of heat, drought, poor soil, and cold, and so can be a useful summer shade tree in difficult situations.

319 W. 5th St., Escondido

Meryta sinclairii
(MAIR-ih-tuh sin-CLARE-ee-eye)
PUKA
Araliaceae
New Zealand

Native only to the tiny Three Kings and Hen and Chicken Islands off the coast of northern New Zealand, the unusual and dramatic Puka is a handsome evergreen for tropical effects. Slow-growing and shrubby when young, it in time becomes a 20' multi-stemmed tree of great beauty. Its main feature is its large, glossy, heavily veined oval leaves that grow to over 1 foot long and densely cover the tree. Flowering on mature plants occurs in summer and consists of large branching clusters of tiny greenish flowers which are followed by black berry-like fruit.

Happiest in coastal gardens, the Puka needs a rich, well-drained soil, regular watering and fertilizing, and protection from frost and strong sun to look its best. It actually prefers partial to full shade, and can make a good-looking tropical background underneath taller trees or in shady entryways. A beautiful variegated-leaf form with leaves boldly splashed with bright yellow is popular in New Zealand but uncommon in California. **B35,QBG**

Casa del Prado Theater, Balboa Park

91

East side of Presidio Park

Metasequoia glyptostroboides
(meh-tuh-seh-KOY-uh   glip-toe-stroe-BOY-deez)

DAWN REDWOOD
Taxodiaceae
Central China

As known from fossil records, the genus *Metasequoia* was an ancient group of conifers that flourished over 200 million years ago. It was always assumed that these trees were long-extinct— until a living tree first noticed by a Chinese botanist in a remote region of central China in 1941 was determined to be the same species as the ancient fossils. More trees were soon discovered, seed was collected and grown, and before long the Dawn Redwood became famous as a "living fossil" that today is enjoyed in gardens throughout the world.

The deciduous Dawn Redwood looks somewhat like its American relative the Bald Cypress (*Taxodium distichum*), from which it differs mainly in having opposite, not alternate, leaves. It is a tall, pyramidal tree that grows at a moderate rate to an eventual 50-80' tall and 20' wide, with a strong, straight trunk that has a textured grayish-brown bark. The delicate foliage of the Dawn Redwood is bright yellow-green when it emerges in the spring and light green in the summer, turning yellow and light bronze before dropping in the fall. Trees also produce small brown cones similar to those of redwood trees. The Dawn Redwood needs regular watering and protection from hot, dry winds, and is completely cold-hardy, to below 0°F.   **B7,QBG**

L'Auberge Hotel,1540 Camino Del Mar, Del Mar

Metrosideros excelsa
(meh-troe-SIH-dur-ose   ek-SELL-suh)

NEW ZEALAND CHRISTMAS TREE
Myrtaceae
New Zealand

The seasons are reversed in the Southern Hemisphere, where Christmas marks the beginning of summer, not winter. That's why the summer-flowering New Zealand Christmas Tree is in full bloom for Christmas in its native land. Here in San Diego, it blooms from May to July, and like many New Zealand natives is especially at home in coastal gardens.

The New Zealand Christmas Tree is a shrubby, round-headed evergreen that grows at a slow to moderate rate to 30' tall and wide. Its dense foliage is composed of 2-4" long leathery gray-green oval leaves. It is showy in bloom, when big, dense clusters of dark red bottlebrush-like flowers open from whitish clusters of flower buds and cover the tree. Although it will bloom inland, the best flowering occurs on trees growing near the coast and in full sun.

The New Zealand Christmas Tree is frost-tender but is very tolerant of coastal winds and salt spray and will also tolerate some drought. A number of superior cutting-grown selections have been developed in New Zealand and are sometimes available here, including varieties with orange-red, pink, and yellow flowers. There is also a variegated selection called 'Goldfinger' that has colorful leaves with yellow centers.   **B30,QBG**

Michelia champaca
(mih-KELL-ee-uh   cham-PAK-uh)
CHAMPAK
Magnoliaceae
Eastern Himalayas

Native to the foothills of the eastern Himalayas, the Champak has been grown for centuries around Hindu temples for its sweetly scented flowers which are used to make perfume. Although it grows larger in its native land, in Southern California it is a shrubby tree to around 20' tall and 10-15' wide. The Champak is evergreen, with a handsome tropical-looking foliage composed of 10" long light green glossy leaves. Its main blooming season here is in the summer, when it produces many 3" fragrant star-shaped flowers with up to 20 segments each. Although there are a number of different color forms grown in India, most trees sold here are seedlings, which typically have orange-yellow flowers and bloom more profusely as the tree matures.

The Champak is best in a frost-free site with protection from strong sun and wind, and thrives in the extra humidity of coastal gardens. It grows in full sun or partial shade, and appreciates a rich soil and regular watering and fertilizing. Of similar culture and also well worth growing is a hybrid of the champak called Pak-lan (*Michelia* x *alba*). The Pak-lan has 3" starry white flowers that are very fragrant and are produced throughout the year. Best in partial shade with no frost, it is usually grown as a grafted plant.   **B30,QBG**

41 I St., Chula Vista

Michelia doltsopa
(mih-KELL-ee-uh   dolt-SOE-puh)
WONG-LAN
Magnoliaceae
Western China, Nepal, and Tibet

With its large, fragrant white flowers and lush evergreen foliage, the beautiful Wong-lan is often mistaken for a true magnolia. Like all michelias, however, it bears its flowers along its branches in the axils of the leaves and not just at the tips of the branches as magnolias do.

The Wong-lan grows slowly here to 25' tall and about half as wide, with glossy, leathery dark green leaves to 9" long and 4" wide. It blooms in mid-winter with 5-7" wide sweetly fragrant magnolia-like white flowers that open from velvety brown buds. Because it is usually sold as a grafted tree, it blooms well even as a young plant, but older trees typically flower even more abundantly and for a longer period of time.

The Wong-lan needs a rich, well-drained soil and regular watering and feeding to look its best. It also needs protection from hot sun and dry winds, growing well in full sun along the coast but probably best in a little shade farther inland. It is cold-hardy to around 25°F., although cold weather may cause young trees to defoliate somewhat just prior to bloom. The most common form of the Wong-lan sold in Southern California has large saucer-shaped flowers with wide petal-like segments. Equally impressive is another selection called 'Silver Cloud' that has more star-shaped flowers with narrower segments.   **B30**

Across from Shamu, SeaWorld, San Diego

93

Montanoa guatemalensis
(mon-tan-OH-uh gwah-teh-mah-LEN-sis)
DAISY TREE
Asteraceae (Compositae)
Central America

Although the sight of "daisies" on a tree is not a common one in Southern California, a number of Central American natives in the genus *Montanoa* are grown here that have daisy-like flowers and attain tree-like proportions. However large, most of these are quite shrubby, typically with a thicket of basal stems that does not train easily into a traditional tree shape. There is one species, however, that can rightfully be called the Daisy Tree because it can be trained as a good-looking multi-trunked small tree, and this species is *Montanoa guatemalensis*.

The Daisy Tree grows fairly quickly to a height of 15-20' with a spread of 10-15'. It has a dense evergreen foliage of 4-8" long light green fuzzy leaves. It blooms in the winter with large clusters of 2" white daisies with yellow centers that cover the tree. Peak bloom on the Daisy Tree often comes right in time for Christmas in Southern California, and it can be one of our showiest trees at that time of year.

The Daisy Tree appreciates a rich, well-drained soil with regular watering, and grows in full sun or partial shade. It should be protected from strong winds and heavy frost, but can survive temperatures as low as 25°F.   **QBG**

Quail Botanical Gardens

745 7th Ave., W. Escondido

Morus alba
(MORE-us AL-buh)
WHITE MULBERRY
Moraceae
China

In China, the White Mulberry is used for many purposes, most importantly as the food tree for silkworms on silk plantations. Here in Southern California, it is a fast-growing deciduous shade tree that is extremely tolerant of tough conditions and grows easily in any climate from desert to mountain to seashore. It grows 30-50' tall and wide, with a dense crown of foliage composed of 6" long bright green lobed leaves. The spring flowers of the White Mulberry are inconspicuous, but they are followed on female trees by fruits that resemble miniature blackberries and are attractive to birds. Male trees do not produce fruit, but they do produce prodigious amounts of pollen in the spring which unfortunately can spell misery for allergy sufferers.

The White Mulberry is tolerant of poor soil and great extremes of heat and cold, and its main virtue is its ability to withstand adversity. It does have heavy surface roots, and mature trees are difficult to garden under. Because its fruits stain pavement and clothing, cutting-grown male trees that do not produce fruit are the most popular varieties for home gardens. These include 'Stribling', which has maple-like leaves and 'Chaparral', which has a weeping habit and deeply cut dark green leaves. For mulberries you can eat, a related species called the Black Mulberry (*Morus nigra*) is a similar but somewhat smaller tree whose selections produce tasty fruit.

94

Myoporum laetum
(mye-AH-por-um LAY-tum)

MYOPORUM
Myoporaceae
New Zealand

Dusty Rhodes Park, Point Loma

The Myoporum is a fast-growing evergreen shrub which can easily be trained to tree form. When grown as a tree, it looks best with multiple trunks and can grow as much as 25' tall by 20' wide, although it may be kept smaller with occasional pruning. The Myoporum forms a dense crown of 3-4" shiny dark green leaves. In summer, it produces small white flowers with purple markings that are attractive at close range, followed by colorful reddish-purple fruits that are attractive to birds.

The Myoporum is hardy to 25°F., and is adaptable to inland areas that do not get heavy frosts. It is most useful, however, as a seaside tree, where it will tolerate even the most challenging of coastal conditions. This is a tree that is tolerant of strong ocean winds and also sandy coastal soils, and can get by with only moderate watering. It is often the first line of defense when wind protection is desired in beachside gardens. Unfortunately, it can reseed itself and become weedy in wild areas, so caution may be advised when considering it. **QBG**

Myrtus communis
(MERR-tuss kuh-MYOO-niss)

COMMON MYRTLE
Myrtaceae
Mediterranean Sea Region

165 Pala Vista Dr., Vista

The aromatic fragrance of the Common Myrtle is legendary, and it is a plant that has been used for centuries in Europe for scent-making, woodworking, leather tanning, and also medicinally. Although frequently thought of as a shrub, it can, with age, be trained as an attractive small multi-trunked tree. The Common Myrtle is of course a mainstay in herb gardens, but also is a good addition to any Mediterranean-style garden, where it blends well with other drought-tolerant plants and can be an attractive centerpiece tree even where space is limited.

The Common Myrtle grows at a moderate rate to an eventual 10-15' tall and wide, and can easily be pruned up as it grows to reveal its handsome branching structure. Its evergreen foliage is dense and bright green, and is composed of 1-2" long pointed oval leaves which are pleasantly fragrant. Also fragrant are its 3/4" wide sweetly-scented white flowers which appear in summer and are followed by aromatic 1/2" bluish-black berries.

The Common Myrtle grows easily in full sun or partial shade, and tolerates a wide variety of soils as long as drainage is good. It thrives with regular watering, but is also drought-tolerant, and is cold-hardy to around 15°F. Besides the typical green-leaved form, there is also a beautiful variegated-leaf variety ('Variegata') that has leaves broadly edged in white and may also be trained as a small tree. Other, smaller-growing varieties of the Common Myrtle are grown, but only the larger varieties grow big enough to be trained as trees. **B8**

Nerium oleander

(NAIR-ee-um oh-lee-AN-dur)

OLEANDER

Apocynaceae
Mediterranean Sea Region to China and Japan

The evergreen Oleander is cultivated throughout the world for its large, colorful flowers. Although there is only one species of Oleander, there are over 400 named cultivars of it that range from dwarf to tall and have either single or double flowers in a wide variety of colors. The Oleander is most commonly grown as a shrub, but the taller varieties are frequently trained as either single or multiple-trunked small trees.

Trained as a tree, the Oleander has a dense, rounded crown of foliage composed of narrow, dark green leathery leaves 8-12" long. From late spring through fall, it bears showy clusters of 2-3" wide flowers in colors ranging from white to pink, salmon, and red. The largest, most vigorous variety grown in California is 'Sister Agnes', which has single pure white flowers and can reach 20' tall. There are also single-pink and single-red flowered varieties that can be trained as 10-15' trees, plus many other varieties that grow somewhat smaller.

The Oleander is a tough plant that needs little water once established but can take regular watering as long as drainage is good. It loves full sun and heat, and will tolerate cold to around 20°F. Unfortunately, a fatal bacterial disease called leaf scorch has attacked Oleanders in some areas, and so far there is no known cure. It is very important to note that all parts of the Oleander plant are extremely poisonous, and so caution is advised when considering this plant.   **B29,QBG**

1718 San Luiz Rey Ave., Coronado

Plaza Camino Real, Carlsbad

Olea europea

(OH-lee-uh yoo-ROE-pee-uh)

OLIVE

Oleaceae
Mediterranean Sea Region

Cultivated since ancient times both for its fleshy fruit and the oil within it, the Olive is synonymous with the Mediterranean Sea Region and its cuisines. In California, it was first introduced into the early Mission gardens and later became an important agricultural crop. Because even fully mature Olive trees can be easily moved, the Olive has in more recent times also become a popular landscape tree in situations where a large, older tree is immediately desired.

The Olive is an evergreen tree with 3" long gray-green willow-like leaves that develops a gnarled, picturesque trunk and branching structure as it matures. It blooms in spring, with clusters of inconspicuous flowers that unfortunately have highly allergenic pollen. Many landscape trees are commercial fruiting varieties which have been transplanted from their original groves—these grow to 25-30' tall and wide and bear 1-2" dark green oval fruit in the summer that ripens to black late in the year. Without processing, however, ripe olives are inedible, and they can be messy when they drop. For this reason, a number of varieties are sold that produce little or no fruit. The Olive tolerates heat and drought, and is cold-hardy to 15°F.   **B27,Q121**

7242 Olivetas Ave., La Jolla

Pandanus tectorius
(pan-DAN-us   tek-TORR-ee-us)
SCREW PINE
Pandanaceae
Western Pacific Ocean Region

From northeastern Australia to Hawaii, the unusual Screw Pine is a familiar sight along tropical shores throughout the western Pacific Ocean region. Here in Southern California, it thrives only in the mildest frost-free gardens, and is happiest in sandy soils along the immediate coast.

Completely unrelated to the true pines in the genus *Pinus*, the evergreen Screw Pine gets its common name from its large pineapple-like fruits and also from the spiral arrangement of its 3' long spiny leaves, which are clustered at the ends of its thick, spreading branches. Also distinctive is its heavy gray trunk, which is supported at the base by thick aerial roots that in the wild help to support the tree in swampy or sandy soils and strong winds. Plants of the Screw Pine may be either male or female, with both male and female trees producing creamy white clusters of tiny flowers. If a pollinating male is present, female trees can produce large orange pineapple-like fruits which are edible when fully ripe.

Although it grows more vigorously in the tropics, the Screw Pine grows fairly slowly here to an eventual 20-25' tall. It likes full sun, regular watering and fertilizing, and must have a well-drained soil. The Screw Pine loves humidity but is intolerant of frost, and is very much at home near the ocean, where it can even grow in beach sand. A widespread form of this species is sometimes listed as *Pandanus odoratissimus*.   **QBG**

258 Kolmar Street, La Jolla

Parkinsonia aculeata
(par-kin-SOE-nee-uh   uh-kew-lee-AY-tuh)
MEXICAN PALO VERDE
Fabaceae (Leguminosae)
Tropical America

Drought and heat tolerant in the extreme, the Mexican Palo Verde is cultivated in many countries throughout the world and has naturalized in many areas, including San Diego County. It grows quickly to 20-30' tall and wide, with a somewhat spiny "see-through" foliage and a picturesque form. Its long compound leaves have many tiny leaflets which are quickly shed in either drought or cold. Many 1/2" wide fragrant yellow flowers appear in loose clusters in spring, with some bloom occurring at other times of the year as well, and the flowers are followed by tan seed pods.

The Mexican Palo Verde likes full sun and is cold-hardy to at least 15°F. It requires little attention and little water once established. Because of its lightweight foliage, it is possible to grow many other drought-tolerant plants underneath it, and it can be a beautiful centerpiece tree in a cactus and succulent garden. Two related trees formerly in the genus *Cercidium* that are of similar culture are the Blue Palo Verde (*Parkinsonia floridum*) and a new hybrid called *Parkinsonia* 'Desert Museum', which is a particularly good small tree for desert gardens.   **B26,Q123**

Desert Gardens, Balboa Park

837 W. 8th Ave., Escondido

Paulownia kawakamii
(paw-LOW-nee-uh   kow-uh-KAH-mee-eye)
SAPPHIRE DRAGON TREE
Scrophulariaceae
Southern China and Taiwan

The remarkable trees in the genus *Paulownia* have been grown for centuries in China, where their timber is highly prized for making fine furniture and musical instruments. Deciduous and fast-growing, they are often farmed together with food crops that thrive in their summer shade. Paulownias are also beautiful flowering trees, and over the years many hybrids and selections have been made for use as ornamentals.

The Sapphire Dragon Tree is a selected form or hybrid of *Paulownia kawakamii* that is renowned for its extremely fast growth and extravagant bloom. In as little as a few years, it can attain its mature size of 25-35' tall and wide. From spring through fall, it has a dense foliage of big, fuzzy heart-shaped leaves 7-12" long and 5-11" across. Its main blooming season is just before the leaves appear in spring, when the entire tree is covered with tall upright clusters of 3" lilac-blue flowers that look like giant foxglove blooms. Sometimes, trees will bloom again in the fall here.

The Sapphire Dragon Tree likes a well-drained soil in full sun. It is deep-rooted as long as it is watered deeply and thoroughly, but shallow watering only can result in heavy surface roots that are prone to suckering. This is a tree that is unusually tolerant of climate extremes, growing mightily in the hottest heat and also withstanding cold down to 0°F.   **B3,QBG**

Persea americana
(PER-see-uh   uh-meh-rih-KAN-uh)
AVOCADO
Lauraceae
Central America

1757 Warmlands Ave., Vista

For over 10,000 years, the Avocado has been cultivated in its native Central America for its nutritious, high-energy fruit. But it was not until 100 years ago that Californians began to grow this evergreen tree with seeds imported from Mexico. Today, the Avocado is much-grown and much-loved in San Diego County, where it is an important commercial crop and a big part of our local economy.

The Avocado is an evergreen tree that grows at a moderate rate to 30-40' tall with an equal or greater spread. It has 4-6" long oval leaves which are dark green above and paler beneath. Flowering occurs in late winter to early spring with terminal clusters of small yellow-green flowers, which are followed by the fruits that ripen at various times of the year depending on the variety grown.

Avocado trees like full sun, good drainage, and regular watering. Although they are cold-hardy to 24°F., temperatures much below freezing when trees are blooming can prevent fruiting. There are a number of fine varieties of Avocado that may be of interest to the home gardener, including but not limited to the commercial 'Hass' (black, pebbly skin) and 'Fuerte' (smooth, green skin).   **QBG**

Phoenix canariensis
(FEE-niks   kuh-nair-ee-EN-sis)
CANARY ISLAND DATE PALM
Arecaceae (Palmae)
Canary Islands

Although originally native to just a few small islands in the eastern Atlantic Ocean, the Canary Island Date Palm is now grown throughout the world, and is especially valued for both its size and its cold-hardiness. In San Diego County, it is the most massive of our commonly grown palms, and many large old specimens are familiar elements in our landscape. Unfortunately, however, a palm disease has in recent times been responsible for the death and removal of some of our finest coastal specimens.

The Canary Island Date Palm is a massive palm to 60-70' tall that grows with a trunk diameter of 3' and a 30' wide crown of gracefully arching dark green leaves. Before they form much of a trunk, young plants tend to look like giant pineapples, and sometimes mature palms are pruned to look like giant pineapples on tall thick stems. Large clusters of golden-yellow fruits can be showy, especially in inland regions.

The Canary Island Date Palm appreciates good drainage and is tolerant of both interior heat and seacoast conditions. It is also cold-hardy to 20°F. Because it is easily transplanted even as a mature specimen, it is often used in commercial landscapes when a big palm is immediately desired. Not for small gardens, it definitely needs plenty of room to grow.   **B21,QBG**

Phoenix dactylifera
(FEE-niks   dak-tih-LIH-fer-uh)
DATE PALM
Arecaceae (Palmae)
Northern Africa and Arabia

The Date Palm is one of the world's oldest food crops, having been cultivated for nearly 6000 years in the Middle East. Within the past century, plantations of the Date Palm were established in the Southern California desert area of Indio, where you can still see their sweet fruit grown and harvested. In recent times, however, a new use for the Date Palm has become established in commercial landscapes here. Because even large specimens are easily transplanted, big mature Date Palms are being moved from the desert plantations and planted around newly built shopping centers, giving the appearance of an established landscape nearly overnight.

The Date Palm can grow as much as 80' tall, with a 20-30' wide crown of stiff gray-green leaves. Naturally multi-trunked, its basal stems are often removed to make a single-trunked tree. This palm is tolerant of both desert and seashore conditions, and is cold-hardy to 15°F. Many selected varieties of the Date Palm are grown commercially for their sweet edible fruit, with the most common being 'Deglet Noor'. However, a desert climate and hand-pollination are necessary for fruit production.   **B37,QBG**

99

Hotel del Coronado, Coronado

5690 Cancha de Golf, Rancho Santa Fe

Phoenix reclinata
(FEE-niks   reh-klih-NAY-tuh)
SENEGAL DATE PALM
Arecaceae (Palmae)
Tropical Africa

With its gracefully-curving multiple trunks and crowns of arching leaves, a mature Senegal Date Palm makes a striking tropical-looking silhouette against the sky. This is a vigorous palm which needs a big space to show off and also needs some early training, but if grown well can produce spectacular results.

The Senegal Date Palm grows at a moderate to fast rate to 20-30' tall and as wide, with individual feather-type leaves 4-10' long. Without training, it grows many suckers from its base and soon becomes an impenetrable thicket, and so for the nicest specimen it is important early-on to encourage just a few or several main stems and remove all others.

The Senegal Date Palm needs full sun, good soil, and generous amounts of water and fertilizer to grow quickly and look its best. It thrives in both inland and coastal areas, including the immediate seacoast, and is cold-hardy to 20°F. Although it is a fairly fast-growing palm, if you are impatient you may want to purchase a fully-trained mature specimen. This is possible because like other date palms, even a big, mature Senegal Date Palm may be dug and transplanted with little setback except to one's pocketbook.   **B21,QBG**

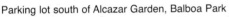

3999 Mission Blvd., San Diego

Parking lot south of Alcazar Garden, Balboa Park

Phoenix rupicola
(FEE-niks   roo-pih-KOE-luh)
CLIFF DATE PALM
Arecaceae (Palmae)
India

The Cliff Date Palm is an elegant, tropical-looking palm which makes an excellent specimen plant in the landscape. With its soft, shiny-green drooping leaflets, it has all the style and grace of the popular Pygmy Date Palm (*Phoenix roebelenii*), but on a larger scale.

The Cliff Date Palm grows in full sun or partial shade, with a single trunk around 10" in diameter. It has long, arching 8-10' long feather-type leaves that are softer than most other date palms, with drooping leaflets that give it a tropical look. Although the Cliff Date Palm ultimately will grow to 25' tall and 12-15' wide, it grows slowly here compared to many other palms we grow, and so will take a number of years to reach full size. Fortunately, it is quite handsome at all stages of development, and makes an attractive garden specimen even when it is small.

The Cliff Date Palm likes regular watering and fertilizing, and grows well in both inland and coastal areas as long as temperatures do not fall below 24°F. When mature, female trees can produce showy clusters of purplish-red fruits.   **B21**

100

Phytolacca dioica

(fye-toe-LAK-uh dye-OY-kuh)

OMBU

Phytolaccaceae

Paraguay, S. Brazil, Uruguay, and N. Argentina

Although more than tree-like in proportions, the unusual Ombu is actually a giant herb, and is related to the eastern U.S. native herb called Pokeweed. This is the only tree that grows in the "pampas," which is an expansive area of grassland in southern South America, and it is a botanical curiosity because its soft "wood" in cross-section actually looks more like rolled-up cardboard than real wood. The Ombu is further distinguished by its huge swollen trunk and surface roots, which store water for survival in times of drought.

The Ombu is an evergreen tree that grows quickly to 30-40' tall with an even wider spread. Its 4-6" oval leaves look somewhat like avocado leaves, but its dominant feature is always its huge swollen whitish-gray trunk base and surface roots. Trees are either male or female, both with 6" hanging clusters of small cream-colored flowers in the spring. On female trees, flowers may be followed by small golden berries which eventually ripen to black, but only if trees of both sexes are in proximity. The Ombu is an easily grown tree that needs only average watering and soil and is hardy to at least 25°F. It needs room to grow, but a mature tree can be spectacular. **B17,QBG**

Cactus Gardens, Balboa Park

West of Botanical Building, Balboa Park

Pinus canariensis

(PYE-nus kuh-nair-ee-EN-sis)

CANARY ISLAND PINE

Pinaceae

Canary Islands

The true pines in the genus *Pinus* are a diverse group of around 110 species of cone-bearing evergreens that are native to both temperate and tropical regions of the Northern Hemisphere. Included in this group is one of the oldest living trees on Earth, which is an ancient Bristlecone Pine (*Pinus longaeva*) growing in the White Mountains of eastern California that is over 4800 years old. The foliage of most pines consists of bundles of 2 to 5 long narrow leaves called "needles," and one way to identify them is to count the number of needles in a bundle. Another identification aid is their woody cones.

Many kinds of pine trees grow well in Southern California and are beautiful additions to our landscape. The Canary Island Pine is one of the most popular here, and is easily grown because it is so well-suited to our climate. This is a tall, slender tree that grows quickly to 50-80' tall and 20-35' wide here, with a graceful foliage of 9-12" long needles in bundles of 3 that are bluish-green when new and dark green when older. It has a handsome fissured reddish-brown bark and shiny brown oval-shaped cones that are 4-9" long. The Canary Island Pine has a distinctive "tiered" look when young, and is especially effective when planted in groups. Although it is somewhat drought-tolerant, it is best with regular irrigation, and is cold-hardy to around 15°F. **B18,QBG**

101

Pinus halepensis
(PYE-nus   ha-leh-PEN-sis)
ALEPPO PINE
Pinaceae
Mediterranean Sea Region

As a native of the Mediterranean Sea region, the Aleppo Pine is well-adapted to our climate of dry summers and wet winters. This is a big evergreen tree that grows fairly quickly to 40-60' tall and 20-40' wide, with an informal branching structure and characteristic light green foliage. The needles of the Aleppo Pine are 3-4" long, and appear in bundles of two or rarely three. Its reddish-brown cones are 3" long, oval to oblong, and often recurved back along the branches, where they can persist for many years.

The Aleppo Pine is a popular landscape plant because it is tolerant of poor soils and climate extremes, and grows well in desert as well as seacoast areas. It is tolerant of drought but will also grow with regular watering, and is hardy to around 10°F.

A related pine of similar culture is the Calabrian Pine (*Pinus brutia*). It is faster growing and somewhat shapelier than the Aleppo Pine when young, with a denser, dark green foliage of 5-6" needles in bundles of two and cones which are not bent backwards along the branches.   **B42,QBG**

158 E. 8th Street, Escondido

522 Tarento Dr., Point Loma

Pinus patula
(PYE-nus   PAT-yoo-luh)
JELECOTE PINE
Pinaceae
Mexico

Although most people think of pines as trees of cold northern forests, there are actually more species of pine trees in Mexico than in the rest of the world combined. Although the Mexican pines are not commonly grown in nurseries, there are a number of them with luxuriant, tropical-looking foliage that make beautiful landscape trees in our climate.

The Jelecote Pine is a long-needled pine with graceful, weeping evergreen foliage and a handsome branching structure. It grows very fast to 50-60' tall and 30-40' wide. Young trees are tall and slender, with widely spaced tiers of branches, but trees become more dense as they mature and may even be multi-trunked. The Jelecote Pine has 12" long apple-green pendulous needles which are typically arranged in bundles of three. Its pale brown cones are 4-5" long, conical in shape, and curved, persisting along the branches in clusters of 2-5.

The Jelecote Pine needs regular watering and enjoys the extra humidity of coastal gardens. It is tolerant of poor soils and is cold-hardy to 15°F. Young or old, it makes a beautiful silhouette against the sky and is an excellent foliage tree.   **B5**

Pinus pinea
(PYE-nus   PYE-nee-uh)
ITALIAN STONE PINE
Pinaceae
Southern Europe and Turkey

The Italian Stone Pine is a big, dominant evergreen tree whose characteristic umbrella shape is a famous component of the Italian landscape. It grows at a moderate rate to an eventual 40-80' tall and 40-60' wide, with a thick, fissured trunk and many spreading branches. Mature trees growing near the coast are typically very broad, dense, and flat-topped, but those farther inland are usually taller, with a more open crown. The dense foliage of the Italian Stone Pine is bright green to olive-green, and is composed of stiff 5-8" long needles arranged in bundles of two. Its 4-6" rounded cones are shiny and light brown and contain edible seeds known as pine nuts.

Although it will ultimately grow too large for small gardens, the Italian Stone Pine is a majestic tree where it has space to grow. It is tolerant of poor soil, drought, summer heat, and winter cold to around 10°F., and will even grow well on the immediate seacoast. **B32,QBG**

1511 Law St., Pacific Beach

3327 Cadencia St., Carlsbad

Pinus radiata var. *radiata*
(PYE-nus   ray-dee-AY-tuh)
MONTEREY PINE
Pinaceae
Coastal Central California

Although the Monterey Pine is rare in the wild, the fact that it grows so fast in cultivation has made it an important timber tree in many parts of the world as well as a popular landscape tree in California. However, its susceptibility to pests, diseases, and wind damage can limit both its lifespan and permanence in the landscape here.

The typical form of the Monterey Pine in cultivation is native to just a few small areas along the central California coast, the most famous of which is the forest on the Monterey Peninsula itself. As a landscape tree, it grows very fast to 50-80' tall here with a spread of 25-35', with a dense, bright green foliage composed of 3-7" needles arranged in bundles of three, and 3-6" light brown cones that are lopsided and persistent in clusters on the tree.

The Monterey Pine can be shallow rooted, and if so older trees may be subject to blowing over in the wind. Good drainage, deep soil, and the avoidance of planting potbound plants will help in establishing a deep root system. The Monterey Pine is cold-hardy to around 18°F. and is fairly drought-tolerant, but to forestall disease and keep an established tree healthy occasional deep watering and feeding are recommended. **B15**

103

699 Rosecrans St., Point Loma

Pinus roxburghii
(PYE-nus roks-BURG-ee-eye)
CHIR PINE
Pinaceae
Himalayas

The long-needled Chir Pine is a handsome evergreen tree with weeping foliage and a dominant presence in the landscape. In youth, it is a slender pyramid, but as it matures it develops a spreading crown. The Chir Pine grows at a moderate rate here to an ultimate height of 60-80' with a spread of 30-40'. It has a light green foliage of 8-12" long pendulous needles that are arranged in bundles of three, and its 4-7" long oval cones are a lustrous brown.

The Chir Pine appreciates regular watering and good drainage, and is cold-hardy to at least 15°F. It has proven successful in both coastal and inland regions, and with adequate water will even grow in desert climates. Its cones contain edible seeds (pine nuts), and in its native Nepal the resinous sap from this tree is used for medicinal purposes. Because of its graceful, weeping foliage, it is a striking foliage tree in all stages of its development. **B29,QBG**

145 Via Vera Cruz, San Marcos

Pinus thunbergii
(PYE-nus thun-BURG-ee-eye)
JAPANESE BLACK PINE
Pinaceae
Japan

The Japanese Black Pine has for centuries been the backbone of Japanese gardens, where it is meticulously pruned in order to imitate the graceful shapes of pines by the sea. Although it can grow to be a tall tree in many climates, in Southern California it is much smaller, growing at a slow to moderate rate here to around 20' tall and 10' wide. Its spreading branches form an irregular shape, often of great character, with evergreen foliage composed of stiff, dark green 3-5" long needles that are arranged in bundles of two. New growth comes from conspicuous upright shoots that are nearly white, and its 3" oval cones are brown.

The Japanese Black Pine grows well in most soils, appreciates regular watering, and is cold-hardy to 0°F. It can easily be trained to almost any size with occasional pruning. To train it in an oriental fashion, prune to emphasize a horizontal branching pattern and create an upswept look by removing twigs and any needles that point downward. **B19,QBG**

Pinus torreyana var. *torreyana*
(PYE-nus tor-ee-AN-uh)
TORREY PINE
Pinaceae
Del Mar and La Jolla

San Diego County is fortunate indeed to be the native home of one of the rarest trees in the world—the majestic Torrey Pine (*Pinus torreyana* var. *torreyana*), which naturally grows only along a few miles of coastline from Del Mar to La Jolla, north of downtown San Diego. This evergreen tree is fast and easy in cultivation here, where it grows to 40-60' tall and 30-50' wide.

When exposed to ocean winds, the Torrey Pine develops a picturesque, open, irregular form, but it is a tall, upright, and spreading tree when grown further inland. Its foliage is composed of 8-12" long gray-green needles which are arranged in bundles of five, and its 4-6" roundish cones are dark brown. The Torrey Pine is tolerant of drought and poor soil, and is cold-hardy to 15°F.

Our rare Torrey Pine has an even rarer relative which is seldom cultivated but has great garden potential. This is the Island Torrey Pine (*Pinus torreyana* var. *insularis*), which exists in the wild as just one tiny grove of trees 175 miles from here, on a remote corner of Santa Rosa Island off the Santa Barbara coast. These island trees are shorter, broader, and bushier than their mainland cousins, and if considered as a distinct group, they might well qualify as the rarest pines in the world. **B42,QBG**

3576 Highland Dr., Carlsbad

Pistacia chinensis
(pis-TASS-ee-uh chi-NEN-sis)
CHINESE PISTACHE
Anacardiaceae
China, Taiwan and Philippines

Although our mild San Diego climate is not noted for its autumn foliage color, there are a few trees that do color up nicely in the fall here even in coastal gardens. The Chinese Pistache is a winter-deciduous tree that grows at a slow to moderate rate to 40' tall and wide. It has a dense, rounded crown of spring and summer foliage composed of 10-12" long compound leaves, each with 10-16 2-4" leaflets. In the fall, these leaves turn scarlet, crimson, orange, and yellow before dropping.

The Chinese Pistache loves full sun and heat, and is cold-hardy to around 10°F. It grows easily in most soils and is fairly drought-tolerant, although it will accept regular watering and grows fine in lawns. Because they are usually grown from seed, not all Chinese Pistache trees are equal in terms of their fall color. Although fall color is likely to be good on most trees in the heat and cold of inland, mountain, and desert climates, gardeners nearer to the coast should choose a tree when it is in fall color to get the best specimen. If you can find one, the very best choice for a garden tree is a grafted plant of a male variety that has been selected for its superior fall color. **B12**

SW corner of College & Hwy. 76, Oceanside

105

799 Cromwell Way, Vista

1739 Village Run North, Encinitas

Pittosporum angustifolium
(pih-tuh-SPORE-um   ang-us-tih-FOE-lee-um)
WILLOW PITTOSPORUM
Pittosporaceae
Australia

The Weeping Pittosporum is an elegant small evergreen tree that makes a good patio, lawn, or street tree and is very well-behaved. Although it is native to hot, dry areas of Australia, it will grow fine under normal garden conditions and is equally at home in desert or coastal gardens.

The Weeping Pittosporum grows fairly slowly here to 15-25' tall and 10-15' wide, with a delicate, willowy foliage of 2-4" long narrow olive-green leaves closely set along pendent branchlets. In late winter and early spring, it bears clusters of small but very fragrant yellow flowers, which are followed by attractive 1/2" yellow-orange fruits.

Best displayed as a specimen tree where its structural form can show off, the Weeping Pittosporum prefers full sun but will also grow in partial shade. Drought-tolerant when established, it is very tolerant of dry heat and is also cold-hardy to 20°F. If drainage is poor, infrequent but deep waterings are recommended, but regular watering is fine as long as drainage is good.

In the past, the Weeping Pittosporum has been confused with *Pittosporum phylliraeoides*, a related species which is not in cultivation. It is still often grown under that name and listed that way in older books.

Pittosporum napaulense
(pih-tuh-SPORE-um   nap-all-ENCE)
GOLDEN FRAGRANCE TREE
Pittosporaceae
Northern India, Nepal, and Bhutan

The Golden Fragrance Tree can be an ideal choice for the gardener who wants a small evergreen tree with fragrant flowers. Although shrubby when young, this Himalayan native grows fairly quickly to 12-20' tall and is easily shaped as it grows into a round-headed multi-trunked tree of great beauty.

The Golden Fragrance Tree has a lush foliage composed of glossy green leaves that are 5-8" long and 2-3" wide. It blooms in late spring or early summer with large, showy clusters of 1/2"golden-yellow flowers that are prominently displayed at the ends of the branches. These flowers are intensely and sweetly fragrant, and a tree in bloom can perfume a large area.

The Golden Fragrance Tree appreciates a rich, well-drained soil in full sun or partial shade, and needs regular watering and fertilizing. Although its foliage may be damaged in a heavy frost, it is cold-hardy to 25°F. It has also been grown under an older name, *Pittosporum floribundum*.

106

Pittosporum tobira
(pih-tuh-SPORE-um   toe-BYE-ruh)
MOCK ORANGE
Pittosporaceae
China and Japan

The Mock Orange is a popular landscape plant because of its glossy evergreen foliage and clusters of fragrant flowers. Although young plants are usually grown as shrubs, an older plant may be trained most effectively as a small tree with multiple trunks and a rounded crown to around 15' tall and 10' wide, or even a little larger with great age. The Mock Orange has a dense foliage composed of whorls of 5" long shiny dark green leathery leaves. It blooms in spring, with clusters of small creamy-white flowers that have the sweet fragrance of orange blossoms.

The Mock Orange is fairly slow-growing, but is tolerant of adverse conditions such as heat, frost, poor soil, and drought. It is cold-hardy to at least 20°F, will grow in sun or shade, and is very tolerant of seacoast conditions and salt wind. For training as a tree, only the full-sized green form of the Mock Orange works best. There is a variegated form, however, with gray-green leaves edged with creamy-white, which grows to 8-10' tall with age and can be trained as a very small tree.   **B1,QBG**

1141 Moana Dr., Point Loma

Old Town, San Diego

Pittosporum undulatum
(pih-tuh-SPORE-um   un-dyoo-LAY-tum)
VICTORIAN BOX
Pittosporaceae
Eastern Australia

The Victorian Box is an easily grown evergreen tree of great beauty. Valuable for its handsome foliage as well as its fragrant flowers, it grows quickly even in tough situations and needs little care.

As a young tree, the Victorian Box grows at a fast rate to 15' tall, then slows conveniently to an eventual 30-40' tall and wide with a dense, rounded crown. Its attractive foliage is composed of whorls of 4-6" long dark green leaves with wavy edges. The Victorian Box blooms in late winter or early spring with terminal clusters of 1/2" bell-shaped creamy-white flowers which are sweetly fragrant and can perfume a large area. Later in the year, 1/2" yellow-orange fruits are produced that contain sticky orange seeds.

The Victorian Box is remarkably tolerant of drought and poor soils, but actually prefers regular watering and good drainage. It will grow in full sun or part shade, and is cold-hardy to around 24°F. It does unfortunately have the capability to escape from cultivation and naturalize in semi-moist areas via bird-distributed seed, as it has done even in its native Australia. For this reason, it is not a good idea to plant it near wild areas where it could invade and overcome native vegetation   **B1,QBG**

107

Pittosporum viridiflorum
(pih-tuh-SPORE-um vih-rih-dih-FLOOR-um)
CAPE PITTOSPORUM
Pittosporaceae
South Africa

The Cape Pittosporum is a small evergreen tree which grows at a slow to moderate rate to 15-25' tall and wide. It can be shrubby as a young plant, but is easily pruned up as it grows, and looks best when allowed to develop multiple trunks. In the landscape, it somewhat resembles the Mock Orange (*Pittosporum tobira*), but on a larger scale.

The Cape Pittosporum has a dense foliage composed of 2-5" long glossy, dark green, leathery oval leaves. In late spring, it produces terminal clusters of 1/2" yellowish-green flowers with a pronounced jasmine-like fragrance. These are followed later in the year by clusters of 1/2" orange fruits.

The Cape Pittosporum grows easily in full sun or partial shade, and prefers regular watering and a well-drained soil. It is very tolerant of seashore conditions, but will also grow well farther inland, and is cold-hardy to at least 24°F. **B35**

757 C Ave., Coronado

918 Lupine Hills, Vista

Platanus x hispanica
(PLAT-uh-nus hih-SPAN-ih-kuh)
LONDON PLANE TREE
Platanaceae
Horticultural Hybrid

Because of its tolerance of heat, cold, drought, and air pollution, the deciduous London Plane Tree is a popular street tree in many cities around the world. This tree originated over 300 years ago at the Oxford Botanic Garden and is reputed to be a hybrid of the Eurasian *Platanus orientalis* and the American *Platanus occidentalis*. By the eighteenth century, it was a popular tree in London, as it still is today. The most up-to-date botanical name for the London Plane Tree these days is *Platanus x hispanica*, but it is still well-known under its former name *Platanus x acerifolia*.

The London Plane Tree grows quickly to 40-60' tall and 30-40' wide here, with an open, spreading crown. Rather formal-looking, it has a straight, stout trunk with cream-colored bark. Its large, bright green maple-like leaves are 3-5" long and 4-10" wide, with wooly hair underneath. Spring flowers are inconspicuous, but they are followed by round bristly seed pods which hang on pendent stalks and persist on the tree throughout the winter. Fall foliage color is yellow to brown, but not particularly showy here.

The London Plane Tree is best rich, deep soil with regular watering, and is cold-hardy to below 0°F. It is unfortunately subject to anthracnose and powdery mildew, which can cause disfigured leaves and premature leaf drop. There are, however, selected varieties available that are somewhat resistant to these diseases. **B40,QBG**

Platanus racemosa
(PLAT-uh-nus ray-see-MOE-suh)
CALIFORNIA SYCAMORE
Platanaceae
California and Baja California, Mexico

Our robust native California Sycamore is a familiar sight along watercourses in undisturbed areas, where its huge, grayish-white twisting trunks dominate the natural landscape. It grows quickly to 30-80' tall and 20-50' wide, with trees in deep, moist soils growing larger while those in more challenging situations stay smaller. Its trunk and branches naturally take on informal, twisted shapes, with attractive gray, white, and brown mottled bark. Deeply lobed maple-like leaves are dark green above and hairy beneath, turning dusty-brown early in the fall. Inconspicuous spring flowers are followed by round seed clusters that hang from the tree in numbers of 3-7 along slender stalks and persist throughout the winter.

The California Sycamore likes regular watering and is cold-hardy to at least 10°F. It is unfortunately very susceptible to powdery mildew and anthracnose, both of which can severely disfigure foliage and cause premature leaf drop. Both this species and the London Plane Tree have hairs on their leaves and fruits that can cause allergic reactions in some people. **B40,QBG**

4351 Pescadero Ave., Point Loma

Plumeria rubra
(ploo-MAIR-ee-uh ROO-bruh)
FRANGIPANI
Apocynaceae
Mexico to Panama

The enchanting fragrance of its flowers has made the Frangipani a favorite garden tree in tropical regions throughout the world, where it is easy to grow and blooms over a long season. Although it is not as vigorous in Southern California as it is in the heat of the tropics, the Frangipani will grow and bloom well here as long as it is given a warm, sunny spot in the garden and is protected from frost.

As a garden tree here, the Frangipani is at its best in mild coastal gardens, where it will grow at a moderate rate to 15-20' tall and 10-15' wide with many thick succulent branches. Deciduous in winter, its tropical-looking foliage emerges in late spring at the ends of the branches and is composed of 8-16" long shiny green leathery leaves with narrow pointed tips. From late spring through fall, showy clusters of 2-4" five-petaled fragrant flowers are produced in colors from white through yellow, gold, and orange to shades of pink and red, depending on the variety grown. There are over 100 named varieties, all varying in flower color and shape, fragrance, and lasting qualities as a cut flower.

The Frangipani needs good drainage and a loose, friable soil. It loves heat and sun and needs regular watering and fertilizing during the warm season but should be kept fairly dry in the winter. Where frost is a problem, it is often grown in a large container that is moved to a protected spot in the winter. **B16,QBG**

1582 Fronde St., Point Loma

Quail Botanical Gardens

Podachaenium eminens
(poe-duh-KEE-nee-um EM-in-nenz)
GIANT DAISY TREE
Asteraceae (Compositae)
Southern Mexico to Costa Rica

Fast-growing and magnificent in bloom, the Giant Daisy Tree is one of the largest "daisies" in the world. Native to mountain forests in Central America, this evergreen grows to 25-30' tall and wide, with multiple stems that arise from a thick gray trunk and tropical-looking aromatic foliage composed of 9-12" wide soft gray-green leaves. The Giant Daisy Tree flowers from April to June, with showy terminal clusters of 1" sweetly scented white daisy-like flowers with yellow centers. Hundreds of these 12-18" wide flower clusters cover the plant in bloom, and a full-sized tree can produce as many as 25,000 flowers all at once. After flowering, clusters of small gray seed heads form that persist on the tree.

The Giant Daisy Tree will grow in full sun or partial shade and likes regular watering. It needs protection from strong wind and frost, but can recover from temperatures as low as 25°F. by quickly resprouting as soon as the weather warms up. Shrubby when young, it may also be grown as a fast-growing tall hedge or screen planting, where it can attain a height of 20' in just 3 years. **B17,QBG**

7733 Ivanhoe Ave., La Jolla

Podocarpus henkelii
(poe-doe-KAR-pus hen-KELL-ee-eye)
LONG-LEAFED YELLOWWOOD
Podocarpaceae
Southeastern Africa

The graceful, luxuriant foliage of the Long-Leafed Yellowwood has made it a popular evergreen tree in gardens here, and it is being used more and more in commercial landscapes as well. Upright and pyramidal when young, it becomes more spreading with age, growing at a slow to moderate rate to 25-35' tall and 15-25' wide. The dense, shiny green foliage of the Long-Leafed Yellowwood is especially striking on young trees, whose narrow, weeping leaves are 5-7" long and pointed at both ends. Older trees have somewhat shorter, narrower leaves, but are still quite dramatic. Clusters of light green new leaves at the ends of the branches contrast nicely with the darker green older growth. On mature female trees, waxy olive-green seeds are produced on small thickened stalks if a pollinating male tree is nearby.

The Long-Leafed Yellowwood grows happily in full sun but will also tolerate considerable shade, and is often more luxuriant in partial shade. It likes well-drained soil and regular watering, and is cold-hardy to 20°F. Although it is easy to grow and practically maintenance-free, it can be disappointing in poorly drained clay soils. **B19,QBG**

110

Podocarpus macrophyllus
(poe-doe-KAR-pus   mak-roe-FILL-us)
YEW PINE
Podocarpaceae
Japan and Eastern China

Popular in Japanese gardens as a clipped specimen, and also grown as a shrubby foundation plant near homes, the Yew Pine makes an interesting evergreen tree when allowed to grow naturally. Although it can grow taller in other climates, it usually grows slowly here to around 25' tall and 10-15' wide, with a stiff, upright growth habit. The foliage of the Yew Pine is composed of whorls of 4" long dark green narrow leaves, with lighter green new growth. It is often multi-trunked, with an ornamental light gray peeling bark. Mature female trees may produce small "fruits" if a pollinating male tree is nearby.

The Yew Pine likes regular watering and full sun, but will also tolerate some shade. It is heat tolerant and cold-hardy to at least 10°F. It makes a good street or lawn tree of manageable size and is easy to grow. A dwarf variety of this species from China is called the Shrubby Yew Pine (*Podocarpus macrophyllus* var. *maki*). This is a dense, columnar shrub with shorter 3" long leaves. The Shrubby Yew Pine grows to just 6-8' tall in ten years and is a better choice for foundation plantings.   **QBG**

Catamaran Hotel, 3999 Mission Blvd., San Diego

Populus fremontii
(POP-yoo-lus   free-MON-tee-eye)
WESTERN COTTONWOOD
Salicaceae
Western United States and Northern Mexico

Although too large for small gardens, our native cottonwood trees can be useful in larger gardens where a fast-growing shelter tree is needed. They also can quickly provide quality habitat for our native birds, and relaxing sight and sound as their leaves rustle in the wind. Two species of Cottonwood are native to San Diego County, both of which may be seen along natural watercourses and in other wet places.

The Western Cottonwood (*Populus fremontii*) is a large deciduous tree which grows very quickly with an upright growth habit to 40-60' tall and 30' wide. It has a dense foliage of glossy bright green 2-4" wide triangular leaves that emerge in spring and turn bright lemon-yellow before dropping in the fall. Somewhat less common here is the Black Cottonwood (*Populus trichocarpa*), an equally large tree with 3-5" wide dark green leaves that are silvery underneath and turn golden-yellow in the fall.

Of our two native species, the Western Cottonwood is the best choice for cultivation because of its stronger wood and better growth habit. It likes regular watering and is cold-hardy to below 0°F., but it has an aggressive root system and should not be planted close to structures or paving. Because the female trees of all cottonwoods release large amounts of white cotton along with their seeds, it is important to plant only cutting-grown male plants, which are often sold as "cottonless cottonwoods."   **B39**

2624 Foothill Dr., Vista

111

Birch St. & Dogwood Way, Vista

Populus nigra 'Italica'
(POP-yoo-lus NYE-gruh ih-TAL-ih-kuh)
LOMBARDY POPLAR
Salicaceae
Horticultural Selection

The Lombardy Poplar has been cultivated in Europe for centuries, and was first brought to North America in the seventeenth century by Thomas Brigham, a member of the Massachusetts colony and an ancestor of the author of this book. Since then, its fast, sturdy growth, cold-hardiness, and ease of propagation have made it a great favorite for planting as a windbreak and along country roads throughout the United States.

The Lombardy Poplar is a beautiful columnar tree that grows quickly to 40-100' tall and 15-30' wide with strongly upright branching. Its dense foliage is composed of 4" bright green triangular to diamond-shaped leaves that turn a striking golden yellow in the fall. Like other poplars, the Lombardy Poplar has strong surface roots and will send up shoots from those roots if they are disturbed, and so is best planted away from buildings and paved areas where it has room to grow. Since it is a male clone, the Lombardy Poplar produces no seed and so is propagated by cuttings. It is cold-hardy to below 0°F., tolerates most any soil, and needs only moderate watering. **B8**

Private residence, San Marcos

Prunus campanulata
(PROO-nus kam-pan-yoo-LAY-tuh)
TAIWAN FLOWERING CHERRY
Rosaceae
Taiwan and Ryukyu Islands

The Taiwan Flowering Cherry is the earliest flowering cherry to bloom here, becoming a riot of color in mid-to-late winter even in frost-free coastal gardens. It is a vigorous deciduous tree to 20-25' tall which is naturally multi-stemmed but often is grafted high to make a single-trunked tree. Flowering is spectacular, with bare branches quickly becoming covered with clusters of bell-shaped pendulous flowers of the brightest magenta-pink color imaginable. The handsome foliage which follows is composed of 4" long dark green pointed oval leaves which can provide good color before dropping in the fall. Because of its low chill requirements and also its tolerance of cool summers, the Taiwan Flowering Cherry is a valuable addition to mild-climate gardens where other varieties of flowering cherry do poorly, but it is also fully cold-hardy to 23°F.

The many showy Japanese Flowering Cherry hybrids that have been derived from *Prunus serrulata* are cold-hardy to 0°F. and are famous throughout the world for their beautiful springtime flowers. These small deciduous trees generally need a lot of winter chill to grow and bloom well, however, and so they are recommended only for our coldest inland areas. One variety that blooms well with less winter chill here is *Prunus* 'Pink Cloud', which has a showy display of large single pink flowers in late winter.

112

Prunus caroliniana
(PROO-nus   kair-oh-lih-nee-AN-uh)
CAROLINA LAUREL CHERRY
Rosaceae
North Carolina to Texas

Spreckels Park, Coronado

There are many members of the genus *Prunus* that are evergreen shrubs or small trees. The Carolina Laurel Cherry can be grown as both, and when it is trained as a tree will grow up to 20-30' high and 15-25' wide, with a dense, rounded crown of foliage composed of 2-4" long glossy green leaves. In late winter and early spring, it blooms with 1' spikes of small fragrant creamy-white flowers which are followed by 1/2" black fruits which attract birds.

The Carolina Laurel Cherry is drought-tolerant but also grows well with regular watering. It grows easily in full sun or partial shade in coastal gardens, but needs protection from hot sun in desert climates, and is cold-hardy to at least 10°F.

Another tough evergreen species of *Prunus* which may be trained as a small tree is the Portugal Laurel (*Prunus lusitanica*), which grows up to 25-30' tall and wide. It has a dense foliage of glossy dark green 5" narrowly oval leaves and 5-10" spikes of small creamy-white flowers in spring and early summer and is cold-hardy to 10°F.   **B22**

Prunus cerasifera 'Atropurpurea'
(PROO-nus   seh-ruh-SIH-fer-uh   at-roe-pur-PURR-ee-uh)
PURPLE-LEAF PLUM
Rosaceae
Horticultural Selection

859 Morning Sun Dr., Encinitas

The genus *Prunus* is best known horticulturally for the hundreds of cultivated ornamental and fruiting varieties of cherries, plums, apricots, peaches, and nectarines. Although the performance of many of these deciduous trees is limited in the mild winter climates of San Diego County, there are still many varieties that do well here and are enjoyed in our gardens for both flowers and fruit.

Particularly in our inland areas that get some winter chilling, one of the most popular spring-flowering deciduous trees is the Purple-Leaf Plum, which has the added bonus of colorful foliage. It grows quickly to around 20-25' tall and wide, with new leaves emerging coppery-red in spring, deepening to a dark purple in summer, then turning reddish-purple before dropping in the fall. The Purple-Leaf Plum has a showy bloom of single white flowers in late winter or early spring, then produces a heavy crop of 1" red cherry plums. All of the flowering plums grow easily in most soils in full sun with regular watering and are cold-hardy to below 0°F. There are a number of varieties grown that differ in their flowers, foliage, and growth habits, some of which also produce fruit while others do not.   **B20,QBG**

Prunus persica
(PROO-nus PER-sih-kuh)
FLOWERING PEACH
Rosaceae
China

The Chinese species *Prunus persica* is the ancestor of our modern-day fruiting peaches and nectarines, and has also been developed into a number of showy varieties that are grown only for their flowers. The Flowering Peach is a deciduous tree that grows to 15-25' tall and wide. In early spring, its bare branches become covered with intensely colored 1-1/2" double flowers in pink, red, or white. Out of bloom, it looks like a fruiting peach, with a dense foliage of pointed green leaves to 6' long.

The best types of Flowering Peach for our mild-winter areas are the "early" varieties that need less winter chill. Although most of these produce either very small fruit or no fruit at all, there are a few hybrids such as 'Red Baron' that also produce high-quality delicious fruit. As with all peach trees, the flowering varieties are cold-hardy to below 0°F. and benefit from annual pruning and leaf-disease control to look their best.

A closely related tree that is also very showy in bloom is the Flowering Nectarine, *Prunus persica* 'Alma Stultz'. It grows to 20' tall, with a bright show of 2" wide ruffled pink flowers that are nicely fragrant. The Flowering Nectarine was first sold by California plant pioneer Luther Burbank 100 years ago, but he supposedly gave up on it because its fruit quality was poor. It was rediscovered 50 years later in a garden in Hollywood by Theodore Payne, who re-introduced it to horticulture. **B3,QBG**

169 Avenida Chapala, San Marcos

6001 Bellevue Ave., La Jolla

Psidium cattleianum
(SID-ee-um kat-lee-AN-um)
STRAWBERRY GUAVA
Myrtaceae
Brazil

Trained as a multi-trunked small tree, the Strawberry Guava is an attractive evergreen ornamental with the added bonus of edible fruit. It grows at a moderate rate to 10-15' tall, with an open branching structure, handsome reddish-brown bark, and 3" shiny green oval leaves. Solitary 1" white flowers are followed by round 1" dark red fruits that have white flesh and a strawberry-like flavor. Rich in vitamin C, they may be eaten fresh but are often made into jams and jellies.

The Strawberry Guava is tolerant of drought and poor soil, but prefers good soil and regular watering for best fruit production. It is cold-hardy to 24°F. A close relative called the Lemon Guava (*Psidium cattleianum* var. *lucidum*) is similar, but has somewhat larger yellow-skinned fruits with a sweet lemony flavor, lighter-green leaves, and a greenish to golden bark. Both the Strawberry Guava and the Lemon Guava are sometimes sold under the name *Psidium littorale*. **QBG**

Psidium guajava
(SID-ee-um gua-YAH-vuh)
TROPICAL GUAVA
Myrtaceae
Tropical America

The Tropical Guava is grown in tropical and subtropical climates throughout the world for its edible fruit, which may be eaten fresh or used to make jellies, jams, chutneys, and juices. Although intolerant of much frost, mature plants of the Tropical Guava will survive temperatures as low as 27°F. and so may be grown in the milder climates of San Diego County. The Tropical Guava grows to 15-20' tall here and is shrubby at first, but later may be trained as a multi-trunked tree with attractive peeling brown bark. Its foliage is basically evergreen, although it may lose some of its 3-6" long strongly veined leaves in the spring before new growth occurs.

The Tropical Guava flowers from spring to fall with 1" wide white flowers which are followed by 2-4" long pear-shaped fruits with yellow skin and white, pink, or yellow flesh. For fruit production, it is best to choose named varieties that grow and produce well in your area. The fruit of some varieties has a sweet flavor that makes them good as a fresh fruit, whereas other varieties have fruits that are more tart and better for juices. Although the Tropical Guava is tolerant of drought and poor soil, it should be grown in rich soil with regular watering for good fruit production. **B14,QBG**

Quail Botanical Gardens

Punica granatum
(POO-nih-kuh gruh-NAH-tum)
POMEGRANATE
Punicaceae
Southeastern Europe to Northern India

The Pomegranate has been cultivated since ancient times for its refreshing fruit and has long been popular throughout the Mediterranean Sea region, where the characteristic crown-like structure on the bottom of its fruit was the inspiration for King Solomon's crown and all European crowns after that.

Shrubby when young, the Pomegranate may with time be trained into an attractive multi-trunked small tree to 12-20' tall and wide, with a dense foliage of narrow 1-3" long glossy-green leaves that turn bright yellow before dropping in the fall. It blooms in spring and early summer, with 1-2" ruffled, waxy flowers which are typically orange-red but can be pink, yellow, orange, or cream in some varieties. These are followed in the fall by round reddish fruits 2-5" in diameter which contain a juicy, sweet-tart pulp that surrounds each of the many seeds within. This pulp may be eaten fresh or used to make jams, jellies, and juices, or fermented to make a cordial known as grenadine.

The Pomegranate tolerates great extremes of cold and heat and is also quite drought-tolerant, although regular watering will encourage better fruit development. There are a number of good fruiting varieties with an assortment of fruit and flower characteristics, and also several varieties which are grown only for their colorful flowers. **B33,QBG**

418 Buena Creek Rd., San Marcos

1250 E. Vista Way, Vista

2510 San Clemente Ave., Vista

Pyrus calleryana
(PYE-rus kal-er-ee-AN-uh)
FLOWERING PEAR
Rosaceae
China, Korea, Japan, and Taiwan

There are many varieties of fruiting pears that are pretty flowering trees in their own right, but there are also a number of ornamental pear trees that are grown just for their flowers and foliage. Particularly in inland climates where they get some winter chill, the various varieties of Flowering Pear that have been selected from the species *Pyrus calleryana* provide a good show of white flowers before their leaves emerge, attractive green foliage throughout the summer, and bright leaf color in the fall.

The Flowering Pear is a deciduous tree that grows to 30-40' tall with a strongly upright branching structure. Some varieties such as 'Bradford' and 'Aristocrat' have a pyramidal growth habit and eventually develop a somewhat rounded crown, whereas others such as 'Whitehouse' are narrow and columnar in shape. In all selections, clusters of white flowers cover the tree in late winter or early spring, followed by a dense foliage of 2-3" long dark green glossy oval leaves which turn bright purplish-red to scarlet in the fall. Flowering Pear trees tolerate a wide variety of soils, need only average watering, and are cold-hardy to below 0°F.   **B14**

Pyrus kawakamii
(PYE-rus kow-uh-KAH-mee-eye)
EVERGREEN PEAR
Rosaceae
China and Taiwan

Although it is not always completely evergreen, the Evergreen Pear is a handsome small tree that is widely used in landscapes here. It grows to 15-30' tall and wide, with a dense foliage of glossy-green 2-4" long oval leaves, and blooms profusely in mid-winter with showy clusters of bright white flowers. In the mildest coastal areas, the Evergreen Pear holds its leaves all year, but in colder inland areas its leaves often turn crimson in early winter before dropping, with bloom immediately following on bare branches. When this happens, it is possible to see a tree full of bright green leaves one week, then with leaves completely crimson the next, then with no leaves but covered in white flowers the week after that, then a few weeks later full of bright green leaves again.

The Evergreen Pear is naturally shrubby, but is usually trained as a single-stemmed tree. Although many trees in commercial landscapes are heavily pruned, established trees look better and bloom better with a minimum of pruning. The Evergreen Pear is tolerant of many soils and climates, is cold-hardy to 10°F., and will bloom well even along the coast. Its major drawback is a susceptibility to a disease called fireblight that can cause its twigs and branches to suddenly die back.   **B21,QBG**

116

Quercus agrifolia
(KWER-kuss ag-ri-FOE-lee-uh)

COAST LIVE OAK
Fagaceae
Central California to Baja California, Mexico

The evergreen Coast Live Oak is our most massive native tree, and is famous for the many old specimens throughout San Diego County that have sheltered humans and served as meeting places for hundreds of years. Older trees in natural habitats can be up to 75' tall and over 100' wide, with heavy, spreading branches and a thick trunk over 20' in circumference.

The Coast Live Oak has a dense foliage of 1-3" long leathery dark green leaves with toothed edges. It blooms in spring with pendent yellowish clusters of tiny flowers, which are followed in the fall by numerous 1" long brown acorns. In cultivation, it can grow quickly if given regular deep watering and a fast-draining soil, but will grow more slowly in heavy soil and drought. The Coast Live Oak is cold-hardy to below 10°F. and is easy to grow, but because of its aggressive root system and leaf drop it can be a difficult tree to garden under.   **B1,QBG**

Marston House, 3525 7th Ave., San Diego

Quercus engelmannii
(KWER-kuss eng-ell-MAN-ee-eye)

MESA OAK
Fagaceae
S. California and N. Baja California, Mexico

Once common from Los Angeles to San Diego, the evergreen Mesa Oak has sadly seen a great reduction in its numbers due to urbanization. Although it is still frequent in many foothill areas of San Diego County, our existing old trees should be considered treasures and preserved at all costs.

Also known as the Engelmann Oak, the Mesa Oak can reach 40-50' tall at maturity, with a spreading crown to 60-80' wide. It has a dense foliage of leathery, bluish-green oval leaves to 2" long that are usually smooth-edged. Flowering occurs in spring, with pendent yellowish clusters of tiny flowers, which are followed in the fall by 1" round-tipped oval acorns that are half-enclosed in a warty cap. Like the Coast Live Oak, the Mesa Oak grows best with occasional deep waterings, and is cold hardy to below 10°F.

Because of their susceptibility to root rot, it is important to keep water away from the base of any of our native oaks, and in particular to avoid overwatering around any existing old tree. Preserving the natural layer of leaf litter underneath mature trees is important for their health as well. Old, established native oak trees are frequently endangered by intrusive human activity, sometimes with tragic results. Even a tree that has been healthy for centuries can die within 10-20 years if mistreated.   **B40**

Felicita Park, Escondido

117

Quercus ilex
(KWER-kuss EYE-leks)
HOLLY OAK
Fagaceae
Mediterranean Sea Region

The evergreen Holly Oak makes a good street or lawn tree, and a good substitute for the Coast Live Oak in situations where that tree would be difficult to maintain. It grows to 30-50' tall and wide, with a dense, rounded, symmetrical crown and a more well-behaved root system than our native oaks. Its 1-3" leaves are variable in shape and size, but usually are oval or pointed and often have toothed margins. Leaf color is dark green on top, with the undersides of the leaves covered with yellowish or silvery hairs. In spring, 3-4" pendent clusters of small cream-colored flowers are produced, followed in the fall by egg-shaped gray-brown acorns half-enclosed in round acorn caps.

The Holly Oak grows well in a variety of climates from seashore to desert, tolerates alkaline soil, wind, and drought, and is cold-hardy to 0°F. It will also succeed with regular watering, and can grow quickly if given a well-drained soil and consistent irrigation. It needs little pruning, but may be sheared into a formal shape if desired. **B3,QBG**

Quince St. & Balboa Dr., San Diego

Old Town Square, San Diego

Quercus suber
(KWER-kuss SOO-ber)
CORK OAK
Fagaceae
Southwestern Europe and Northern Africa

As most people know, corks that are used to cap wine bottles are a natural product that literally grows on trees—in this case the bark of the Cork Oak. Native to the western Mediterranean Sea region, this beautiful evergreen tree is cultivated extensively on plantations in Portugal and Spain, where the bark of mature trees is harvested every 8-10 years with no ill effects. In nature, the thick corky bark of the Cork Oak is a protection against fire. In the garden, it is quite ornamental and always a conversation piece.

The Cork Oak grows at a moderate rate to 30-60' tall and wide, gradually developing a thick trunk and heavy branches covered with thick gray fissured bark. It has a dense foliage of 3" long toothed oval leaves which are dark green above and gray beneath. Clusters of cream-colored pendent flower clusters are produced in the spring, followed in the fall by egg-shaped acorns which are half-covered by a bowl-shaped cap.

The Cork Oak needs good drainage and is drought-resistant once established. It prefers deep but infrequent irrigation, and it is important to keep water away from the base of mature trees so that they do not fall victim to root rot and premature death. The Cork Oak succeeds in all climates from seashore to desert, tolerating high heat and also cold temperatures to at least 10°F. Its soft bark can provide a wealth of opportunity to our native Acorn Woodpeckers and other birds who will store acorns in it. **B2,QBG**

118

Quercus virginiana
(KWER-kuss ver-jin-ee-AN-uh)
SOUTHERN LIVE OAK
Fagaceae
Southeastern United States, Mexico, and Cuba

Although it is partially deciduous where winters are very cold, the Southern Live Oak is completely evergreen in Southern California. Because it prefers regular watering, it is a good substitute for our native species of evergreen oaks in landscapes that receive regular irrigation.

The Southern Live Oak grows at a moderate to fast rate, eventually reaching 40-70' tall with a wider spread. It has a dense foliage of leathery, 2-5" long oval leaves which are shiny dark green above, whitish beneath, and normally smooth-edged. Oval acorns are 1" long with a sharp spine at the tip, and enclosed by one-fourth in a bowl-shaped cap with hairy scales.

The Southern Live Oak grows best in full sun with regular watering, and likes a deep, rich soil. It grows well in every Southern California climate, from desert to mountain to coast, and even succeeds as a lawn tree. As a landscape tree, it is faster-growing and longer-lived than our native species of evergreen oaks, and is also hardier to extremes of cold (to at least 0°F.) and heat. **QBG**

Quail Botanical Gardens

Radermachera sinica
(ray-der-MACK-er-uh SIN-ih-kuh)
CHINA DOLL TREE
Bignoniaceae
Southeast Asia

The China Doll Tree caused quite a stir in the 1980's when it was first introduced here—as a house plant! Naturally, a few of them eventually started making their way into gardens, with surprising results. Originally thought to be too tropical for outdoor use in Southern California, it has proven to be an excellent and very ornamental evergreen tree that is easy to grow and quite hardy to cold.

The China Doll Tree grows quickly to 30-40' tall and 20-30' wide, and looks best with multiple trunks. It is a beautiful tree for its bright green tropical-looking foliage alone, which is composed of divided leaves to 3" long, each with many 1" long nearly triangular leaflets. The China Doll Tree also produces clusters of beautiful fragrant flowers, which appear in late summer. These 3" funnel-shaped flowers open at night, lasting into the next morning, and are usually pure white, although there is a light yellow flowered form.

The China Doll Tree grows easily in full sun or partial shade, and prefers a rich, well-drained soil away from strong winds. It likes regular watering and fertilizing, but mature trees are also fairly drought-tolerant. Somewhat frost-tender when very young, it has proven surprisingly cold-hardy as it matures, with established trees tolerating temperatures as low as 20°F. If heavy frosts do occur, however, this tree may go deciduous for a brief period of time. **B24,QBG**

937 San Pablo Dr., San Marcos

119

1115 Savoy St., Point Loma

Rauvolfia samarensis
(rau-VOL-fee-uh   sam-ar-EN-sis)
RAUVOLFIA
Apocynaceae
Philippines

The tropical-looking leaves of the Rauvolfia look somewhat like Plumeria leaves, and in fact these two trees are related. The Rauvolfia, however, is a bigger tree that is grown mostly for its foliage, since its flowers are quite small. It grows fairly quickly to 25-40' tall, upright at first but with a wide-spreading crown as it matures. It has a dense foliage of narrow, 6-12" long shiny green leaves which are arranged in whorls of 3-6 and are pointed at their tips. The foliage of the Rauvolfia is evergreen in the mildest frost-free areas, but partially to completely deciduous in winter with cooler temperatures. Flowering occurs in spring at the tips of the branches, with 6-10" wide clusters of tiny white 3/16" wide flowers. Fruits which may follow are olive-shaped 1/2" long purple berries.

The Rauvolfia likes a rich well-drained soil and regular watering, but does not like frost. Young trees are especially frost-sensitive, but mature trees can recover from temperatures as low as 26°F. Like many members of its family, all parts of the Rauvolfia are poisonous if eaten. Although not a common tree, it has been grown in California since 1908.   **QBG**

140 11th St., Del Mar

Ravenala madagascariensis
(rav-en-AY-luh   mad-uh-gas-kar-ee-EN-sis)
TRAVELER'S TREE
Strelitziaceae
Madagascar

Anyone who has visited the tropics and has seen a large Traveler's Tree knows that it is an unforgettable sight. This remarkable relative of our commonly grown Giant Bird of Paradise (*Strelitzia nicolai*) has long banana-like leaves that form gigantic flat fans atop palm-like trunks, and is one of the most dramatic landscape plants imaginable. Tropical in nature and tender to cold, the Traveler's Tree succeeds in Southern California only in the mildest frost-free gardens, but even young plants are distinctive and strikingly ornamental.

In the tropics, the evergreen Traveler's Tree can grow to 30-40' tall and 25-30' wide, but large specimens are rare here. With age, it naturally forms a clump of upright trunks, although it is sometimes trained to a single trunk for dramatic effect. The large banana-like leaves of the Traveler's Tree are arranged oppositely on long leaf stalks, forming a flat crown of foliage. Clusters of white flowers emerge in summer from large greenish boat-shaped bracts that form in the crown of the tree.

The Traveler's Tree must have a frost-free location and prefers a rich, well-drained soil in full sun with regular watering and fertilizing. It grows best near the coast in a protected site away from strong winds that will shred its leaves. Both the flower bracts and the leaf bases hold good quantities of rainwater as a possible aid to travelers in remote areas, hence the tree's common name.

Ravenea rivularis
(ruh-VEE-nee-uh   riv-yoo-LAIR-iss)
MAJESTY PALM
Arecaceae (Palmae)
Madagascar

The Majesty Palm is often sold as a house plant here, but it has also proven to be an excellent outdoor palm that is more adaptable than originally thought. Given good drainage and adequate water and fertilizer, it grows fairly quickly in full sun or filtered shade. Although it appreciates the extra humidity of coastal gardens, it will also grow farther inland and is tolerant of heat as well as light frost.

The Majesty Palm grows to an ultimate height of around 40' here, with a bold, thick white trunk and a 12' wide crown of 7' long bright green feathery pinnate leaves. Young plants have upright, arching fronds and are very attractive in their own right, but as trees mature they develop great character with their dominant trunk and a more-rounded crown. The Majesty Palm makes a dramatic specimen plant planted singly, and is also effective when planted in groups. Young plants are excellent in containers, and will grow more slowly when so confined. The Majesty Palm is cold-hardy to at least 27°F. and likes regular watering and fertilizing to look its best. **B23,QBG**

Upper Palm Canyon, Balboa Park

Rhopalostylis sapida
(roe-pal-oh-STY-lis   SAP-ih-duh)
SHAVING BRUSH PALM
Arecaceae (Palmae)
New Zealand

The remarkable Shaving Brush Palm is the southernmost naturally occurring palm in the world. It is the only palm native to New Zealand, where it is known as the Nikau Palm and is an important plant in the Maori culture. Dramatic in form, this single-trunked feather palm has strongly upswept fronds and a bulbous crownshaft that give it its English name.

The Shaving Brush Palm is slow-growing when young, taking 15 years from seed before it forms a trunk. But it grows at a moderate rate after that to around 30' tall in gardens here. Its 6-8' long pinnate leaves are a rich green and form a graceful crown of evergreen foliage to 10-12' wide. It has an attractive, conspicuously ringed trunk, with older plants producing showy branched clusters of small pinkish flowers which are followed by small bright red fruits.

Somewhat faster growing is the related Feather Duster Palm (*Rhopalostylis baueri*) from Norfolk Island. It has a more spreading crown of foliage and lacks the bulbous crownshaft of its New Zealand cousin, but is otherwise similar. Both species are forest dwellers that need partial shade, protection from wind and dry heat, and regular watering and fertilizing to look their best. They do not like heavy frost, but are cold-hardy to 27°F. **B23,QBG**

Upper Palm Canyon, Balboa Park

121

1720 Monte Vista Dr., Vista

Rhus lancea
(ROOCE LAN-see-uh)
AFRICAN SUMAC
Anacardiaceae
South Africa

The African Sumac is a popular street and lawn tree because of its evergreen habit, manageable size, and tolerance of adverse conditions. Its main horticultural feature is its dark green, willowy foliage that looks attractive all year, as well as its durability. This tree grows at a moderate rate to 20-30' tall and wide, with a dense, rounded crown that may be kept smaller with pruning. It may be trained to either single or multiple trunks, and has distinctive dark reddish-brown rough bark.

The foliage of the African Sumac is composed of dark green leathery leaves which are divided into three 4-5" long by 3/8" wide narrow leaflets, creating a graceful effect as the leaves hang from the weeping outer branches. Trees grown from seed may be either male or female, with inconspicuous early spring flowers followed on female trees by yellow or red pea-sized fruits.

The African Sumac is very tolerant of dry heat, wind, and poor soils, and is cold-hardy to 10°F. It is drought-tolerant when established, but grows well with regular watering. In addition to its use as a specimen tree, it is also suitable for a tall background or screen planting. **B37,QBG**

4th & Tulip St., Escondido

Robinia pseudoacacia
(roe-BIN-ee-uh soo-doe-uh-KAY-shuh)
BLACK LOCUST
Fabaceae (Leguminosae)
Eastern and Central United States

The Black Locust is a very durable deciduous tree that was long ago brought to California by the early settlers as they moved west. In San Diego County old trees of this original species form can be seen persisting near old homestead sites and also in older gardens. It grows quickly to 40-70' tall and 30-50' wide with an open habit, thorny branches, and divided leaves with 7-19 leaflets each 1-2" long. In spring bloom, it looks like a giant white wisteria tree, with hanging 4-8" long clusters of fragrant sweet pea-shaped flowers. The Black Locust tolerates heat, drought, and poor soil. Root suckers can be a problem in dry soils, however, and trees look much better with regular watering.

Modern selections and hybrids of the Black Locust are popular garden plants in many areas of California. For interesting foliage color, *Robinia* 'Frisia' is a worthwhile selection that grows to 50' tall by 25' wide with yellow-orange new growth and chartreuse-yellow summer foliage. For showy flower color, the *Robinia* x *ambigua* hybrids are shapely trees that grow to 40' tall and 30' wide with big, spectacular 8" hanging flower clusters in spring. The two most popular cultivars are 'Idaho', with bright magenta-rose flowers, and 'Purple Robe', with purple flowers and a long blooming season. All are cold-hardy to below 0°F. and flower best in inland areas that get some winter chill. **B38**

Roystonea regia
(roy-STONE-ee-uh   REE-jee-uh)

CUBAN ROYAL PALM
Arecaceae (Palmae)
Cuba

With its massive concrete-white trunk, the Cuban Royal Palm is one of the most popular palms in tropical gardens throughout the world. Even though our climate is something less than tropical, we can grow the national tree of Cuba successfully in Southern California in our coastal gardens where winter nights are warmer and the humidity is higher than farther inland.

The Cuban Royal Palm is a single-trunked feather palm that grows slowly when young here but eventually grows at a moderate rate to 50-60' tall and 20' wide. As it grows, it develops a dominant thick grayish-white trunk to 2' in diameter and a spreading crown of graceful 10-15' long bright green fronds that arch gracefully in all directions. It needs a well-drained soil in full sun and regular watering, and tolerates coastal conditions well. It does not like frost, but mature trees have survived temperatures as cold as 27°F.

The "true" Cuban Royal Palm is *Roystonea regia* var. *regia*. Other related palms grown here that are similar but with less-spectacular trunks include other varieties of this species and also the Florida Royal Palm (*Roystonea elata*), which some botanists consider to be another variety of *Roystonea regia*.   **B29,QBG**

Catamaran Hotel, 3999 Mission Blvd., San Diego

Salix babylonica
(SAY-liks   bab-il-AH-nih-kuh)

WEEPING WILLOW
Salicaceae
China

There are nearly 400 species of willows worldwide, most of them native to the temperate and colder climates of the Northern Hemisphere. In San Diego County they are familiar trees, with several types that grow naturally along streams and in wet places. Many species of willows are grown in gardens throughout the world, the most popular of which is the Weeping Willow. This graceful tree differs from most willows in its strongly pendent branchlets that hang straight down, and has been grown for centuries for its beautiful form and foliage.

The Weeping Willow is a deciduous tree that grows quickly to 30-50' tall and at least as wide. It has a bright green foliage of 3-6" long narrow leaves that densely clothe its weeping branchlets, creating a strongly vertical effect. It leafs out early in the spring and holds its foliage late into the fall, when its leaves turn yellow before dropping. This is a tree that loves moisture and is ideally suited to planting near a lake or stream. It can also with some training be grown to provide quick shade for a patio or other garden area. Like all willows, the Weeping Willow has weak wood and an aggressive shallow root system that is difficult to garden under. Although it is likely to be somewhat short-lived, it does grow very quickly, and is cold-hardy to below 0°F.   **B14**

Sycamore Ave. & Lobelia Dr., Vista

2013 Coast Blvd., Del Mar

Schefflera actinophylla
(SHEF-ler-uh   ak-ti-noh-FILL-uh)

QUEENSLAND UMBRELLA TREE
Araliaceae
Northeastern Australia and New Guinea

The beautiful tropical-looking foliage of the Queensland Umbrella Tree has made it one of the most popular indoor plants in the world. But if you're familiar with it only as an indoor plant, you'll be amazed at what it can do as a garden tree. Formerly known as *Brassaia actinophylla*, this evergreen rainforest tree grows quickly to 20-35' tall here, performing best in frost-free coastal gardens. The Queensland Umbrella Tree gets its common name from the shape of its large glossy-green compound leaves, which are composed of 7 to 16 foot-long leaflets that radiate outward from a central point like the ribs of an umbrella.

Although the Queensland Umbrella Tree as a houseplant is grown just for its foliage, as a garden tree it also produces spectacular clusters of flowers. From late fall to spring, 3' long twisting stems of small bright red flowers appear in bunches at the ends of its vertical branches, looking like the tentacles of a red octopus (which gives this tree its other common name, the Octopus Tree). Especially when in bloom, this is a tree that makes a striking silhouette against the sky.

The Queensland Umbrella Tree grows in full sun or partial shade, but is best with a little shade in inland gardens. It likes regular watering and fertilizing and a rich, well-drained soil. It should be protected from frost, but mature trees will recover from temperatures as low as 25°F.   **B23,QBG**

Juvenile foliage

Adult foliage

2700 Second Ave., San Diego

Schefflera elegantissima
(SHEF-ler-uh   e-leh-gan-TIH-sih-muh)

FALSE ARALIA
Araliaceae
New Caledonia

As a young plant, the evergreen False Aralia is a popular houseplant that is grown for its lacy-looking juvenile foliage, which some people think looks like marijuana leaves. As it matures, however, its foliage looks very different, and it makes an attractive small garden tree. A young False Aralia is single-stemmed, with dark green leaves composed of 7 to 11 long narrow leaflets that are deeply serrated. As the plant matures, it begins to branch and produces leaves with leaflets that are much wider, thicker, and lighter green. Mature plants produce long clusters of small greenish-yellow flowers, followed by black berries.

The False Aralia grows fairly slowly to around 15' tall and wide in full sun or partial shade near the coast, but is better with some shade farther inland. It likes regular watering and fertilizing, and a rich well-drained soil. Best in frost-free coastal gardens, it should be protected from frost, but older plants will recover from temperatures as low as 27°F. Formerly known as *Dizygotheca elegantissima*, the False Aralia is still sometimes sold under that name but is now classified as a *Schefflera*.   **B35,QBG**

124

Schefflera pueckleri
(SHEF-ler-uh   PYOO-kler-eye)

TUPIDANTHUS

Araliaceae
Tropical Asia

Formerly known as *Tupidanthus calyptratus* (and still often sold under that name), the Tupidanthus has recently been reclassified as a member of the genus *Schefflera*. Shrubby at first, it makes a handsome multi-trunked small tree with beautiful evergreen tropical-looking foliage that is particularly effective when planted near buildings. The Tupidanthus grows at a moderate rate to 15-25' tall and wide, with glossy dark green leaves that are composed of 7 to 9 slightly pendulous leaflets, each to 10" long and 3-4" wide. It blooms in winter, with 1/2" green flowers which are followed by clusters of 1" long mallet-shaped green fruits.

Because their leaves resemble each other's, the Tupidanthus is sometimes confused with the Queensland Umbrella Tree (*Schefflera actinophylla*). It is very different in flower, however, and also in its habit of branching from its base to make a multi-stemmed clump. The Tupidanthus likes regular watering and good drainage and is cold-hardy to 27°F. It grows in full sun or partial shade near the coast, but is best with some shade inland. A handsome variegated form is also grown with leaflets boldly splashed with creamy-yellow.   **B35,QBG**

Casa del Prado, Balboa Park

Schinus molle
(SKY-nus   MOE-lay)

CALIFORNIA PEPPER TREE

Anacardiaceae
Peru

In 1830, Father Antonio Peyri of Mission San Luis Rey planted some seeds which had been given to him by a sailor who knew only that "they came from South America." This was the first planting in California of a tree that came to be known as the California Pepper Tree, and one of Father Peyri's original seedlings survives to this day in the mission gardens in Oceanside. Native to the Andes Mountains of Peru, the evergreen California Pepper Tree is renowned for its fast growth, graceful form, and extreme tolerance of heat and drought, and so has been a popular landscape tree here for over 150 years.

The California Pepper Tree grows quickly to 40' tall, spreading wider with age. It has a thick gnarled trunk with rough grayish bark, heavy main limbs, and weeping branchlets. Its bright green, aromatic foliage is composed of compound leaves with many narrow 2" long leaflets. In spring and summer, it blooms with 4-6" hanging clusters of tiny pale yellow flowers, which on female trees are followed in the fall and winter by clusters of rose-pink to rose-red fruits that look and smell like peppercorns and are attractive to birds.

The California Pepper Tree has aggressive surface roots and drops large quantities of leaves and fruits, but it is a handsome tree that is very tough. It tolerates most any soil, desert heat, and cold temperatures down to 10°F. It prefers not to be overwatered, and too much water too close to its trunk will shorten its life.   **B36,QBG**

Wallace St., Old Town, San Diego

125

Carlsbad Village Dr. & Roosevelt St., Carlsbad

Schinus terebinthifolius
(SKY-nus teh-reh-bin-thi-FOE-lee-us)

BRAZILIAN PEPPER TREE
Anacardiaceae
Brazil

Because of its dense evergreen foliage, strong growth, and manageable size, the Brazilian Pepper Tree is frequently planted as a street tree in Southern California. Most trees are grown from seed, however, and seedlings of this species vary in their growth habits and fruiting characteristics. This tree is a bad weed in many parts of the world, and although it is not as aggressive here, it still can seed itself into places where it is not wanted.

The Brazilian Pepper Tree grows at a moderate rate to 30-40' tall, with a wider spread as it matures. It has a rounded canopy of dark green foliage composed of compound leaves to 8" long with 5-13 oval 1-3" long leaflets. Clusters of small cream-colored flowers are produced from spring through fall, followed in winter on female trees by pink to red berry-like fruits which are attractive to birds but poisonous to humans. Female trees vary in both the size and quantity of fruits they produce, and male trees set no fruit but often have a tidier growth habit.

The Brazilian Pepper Tree prefers regular watering and is tolerant of poor soil, heat, and cold temperatures down to 20°F. Whether you grow it for its colorful fruits or prefer a tree that sets no fruit (and so will not be weedy), it is a good idea to select a tree during fruiting season to get the characteristics you want. **B36**

Quail Botanical Gardens

Schizolobium parahyba
(skiz-oh-LOE-bee-um pair-uh-HYE-buh)

BRAZILIAN FERN TREE
Fabaceae (Leguminosae)
Southern Mexico to Southern Brazil

Unusual and spectacular, the Brazilian Fern Tree is not a fern at all but is a member of the legume family allied to both *Cassia* and *Senna*. This is a tall, fast-growing tree that loves heat and is evergreen in the mildest climates but goes deciduous with winter cold. The Brazilian Fern Tree has a dramatic growth habit, with a single straight trunk that grows up to 30' tall before it branches. Atop this dominant trunk is a bright green, open crown of large 3' long fern-like leaves composed of many 3/4" to 1" long narrow leaflets. Flowering on mature trees may occur in spring or summer, and is an impressive show of large spikes of 1" light yellow flowers at the ends of the branches. Flowering is followed by 5" long by 2" wide seed pods, each containing a single large seed.

The Brazilian Fern Tree grows to 100' tall in the tropics, but it is likely to grow only half that tall here. It likes full sun, regular watering and fertilizing, and good drainage, but dislikes cold wet soils. Because its wood is somewhat brittle, it is best grown in a spot that is protected from strong winds. Although it is a tropical tree, the Brazilian Fern Tree has proven to be hardy to at least 25°F. in inland areas where it gets lots of summer heat. **B24,QBG**

Schotia brachypetala
(SKOE-tee-uh brak-ee-PET-uh-luh)
TREE FUCHSIA
Fabaceae (Leguminosae)
Zimbabwe, Mozambique, and South Africa

The Tree Fuchsia is a subtropical African tree of great character that is native to semi-desert areas and is tolerant of drought and heat. In a warm spring following a dry winter, it can be spectacular in bloom. This is a small tree here which grows at a moderate rate to 20-25' tall and wide, often with multiple trunks. Its glossy foliage is composed of compound leaves with oval leaflets to 3" long. The Tree Fuchsia is mostly evergreen, but it may drop all or most of its leaves for a brief time just before it flowers in May or June. New foliage is quickly produced, however, and is a colorful pink or red color before aging to copper and then to dark green. The Tree Fuchsia is showy in bloom, with large clusters of fragrant waxy bright crimson flowers produced along the branches and even out of hard wood. The flowers are rich in nectar, attracting birds and also baboons and monkeys in the tree's native land, and are followed by flat, dark brown 5" long seed pods.

The Tree Fuchsia likes full sun and heat, and will grow with regular or just occasional watering. Young plants are tender to frost, but mature trees are cold-hardy to at least 25°F. A related species that is sometimes grown here is *Schotia latifolia*, which differs in its clusters of pink flowers which are produced at the ends of the branches only. **B4,QBG**

Quail Botanical Gardens

Senna spectabilis
(SEN-uh spek-TAB-ih-lis)
CROWN OF GOLD TREE
Fabaceae (Leguminosae)
South America

The Crown of Gold Tree is spectacular in late summer when it is covered with showy clusters of bright yellow flowers. Over the years, it has been known and grown as *Cassia excelsa*, *Cassia carnaval*, and *Cassia spectabilis*; now, due to a recent revision of that genus, it is classified as *Senna spectabilis*.

The Crown of Gold Tree is a medium-sized tree that grows fairly quickly to 25-35' tall with an equal spread. It has a dense, rounded crown of bright green tropical-looking foliage composed of 7-18" long compound leaves with pairs of 1-3" long leaflets. In late summer and early fall, it blooms with large 12-16" tall upright spikes of 1" wide bright yellow flowers which create a colorful show above the foliage, with a mature tree in bloom completely covered with flowers. After flowering, 6-12" long black seed pods are produced.

The Crown of Gold Tree loves heat and tolerates cold down to 26°F. It can be completely evergreen in the mildest climates, but in colder areas usually loses all or part of its leaves for a brief time in late winter or early spring. It loves full sun, good drainage, and regular watering, but dislikes cold wet soils.

554 Arden Dr., Encinitas

Sequoia sempervirens
(seh-KOY-uh sem-per-VEER-enz)
COAST REDWOOD
Taxodiaceae
Southern Oregon to Central California

In cool Northern California coastal forests, native stands of the Coast Redwood contain the tallest trees on Earth, with some individuals exceeding 350' in height. Although it won't grow that tall here, this majestic evergreen conifer grows well in Southern California gardens, especially if you choose a named variety that has the vigor to withstand our more-challenging climate.

In cultivation here, the Coast Redwood grows fairly quickly when young, slowing to an eventual 50-60' tall and 25-30' wide at maturity. Its growth habit is elegant, with a tiered branching structure that forms a symmetrical pyramid of soft-looking dark green to bluish-green foliage composed of flat, narrow 1" long leaves (not leaflets) that grow in a flat plane on both sides of slender stems. Older trees develop thick trunks with characteristic fibrous reddish-brown bark and produce 1" long roundish brown cones.

The Coast Redwood loves water, does well in lawns, and is very effective when planted in groups. It is cold-hardy to at least 10°F., but does not like heat or dry winds. For the best performance in our climate, choose a cutting-grown variety with a vigorous growth habit and thick foliage that can withstand heat and dry air. One of the best is 'Majestic Beauty', which has dense bluish-green foliage. **B7,QBG**

1621 Rudd Rd., Vista

2606 Evergreen St., Point Loma

Spathodea campanulata
(spath-OH-dee-uh kam-pan-yoo-LAY-tuh)
AFRICAN TULIP TREE
Bignoniaceae
Tropical Africa

The African Tulip Tree is known throughout the world as one of the most beautiful of all flowering trees. At its best in frost-free areas only, it grows at a moderate rate here to 30-40' tall and 30' wide, with a dense, rounded crown of dark green tropical-looking foliage. Its large compound leaves are 18-24" long and composed of 7-19 oval leaflets each up to 6" long by 2" wide. In late summer and fall, this amazing tree produces spectacular football-sized flower clusters at the ends of its branches, with many pointed flower buds opening into frilly 4" tulip-shaped red-orange flowers. This bloom is not only showy but entertaining as well, since the unopened flower buds are full of watery nectar and make excellent water pistols when squeezed. Fully open flowers also make colorful hanky-like pocket ornaments.

The African Tulip Tree likes full sun, regular watering, and a rich, well-drained soil away from cold ocean winds. It is very tender to frost when young, but mature trees will recover from temperatures as low as 27°F. Although it may be evergreen in the mildest coastal gardens, it is usually winter-deciduous in colder areas here. There is also a beautiful golden-yellow flowered form which is usually sold as 'Aurea'. **B22,QBG**

Stenocarpus sinuatus
(steh-noe-CAR-pus sin-yoo-AY-tus)
FIREWHEEL TREE
Proteaceae
Eastern Australia

Native to subtropical rainforests of Queensland and New South Wales, the remarkable Firewheel Tree is one of Australia's most distinctive flowering trees. Also called the Rotary Tree, its rather fantastic scarlet-red and yellow flowers are arranged like the spokes of a wheel, which has led to its adoption as a mascot of Rotary Clubs around the world.

The Firewheel Tree is a slow-growing, densely foliaged evergreen, ultimately to 25-30' tall and 15' wide. Its shiny, dark green leathery leaves are up to 12" long and deeply lobed on young trees, becoming smaller and unlobed as the tree matures. Flowering may occur at any time of the year, but it is usually heaviest in fall and winter, when large clusters of 3" wide "wheels" provide a bright show of color. Trees are typically grown from seed, and should be expected to take a number of years to reach maturity and flower well.

The Firewheel Tree is tender to frost when young, but older trees will tolerate temperatures as low as 25°F. It grows best with regular watering in a deep, rich, well-drained acid soil with protection from salty ocean winds, and benefits from occasional feeding with micronutrients. The Firewheel Tree resents being moved and is typically slow to establish after planting. Particularly in coastal areas, however, older trees can be magnificent and are well worth the wait. **B8,QBG**

East of Carlsbad Train Station, Carlsbad

Strelitzia nicolai
(streh-LIT-zee-uh NIH-koe-lye)
GIANT BIRD OF PARADISE
Strelitziaceae
Southeastern Africa

To someone unfamiliar with the Giant Bird of Paradise, the first encounter with a mature specimen is likely to be a memorable event. With its tall, palm-like trunks, banana-like leaves, and unusual flowers, this clumping tree-like plant looks like it was designed in a studio, not taken from nature. If nothing else, just the sheer size of a fully grown plant is impressive. The Giant Bird of Paradise grows at a moderate rate to 30-35' tall, with a dramatic evergreen foliage of long-stalked 5-10' gray-green leathery leaves arranged in a fan shape on thick erect or curving trunks. It blooms in spring or early summer, with clusters of 8" white and lavender-blue flowers emerging from 16-18" long boat-like purple spathes that grow from each crown of leaves.

The Giant Bird of Paradise grows in full sun or partial shade with regular watering, but will tolerate some drought once established. It is cold-hardy to around 26°F, but since frost will damage its leaves a protected location is best. Strong winds can also cause leaf damage, so a wind-protected spot is ideal. Generous fertilizing will help young plants grow quickly, but fertilizer should be withheld for slower growth. **B22,QBG**

1390 Park Row, La Jolla

129

Syagrus romanzoffiana
(sye-AG-rus roe-man-zoff-ee-AN-uh)
QUEEN PALM
Arecaceae (Palmae)
South America

Because of its fast growth, graceful habit, and all-around toughness, the Queen Palm is the most popular "feather palm" in California. Even when planted as a young plant, it quickly makes a strong straight trunk and a handsome crown of foliage, creating a bold, tropical look in a short period of time. Native to Brazil, Argentina, Paraguay, and Uruguay, the Queen Palm grows to 50' tall, with a thick gray trunk and a 20' wide crown of dark green, arching fronds that have long slender leaflets. Older trees produce large hanging clusters of creamy-yellow flowers which are followed by showy orange fruits in summer.

The Queen Palm tolerates heat as well as cold, and grows well in a wide variety of climates. Although it may suffer some damage at 25°F., mature trees have survived temperatures as low as 16°F. Regular watering is best, but trees can be quite drought-tolerant when mature. Nitrogen fertilizers will make young trees grow even faster.

When a common landscape plant's botanical name is changed, gardeners and nurserymen are often dismayed—but there are usually good reasons for the new name. Long known as *Cocos plumosa*, then reclassified as *Arecastrum romanzoffianum*, the Queen Palm has now been reclassified again as *Syagrus romanzoffiana* because it was decided that it was not sufficiently distinct from other palms to have a genus of its own (note that the spelling of the species name changes slightly in the new name because of the rules of Latin grammar).   **B9,QBG**

758 J Ave., Coronado

Quail Botanical Gardens

Syzygium jambos
(sih-ZIH-jee-um JAM-boce)
ROSE APPLE
Myrtaceae
Southeastern Asia

Nearly 1000 species make up the large Old World genus *Syzygium*, which was separated some time ago from the related but now mostly New World genus *Eugenia*. Many species in both genera are not only ornamental but also produce edible fruit, and grow well in gardens where frost is not severe.

The Rose Apple is a spreading evergreen tree that grows at a moderate rate to 25-30' tall and wide, with a handsome dark green foliage of 4-7" long leathery leaves that are crimson-red when young. It blooms in spring with attractive clusters of 2-3" flowers composed of many creamy-white stamens, followed in summer by round 2" pinkish-yellow fruits that have a firm, edible pulp.

The fruit of the Rose Apple has a delicious fragrance just like roses—but the surprise is that it actually tastes like roses, too. It may be eaten fresh, but is most popular in the tropics for use in jellies and preserves. The Rose Apple grows best in full sun with good drainage and regular watering. It is tender to frost when young, but established trees will tolerate cold down to 27°F.   **B14,QBG**

Syzygium paniculatum
(sih-ZIH-jee-um pan-ik-yoo-LAY-tum)
AUSTRALIAN BRUSH CHERRY
Myrtaceae
Eastern Australia

Long popular in California as a clipped hedge, the Australian Brush Cherry is actually a rainforest tree that is native to coastal areas of eastern Australia. Allowed to grow naturally, it is a broadly columnar evergreen to 30-50' tall and 10-20' wide with either single or multiple trunks, strongly vertical branching, and a dense crown of glossy-green to bronzy-green foliage composed of 2-3" long oblong leaves which are reddish-bronze when young. The Australian Brush Cherry blooms in summer with clusters of small creamy-white flowers that are composed of numerous stamens. Flowers are followed by showy 3/4" rosy-purple berries that are attractive to birds. Although this fruit is not tasty when fresh, it is edible and may be made into jams and jellies.

The Australian Brush Cherry is fast-growing, but it needs protection from strong winds when grown as a tree. It likes regular watering and a well-drained soil, and is cold hardy to 25°F. It is still sometimes sold as *Eugenia myrtifolia*, which is an older name. The Australian Brush Cherry is unfortunately susceptible to a leaf-disfiguring pest called eugenia psyllid. Although efforts to control this pest through the release of predatory insects have had fair results, some infestation still persists.   **B33,QBG**

Tabebuia chrysotricha
(tab-eh-BOO-ee-uh krye-so-TRY-kuh)
GOLDEN TRUMPET TREE
Bignoniaceae
Colombia and Brazil

The spectacular trumpet trees in the genus *Tabebuia* are surely among the most beautiful flowering trees in the world. In Southern California, there are two species of these Jacaranda relatives that out-perform the rest, both of which were first introduced here by the Los Angeles County Botanic Garden in 1964.

The Golden Trumpet Tree is a briefly deciduous small tree that grows fairly slowly here to 25' tall and 20' wide. It has an open, irregular shape when young, but becomes rounded and spreading with age. Foliage is composed of light green, fuzzy leaves which are divided into five leaflets, each to 5" long by 2" wide. In late winter or early spring, the leaves drop just before flowering, when an impressive show of large clusters of 3-4" long bright yellow trumpet-shaped flowers can cover a mature tree for 4-6 weeks. Flowers are followed by a fresh new growth of foliage and also long, narrow, fuzzy seed pods that split open to shed papery seeds.

The Golden Trumpet Tree loves full sun and heat and is cold-hardy to 25°F. It grows best with regular watering and fertilizing, but is drought-tolerant once established. It will bloom as a young tree, but it produces many more flowers over a longer period of time as it matures, with trees becoming showier the older they get.   **B26,QBG**

3566 7th Ave., Uptown

9877 Waples St., Mira Mesa

131

West side of Presidio Park, San Diego

Tabebuia impetiginosa
(tab-eh-BOO-ee-uh   im-peh-ti-ji-NOH-suh)
PINK TRUMPET TREE
Bignoniaceae
Mexico to Argentina

With its graceful branching structure, attractive foliage, and extravagant show of spring flowers, the Pink Trumpet Tree is an outstanding small tree for the landscape. It grows fairly quickly as a young tree, slowing to a moderate rate as it attains its mature size of 25-30' tall and wide. Its leaves are divided into 3-7 shiny olive-green leaflets, each to around 4" long by 2" wide. Foliage is shed in early spring just before flowering, the timing of which may vary according to weather, microclimate, and individual tree. Mature trees can bloom for 4-6 weeks with large round clusters of 3" long fragrant, ruffled, trumpet-shaped flowers which vary from pink to lavender-purple and develop a yellow throat as they age. Flowers are followed by a fresh growth of foliage and long, narrow seed pods, and some trees can even bloom again in the fall.

The Pink Trumpet Tree likes a well-drained soil in full sun and is cold-hardy to 25°F. It loves heat and typically blooms most profusely in warmer inland climates. This is a tree that needs to be established for a number of years before it blooms well, but after that it just gets better and better as it gets older.

As currently defined, the species *Tabebuia impetiginosa* includes a wide range of forms which differ significantly in their growth habits and flowering characteristics. Two superior selections that are grown as grafted plants are 'Pink Cloud', a 25' spreading tree with especially fragrant rose-pink flowers, and 'Raspberry', a tall tree to 40-50' that is sometimes classified as *Tabebuia avellanedae*. **B26,QBG**

East side of Presidio Park, San Diego

Taxodium distichum
(taks-OH-dee-um   DISS-tih-kum)
BALD CYPRESS
Taxodiaceae
Southeastern United States

Native to swamps and streamsides from Delaware to Florida to Texas, the Bald Cypress is a stately deciduous conifer that tolerates a wide variety of growing conditions. Although old trees in habitat are much larger and broad-topped, in cultivation here it grows to around 50-70' tall and 20-30' wide with a pyramidal habit of growth. The Bald Cypress is related to the Dawn Redwood (*Metasequoia glyptostroboides*), and like it has small roundish cones and a dense, feathery summer foliage composed of bright green 1/2" long narrow leaves which age to a deeper green before turning bronzy-orange and dropping in the fall. In winter, it presents an attractive silhouette that shows off its tall, straight trunk and symmetrical branches.

The Bald Cypress grows quickly in a wide variety of soils and climates, and is cold-hardy to 0°F. It is famous for tolerating extremely wet conditions, and will even grow in waterlogged soil, where it develops knobby root growths called "knees" that help its roots to breathe. It also grows well in ordinary garden conditions, however, and will even tolerate slightly dry soil. **B30,QBG**

132

Taxodium mucronatum
(taks-OH-dee-um myoo-kro-NAY-tum)
MONTEZUMA CYPRESS
Taxodiaceae
Mexico

The Montezuma Cypress is an elegant, long-lived conifer that is well-adapted to our climate and deserves more widespread use. This tree is famous for its largest living representative, which is an ancient wild specimen in Oaxaca with a trunk over 150' around that makes it the world's fattest tree. In cultivation, the Montezuma Cypress can grow to an eventual 75' tall and 50' wide if given adequate water, although many older trees here are not nearly that tall. It is distinguished by its graceful, spreading form and strongly weeping branches, with a dense foliage of 1/2" narrow leaves that are lighter green and finer in texture than the related Bald Cypress (*Taxodium distichum*). Its small round cones are similar to the Bald Cypress but slightly larger.

The Montezuma Cypress grows quickly with regular watering, but slowly in drier conditions. It is evergreen in Southern California coastal climates, but can shed some or all of its leaves in cold-winter climates, where it is cold-hardy to around 10°F. This is an excellent tree for big lawns that deserves to have the space to show off its attractive form. Spectacular old specimens of this tree may be seen at the Huntington Botanical Gardens in San Marino, where they are beautifully displayed. **B18,QBG**

East side of Presidio Park, San Diego

Old Town, San Diego

Tecoma stans
(teh-KOE-muh STANS)
YELLOW BELLS
Bignoniaceae
Southern U.S., Mexico, Central and South America

Shrubby at first, the Yellow Bells can be trained into a beautiful small tree in any garden where frosts seldom occur. In mild coastal gardens, it is not only evergreen but also nearly everblooming, and always attracts attention. The Yellow Bells grows at a moderate rate to 15-25' tall and 10-20' wide, and may be trained to either a single trunk or multiple trunks. It has a bright green foliage of compound leaves with 5 to 13 leaflets each 3-5" long by 1-2" wide. Flowering occurs nearly all year in the mildest microclimates, and from late spring through fall in colder areas, with large clusters of 2" long, bright yellow, sweetly fragrant trumpet-shaped flowers followed by narrow seed pods that contain small papery seeds. Even young plants bloom, but flower clusters get bigger and more numerous as trees mature.

The Yellow Bells likes a well-drained soil in full sun and regular watering and feeding. It loves heat but does not like frost, and will suffer damage below 27°F. As a species it is quite variable, and the best garden trees are propagated from large-leaved, large-flowered plants. If you purchase a young seedling tree, remember that seedlings with the largest leaflets will have the best flowers when they bloom. **B1,QBG**

133

Thevetia thevetiodes
(theh-VEE-tee-uh   theh-vee-tee-OY-deez)
GIANT THEVETIA
Apocynaceae
Mexico

The Giant Thevetia looks something like a large yellow-flowered Oleander, and in fact the two are related. This fast-growing evergreen is shrubby at first, but is easily trained as a muliti-trunked spreading tree to 15-20' tall and wide. The Giant Thevetia has an open foliage composed of dark green narrow leaves to 6" long and 1/2" wide. The upper sides of the leaves are glossy, with a heavily corrugated texture. Flowering occurs in summer and fall, with 4" wide brilliant yellow funnel-shaped flowers that are prominently displayed on the ends of the branches, followed by 2-3" wide green fruits that ripen to black. These fruits are poisonous, as are all parts of this tree.

The Giant Thevetia likes a well-drained soil in full sun and regular watering and fertilizing. It loves heat and does not like frost, but is cold-hardy to 27°F. A related species that may also be trained as a tree in frost-free areas is the Yellow Oleander (*Thevetia peruviana*). The Yellow Oleander grows to 20-25' tall, and blooms from spring through fall with 2-3" long yellow, peach, or white flowers. **B17,QBG**

3658 Park Blvd., San Diego

Tipuana tipu
(tih-poo-ah-nuh   TEE-poo)
TIPU TREE
Fabaceae (Leguminosae)
Brazil, Bolivia, and Argentina

The tropical-looking Tipu Tree is remarkably fast-growing and also very tolerant of a wide variety of soils and growing conditions. In a new garden, it can be invaluable for its ability to quickly create a canopy of foliage to cool a house, shade a patio, or protect other plants. Because of its toughness, it is also becoming increasingly popular as a street tree.

The Tipu Tree can grow to 25' tall and wide in just a few years, ultimately growing to 40-50' tall with a wide, spreading crown. It has a dense foliage of 10" long light green divided leaves composed of 11-21 rounded 1-2" long leaflets, which is at least partially deciduous for a short time in late spring. Trees are showy in bloom in late spring and early summer with clusters of 1/2" yellow-orange pea-shaped flowers which are followed by 2-1/2" long winged seeds.

The Tipu Tree grows well with regular watering, but will also tolerate some drought. It accepts most any soil and is cold-hardy to 25°F., although mature trees can recover from temperatures as low as 18°F. This was a favorite tree of pioneer San Diego horticulturist Kate Sessions, who planted the specimen in the photo at left ninety years ago. Today, this tree is a California Registered Historical Landmark, and a bronze plaque commemorates the long and wonderful career of the "Mother of Balboa Park." **B11,QBG**

2500 Garnet Ave., Pacific Beach

134

Trachycarpus fortunei
(trak-ee-KAR-pus   for-TYOO-nee-eye)
WINDMILL PALM
Arecaceae (Palmae)
China

The Windmill Palm is a medium-sized fan palm from the mountains of China that is very tolerant of adverse conditions. Practically maintenance-free, it is often planted as a street tree here, where it survives even in the most challenging of sites. Growing at a slow to moderate rate to 30' tall, the Windmill Palm has a small, rounded crown of 3' wide dark green fan-shaped leaves with 18" long leaf stalks. These stiff, deeply cut leaves move windmill-like in the breeze, giving the tree its common name. The Windmill Palm has a distinctive trunk that is thicker towards the top of the tree and is covered by dark brown to black hairy fibers that persist for many years. It flowers in the spring with showy clusters of small pale yellow flowers that hang from long branching stalks, with the flowers sometimes followed by small bluish fruits.

The Windmill Palm likes full sun and is tolerant of poor soil, drought, and heat. One of the cold-hardiest palms, it can tolerate temperatures as low as 5°F. The fibers from the trunk of the Windmill Palm can be stripped off in sections and used to line hanging baskets, and is also used to make a variety of products in China. This palm is sometimes incorrectly sold in nurseries as *Chamaerops excelsa*.   **B18,QBG**

1561 Thomas Ave., Pacific Beach

East side of Ranch House, SeaWorld, San Diego

Tristaniopsis laurina
(tris-tan-ee-OP-sis   lor-EYE-nuh)
WATER GUM
Myrtaceae
Eastern Australia

Formerly known as *Tristania laurina*, the Water Gum is an attractive small evergreen that grows slowly and is very well-mannered. Shrubby when young, it grows to just 10' tall and 5' wide in 8 years, eventually reaching around 20' tall and 8' wide here. The Water Gum has a formal, somewhat columnar growth habit, with a dense foliage of leathery dark green leaves to 4" long and 1" wide that are coppery-red when young. It blooms in late spring and early summer with showy clusters of small, lightly fragrant yellow flowers that are held tightly along the twigs and young branches. Flowers are followed by small 1/2" seed capsules. Older trees have attractive mahogany-colored bark that peels off to reveal white new bark underneath.

The Water Gum grows in full sun or partial shade and is cold-hardy to around 20°F. It likes regular watering and will tolerate wet conditions as long as drainage is good. Trees are often trained with multiple trunks, and can even make good container plants. This is a neat, litter-free tree that can be useful in confined spaces. A cutting-grown selection called 'Elegant' has improved foliage, with broader leaves which are bright red when young and darker green when mature.   **QBG**

Ulmus parvifolia
(UL-mus   par-vi-FOE-lee-uh)
CHINESE ELM
Ulmaceae
China, Korea, and Japan

Sometimes called the Evergreen Elm, the Chinese Elm is a highly variable species which can actually be deciduous in some forms and also in cold winters. In Southern California, it is a common shade and street tree that is most popular for its evergreen or nearly evergreen varieties.

The Chinese Elm is a fast-growing tree that can reach 30' tall in as little as 5 years. Ultimately, it grows to 40-60' tall and 50-70' wide. Its form is variable, but trees are generally spreading, with long arching branches and a weeping habit. Trunks of older trees have a brownish bark that sheds in small patches to create a mottled effect. The foliage of the Chinese Elm is dense and dark green, composed of leathery toothed leaves 1-2" long and 1/2" to 3/4" wide. Inconspicuous green flowers in late summer are followed by clusters of small tan-colored winged fruits in the fall.

The Chinese Elm grows easily in nearly any soil and any climate and is cold-hardy to below 0°F. Because of its rapid growth, it may need occasional pruning to strengthen its structure, particularly in windy areas. Many named varieties are grown with different foliage and growth characteristics, and there are even dwarf.and miniature varieties that are used for bonsai. All types of Chinese Elm are resistant to Dutch Elm disease.   **B15**

930 Morse St., Oceanside

Vitex lucens
(VYE-teks   LOO-senz)
PURIRI
Lamiaceae (Labiatae)
New Zealand

The Puriri is an elegant small to medium-sized evergreen tree with attractive glossy foliage and interesting flowers. It grows fairly quickly to 25-30' tall and wide here, with a rounded or spreading crown of bright green tropical-looking foliage. The leaves of the Puriri are very shiny and are composed of 3-5 wavy-edged 5" long leaflets that are arranged in a fan shape. In fall and winter, trees produce clusters of 1" pink to reddish flowers, with older trees blooming more heavily than younger ones.

The Puriri likes regular watering and fertilizing and a rich, well-drained soil in full sun or partial shade. It looks its best with protection from strong winds and frost, but is cold-hardy to 25°F.

A related but very different plant is the Chaste Tree (*Vitex agnus-castus*). Sometimes grown as a large shrub, this fast-growing deciduous native of southern Europe may be trained into a multiple-trunked tree 15-20' tall and wide. The Chaste Tree has a dense summer foliage of grayish-green divided leaves that look a little like marijuana leaves, and blooms in late spring and summer with showy 6-8" long spikes of tiny lavender-blue flowers at the ends of its branches. Grown as a tree, it is cold-hardy to around 20°F.   **B8,QBG**

NW side of SeaWorld, San Diego

Washingtonia filifera
(wah-shing-TOE-nee-uh   fih-LIH-fer-uh)
CALIFORNIA FAN PALM
Arecaceae (Palmae)
Southern California, southwestern Arizona, and
northern Baja California, Mexico

The imposing California Fan Palm is the only palm native
to California, and is further distinguished (along with the
Mexican Fan Palm below) by being named in honor of the
first president of our country, General George Washington.
This is the palm of Palm Springs, and it can be seen growing
naturally near wet places in canyons and washes of our San
Diego County desert areas as well.

The California Fan Palm grows at a moderate rate to 60-
70' tall with a thick columnar trunk that is smooth and dark
gray. It has a 15' wide evergreen crown of large, fan-shaped
light green leaves with long leaf stalks and cottony threads
that hang from the leaf tips. Older leaves persist on the tree,
forming a "skirt" of brown thatch. Flowering occurs in spring,
with large hanging clusters of tiny white flowers followed in
winter by small black fruits.

Well-adapted to desert and inland areas, the California
Fan Palm needs full sun and tolerates extreme heat and
drought, but will grow faster with regular watering. It is cold-
hardy to 15°F.   **B43,QBG**

1910 S. Ditmar St., Oceanside

915 Alameda Blvd., Coronado

Washingtonia robusta
(wah-shing-TOE-nee-uh   roe-BUS-tuh)
MEXICAN FAN PALM
Arecaceae (Palmae)
Northwestern Mexico and Baja California, Mexico

Although it occurs naturally only in Mexico, the Mexican
Fan Palm is practically emblematic of Southern California and
has been planted here in great numbers for well over a century.
It is our most dominant skyline tree, and by far the most
common palm we grow.

The Mexican Fan Palm is our fastest-growing palm and also
our tallest, ultimately reaching a height of 100'. It has a
distinctively slender trunk that is studded with reddish-brown
leaf bases on young fast-growing trees but smooth and gray on
older trees. Its evergreen crown of foliage is composed of large,
glossy, bright green fan-shaped leaves with leaf stalks that have
a red streak underneath. Older leaves persist, forming a "skirt"
of brown thatch on unpruned trees. Flower clusters are 2-3'
long, with tiny creamy-white flowers followed by small
purplish-blue fruits. The single seeds within are likely to be
spread by birds, resulting in "volunteer" palms that come up by
themselves under trees in gardens.

The Mexican Fan Palm grows quickly and easily in nearly
any situation. It is tolerant of drought, and is cold-hardy to
20°F. Sometimes confused with the California Fan Palm
(above), the Mexican Fan Palm grows taller, with a much more
slender trunk and a more compact crown of brighter green
foliage. Hybrids between the two are grown, however, with
intermediate characteristics.   **B23,QBG**

137

Xylosma congestum
(zye-LOZ-muh   kon-JES-tum)
SHINY XYLOSMA
Flacourtiaceae
China

The Shiny Xylosma is well known in California as a basic landscape foliage plant. Often grown as a large shrub, this evergreen may also be trained as a single or multi-trunked small tree. Trained as a tree, the Shiny Xylosma grows at a moderate rate to 15-25' tall with an equal or greater spread. It has a loose, gracefully mounding canopy of foliage composed of shiny 2-3" long yellow-green leaves and reddish-bronze new growth. The Shiny Xylosma can produce clusters of small yellow flowers in the fall, but it is a shy bloomer.

The Shiny Xylosma grows in full sun or partial shade, and is adaptable to most soils and climates. It is drought-tolerant when established, but looks better with regular watering. It is cold-hardy to 10°F., but trees may lose some or all of their leaves after a heavy frost. The Shiny Xylosma should be pruned occasionally to maintain a sturdy structure and pleasing form. Unfortunately, an insect pest called Giant Whitefly can be a problem for this tree—frequent spraying with a hard jet of water from the hose is one way to discourage this pest.　　　　**B36,QBG**

3750 Trudy Lane, Point Loma

1902 Ditmar St., Oceanside

Yucca elephantipes
(YUK-uh   el-ef-an-TYE-peez)
GIANT YUCCA
Agavaceae
Mexico and Central America

The genus *Yucca* is composed of about 40 species of plants which are native to dry areas of North America, Central America, and the West Indies. Within this group are a number of tree-like species, including our Mojave Desert native Joshua Tree (*Yucca brevifolia*). Although the Joshua Tree is very difficult in cultivation and extremely slow-growing, a few of its more southerly relatives are fast and easy here, and may be seen in many gardens. Of these, the Giant Yucca is the largest and most tree-like of them all.

Native to Mexico and Central America, the Giant Yucca grows quickly to an eventual 15-30' tall and half as wide. It often develops several trunks from a large, woody base, but may also have a single trunk which branches higher up. The Giant Yucca is evergreen, with a dominant silhouette of thick gray branches that are densely clothed with stiff, dark green sword-shaped leaves. In late summer and fall it is spectacular in bloom, with tall spikes of many 2" long creamy-white pendent flowers.

The Giant Yucca likes a well-drained soil in full sun, and is cold-hardy to around 25°F. It is quite drought-tolerant, but grows best with moderate to regular watering. A number of hybrids or forms of it are grown, including the plant that is often called the Spanish Dagger and is sold as *Yucca gloriosa*.

138

About the San Diego Horticultural Society

Since our founding in 1994 the SDHS has grown to over 1200 members, including passionate backyard gardeners, garden designers, nursery owners, garden writers, landscape architects, and other horticultural professionals. Our mission is to promote the enjoyment, art, knowledge and public awareness of horticulture in the San Diego area, while providing the opportunity for education and research. Our motto, Let's Talk Plants!, perfectly sums up what most members like best about the SDHS – it provides a forum for plant enthusiasts to share their knowledge. Free friendly monthly meetings include professional speakers, plant sales, opportunity drawings, plant descriptions by experts and much more. They attract over 350 people, from the beginning gardener to the experienced orchid hybridizer.

Membership benefits include our monthly 26-page newsletter of locally-relevant gardening information. We have an extensive lending library of books and videos, including videos of our speakers. We organize garden tours, have a user-friendly website, and annually host an evening with world-famous horticulturists like Christopher Lloyd, Rosalind Creasy and Dan Hinkley. We give "Excellence in Horticulture" awards at the San Diego County Fair, plus cash prizes to horticultural projects at the Greater San Diego High School Science and Engineering Fair. We award three annual $1000 scholarships to horticulture majors at local colleges, and provide financial support to Quail Botanical Gardens and other institutions. Our Plant Forum Compilation, with descriptions of thousands of plants displayed at our meetings, is edited by Kathy Musial, Curator of Living Collections at The Huntington Botanical Gardens. Each year we honor a local Horticulturist of the Year.

In our second decade we find that what mattered most in the beginning is still of prime importance, namely the delight in sharing our knowledge of plants and learning more about all aspects of horticulture. The SDHS is a friendly, happy group that reaches and serves the average gardener as well as the professional, yet still gives correct and dependable information. This book is a fine example of how we accomplish our mission, and it will help you learn more about the outstanding trees that can grow in your garden.

Susi Torre-Bueno, President
Encinitas, California
September, 2005

Callistemon 'Jeffers' displayed at our April 2005 meeting. Bonsai specimen trained by Phil Tacktill. Photo by Ken Brit

SDHS award-winning display garden at the 2005 San Diego County Fair. Garden designed by Bill Teague. Garden sculpture by Rick Hartner, Sitting Duck Studio, Vista.

How to Select a Tree for the Garden

San Diego's mild Mediterranean climate gives us a wonderful selection of potential trees from which to choose. This book will hopefully make those decisions a little easier. Planting a tree is an important consideration that can have long-reaching results. Many things need to be factored in when making that selection, such as whether the tree is evergreen or deciduous, drought-tolerant, and the amount of maintenance required. Flower color, time of flowering, bark interest, fall color, winter structure and fruit are also important considerations. San Diego is one of the few places where, with a varied planting, one can have trees with color all year long.

The most important consideration is the eventual size of the tree. The needs of the space should be the determining factor in which tree is chosen. This kind of forethought can minimize future maintenance and water consumption. The eventual size and shape of each tree is genetically predetermined. In addition, the genetic code also determines the life span and speed at which a tree grows. Slower plants are usually better long-term picks to minimize maintenance, while fast trees have a tendency to have weak wood and be short-lived.

Trees provide the backbone and main structure in our gardens, and should be one of the first considerations when designing a garden. The placement of a tree can be critical. If planting a tree near a structure, choose a site such that no major limbs will be within four feet of the roofline. Also consider the root structure of the mature tree. Large trees have large roots, and should not be planted near foundations, sidewalks or patios. Working with nature is always easier than fighting it.

One should not overlook the cooling benefits of trees. A deciduous tree planted on the south or west side of a home can greatly cool in the summer, while in the winter, the open canopy can let in all the winter sun. Utility bills can be greatly reduced while at the same time creating great beauty in the garden. The canopy of a mature tree can also make a microclimate, which lets us grow plants from an even wider climatic range.

Landscaping is meant to compliment the architectural style with which we are working. Much of San Diego's architecture is Mediterranean and likewise a Mediterranean plant palette suits it well. But, tropical or more correctly semi-tropical plantings are also widely used in San Diego. Temperate plants are also popular here. Using style as a guideline can help unify a landscape and its surrounding structures. Our limitations are few, and in the end we are afforded the opportunity to combine things unlike anywhere else in the world, making our landscapes unique.

Some of the very best trees may be difficult to find for sale because they do not bloom when young, may not present well in a nursery container or may be slow. These trees may be overlooked or less frequently used than perhaps they should be, and may need to be special ordered.

This book showcases mature specimens of many of the trees that can be grown in San Diego and locations to view them. I greatly recommend getting out to see the trees in real life when possible.

Tom Piergrossi
July 2003

Color Chart of Showy Flowering Trees

There are many kinds of ornamental trees that provide significant color in our landscapes, a number of which are absolutely sensational in bloom. By choosing the right tree, it is possible to have flower color all year. This color chart may be used as a guide when selecting trees for your garden, and also as a quick reference to see which trees bloom when (remember that blooming time may vary somewhat in different years and in different microclimates). Size and climate adaptability is also indicated for each tree, as is whether the tree is evergreen or not.

Botanical Name	Month (Jan–Dec bloom period)	Color	Size	Location
Acacia baileyana	Jan–Mar	Yellow	15' to 30'	Evergreen, Coast, Inland, Mountain
Acacia cognata	Mar–May	Yellow	15' to 30'	Evergreen, Coast, Inland, Mountain
Acacia podalyriifolia	Jan–Mar, Dec	Yellow	15' or less	Evergreen, Coast, Inland
Acacia stenophylla	—	Cream	15' to 30'	Evergreen, Coast, Inland, Mountain, Desert
Acacia xanthophloea	—	Yellow	30' – up	Evergreen, Coast, Inland, Desert
Acca sellowiana	May–Jun	White	15' or less	Evergreen, Coast, Inland, Desert
Acrocarpus fraxinifolius	Mar–Apr	Red	30' – up	Coast, Inland
Aesculus californica	May–Jun	Cream	15' to 30'	Coast, Inland, Mountain
Agonis flexuosa	May–Jun	White	15' to 30'	Evergreen, Coast, Inland
Albizia julibrissin	Jun–Aug	Pink	15' to 30'	Coast, Inland, Mountain, Desert
Aloe barberae	May–Jul	Pink	15' to 30'	Evergreen, Coast, Inland, Desert
Angophora costata	Jun–Jul	White	30' – up	Evergreen, Coast, Inland, Mountain
Arbutus unedo	Jan–Feb, Oct–Dec	White/Pink	15' to 30'	Evergreen, Coast, Inland, Mountain
Auranticarpa rhombifolia	Jun–Jul	Cream	15' to 30'	Evergreen, Coast, Inland
Banksia integrifolia	Jan–Feb, Sep–Dec	Chartreuse	30' – up	Evergreen, Coast, Inland
Bauhinia x blakeana	Jan–Feb, Jul–Aug	Purple	15' to 30'	Evergreen, Coast, Inland, Desert
Bauhinia forficata	Jul–Sep	White	15' to 30'	Coast, Inland, Desert
Bauhinia variegata	Feb–Apr	Pink	15' to 30'	Coast, Inland, Desert
Bocconia arborea	Apr–Jun	Chartreuse	15' to 30'	Evergreen, Coast, Inland, Desert
Brachychiton acerifolius	May–Jun	Red	30' – up	Coast, Inland, Desert
Brachychiton discolor	Jun–Aug	Pink	30' – up	Coast, Inland, Desert
Brachychiton populneus	Jun–Jul	White	30' – up	Evergreen, Coast, Inland, Desert
Brachychiton rupestris	Jun–Jul	Cream	15' to 30'	Evergreen, Coast, Inland, Desert
Brugmansia versicolor	May–Nov	Apricot	15' or less	Coast, Inland
Calliandra surinamensis	Jan–Dec	Pink	15' or less	Evergreen, Coast, Inland
Callistemon citrinus	Jan–Mar, Jul, Oct–Nov	Red	15' to 30'	Evergreen, Coast, Inland, Desert
Callistemon viminalis	Jan–Mar, Jul, Sep–Nov	Red	15' to 30'	Evergreen, Coast, Inland, Desert
Calodendrum capense	May–Jul, Sep	Pink	30' – up	Coast, Inland
Cassia leptophylla	Jun–Sep	Yellow	15' or less	Evergreen, Coast, Inland
Catalpa bignonioides	May–Jun	White	30' – up	Coast, Inland, Mountain, Desert
Ceiba insignis	Sep–Nov	White	30' – up	Coast, Inland, Desert
Ceiba speciosa	Sep–Nov	Pink	30' – up	Coast, Inland, Mountain, Desert
Ceratonia siliqua	Apr–May	Red	30' – up	Evergreen, Coast, Inland, Desert
Cercis canadensis	Mar–Apr	Pink	15' to 30'	Coast, Inland, Mountain, Desert
Chionanthus retusus	May–Jun	White	15' to 30'	Coast, Inland, Mountain
Chiranthodendron pentadactylon	Apr–Jul	Red	30' – up	Evergreen, Coast, Inland, Desert
x Chitalpa tashkentensis	May–Sep	Pink	15' to 30'	Coast, Inland, Mountain, Desert
Citrus x aurantium	Mar–May	White	15' or less	Evergreen, Coast, Inland, Desert
Cornus florida 'Cloud Nine'	Apr–May	White	15' to 30'	Coast, Inland, Mountain
Corymbia calophylla	—	Cream	30' – up	Evergreen, Coast, Inland
Corymbia citriodora	—	Cream	30' – up	Evergreen, Coast, Inland, Desert
Corymbia ficifolia	May–Jul	Red	30' – up	Evergreen, Coast, Inland
Dombeya cacuminum	Feb–Mar	Pink	15' to 30'	Evergreen, Coast, Inland, Desert

141

Color Chart of Showy Flowering Trees

Botanical Name	Month												Color	Size			Location				
	Jan	Feb	Mar	Apr	May	Jun	Jul	Aug	Sep	Oct	Nov	Dec		15' or less	15' to 30'	30' - up	Evergreen	Coast	Inland	Mountain	Desert
Dombeya x cayeuxii								■	■				Pink	■			■	■	■		
Dombeya rotundifolia			■										White	■			■	■	■		■
Duranta erecta	■	■	■	■	■	■	■	■	■	■	■	■	Lt. Blue				■	■	■		■
Eriobotrya deflexa													Cream				■	■	■	■	
Eriobotrya japonica													Cream				■	■	■		
Erythrina x bidwillii					■	■	■	■	■				Red					■	■		■
Erythrina caffra	■	■	■	■							■	■	Red					■	■		■
Erythrina corralloides				■	■								Red					■	■		■
Erythrina crista-galli					■	■	■	■	■				Red	■				■	■		■
Erythrina falcata				■	■								Red					■	■		■
Erythrina humeana							■	■	■	■			Red					■	■		■
Erythrina lysistemon	■	■											Red					■	■		■
Erythrina speciosa				■	■								Red	■				■	■		■
Erythrina x sykesii	■	■								■	■		Red					■	■		■
Eucalyptus cinerea													Cream				■	■	■		■
Eucalyptus cladocalyx													Cream				■	■	■		■
Eucalyptus conferruminata					■	■							Chartreuse				■	■	■		
Eucalyptus erythrocorys	■								■	■			Yellow		■		■	■	■		■
Eucalyptus globulus													Cream				■	■	■		
Eucalyptus leucoxylon	■	■	■	■	■	■	■					■	Cream/Pink				■	■	■		■
Eucalyptus nicholii													White				■	■	■		■
Eucalyptus polyanthemos													Cream				■	■	■		■
Eucalyptus sideroxylon	■	■	■								■	■	Pink				■	■	■		■
Eucalyptus torquata	■	■	■	■	■	■	■	■	■				Pink		■		■	■	■		■
Grevillea robusta					■	■							Gold				■	■	■		■
Heteromels arbutifolia													White	■			■	■	■	■	
Hibiscus rosa-sinensis	■	■	■	■	■	■	■		■			■	Many Colors	■			■	■	■		■
Hymenosporum flavum					■								Gold		■		■	■	■		
Inga affinis													White				■	■	■		
Jacaranda mimosifolia					■	■							Purple					■	■		■
Kigelia africana						■	■	■					Red				■	■	■		■
Koelreuteria bipinnata						■							Yellow					■	■		■
Lagerstroemia indica						■	■	■					Pink Red					■	■	■	■
Lagunaria patersonii						■							Pink				■	■	■		■
Leptospermum laevigatum													White				■	■	■		■
Leptospermum petersonii													White	■			■	■	■		
Ligustrum lucidum													White				■	■	■		■
Liriodendron tulipifera					■								Chartreuse		■			■	■		
Lophostemon confertus													Cream				■	■	■		
Lyonothamnus floribundus													White				■	■	■		
Macadamia integrifolia													Cream		■		■	■	■		
Magnolia grandiflora													White				■	■	■		■
Magnolia grandiflora 'Little Gem'													White	■			■	■	■		■
Magnolia x soulangiana		■	■										Pink	■				■	■		
Markhamia lutea													Yellow				■	■	■		
Melaleuca armillaris													White				■	■	■		■
Melaleuca linariifolia													White				■	■	■		
Melaleuca nesophila	■	■	■										Lavender	■			■	■	■		■

Color Chart of Showy Flowering Trees

Botanical Name	Jan	Feb	Mar	Apr	May	Jun	Jul	Aug	Sep	Oct	Nov	Dec	Color	15' or less	15' to 30'	30' - up	Evergreen	Coast	Inland	Mountain	Desert
Melaleuca quinquenervia													Cream			█	█	█			█
Melaleuca styphelioides													White		█		█	█	█		█
Melia azedarach			█	█									Lavender			█		█	█		█
Metrosideros excelsa						█	█	█					Red		█		█	█			
Michelia champaca					█	█	█	█					Gold		█		█	█	█		
Michelia doltsopa													Cream		█		█	█	█		
Montanoa guatemalensis													White		█		█	█	█		
Myrtus communis													White	█			█	█	█		
Nerium oleander				█	█	█	█	█	█	█	█		Many Colors		█		█	█	█		█
Parkinsonia aculeata		█	█	█									Yellow		█			█	█		█
Paulownia kawakamii			█	█									Lavender			█		█	█	█	
Pittosporum angustifolium													Yellow	█			█	█	█		█
Pittosporum napaulense					█								Gold		█		█	█	█		█
Pittosporum tobira													Cream	█			█	█	█		█
Pittosporum undulatum													Cream		█		█	█	█		
Pittosporum viridiflorum					█								Chartreuse	█			█	█	█		█
Plumeria rubra					█	█	█	█	█	█			Many Colors		█			█	█		█
Podachaenium eminens													Cream		█		█	█	█		
Prunus campanulata	█	█											Pink	█				█	█	█	
Prunus cerasifera 'Atropurpurea'		█											Pink		█			█	█	█	█
Prunus persica		█	█										Pink Red		█			█	█		█
Psidium cattleianum													Cream	█			█	█	█		
Psidium guajava													Cream		█		█	█	█		
Punica granatum					█	█	█						Orange		█			█	█		█
Pyrus calleryana													Cream			█		█	█	█	
Pyrus kawakamii													Cream		█		█	█	█		
Radermachera sinica													White		█		█	█	█		
Robinia pseudoacacia													White			█		█	█	█	█
Schefflera actinophylla		█	█						█	█			Red			█	█	█	█		
Schizolobium parahyba													Yellow			█		█	█		
Schotia brachypetala					█	█							Red		█		█	█	█		
Senna spectabilis													Yellow		█			█	█		█
Spathodea campanulata							█	█	█				Orange			█	█	█	█		
Stenocarpus sinuatus	█							█	█	█	█		Red		█		█	█	█		
Strelitzia nicolai													White		█		█	█	█		
Syzygium jambos													Cream		█		█	█	█		
Syzygium paniculatum													Cream		█		█	█	█		
Tabebuia chrysotricha			█										Yellow		█			█	█		
Tabebuia impetiginosa			█	█									Pink			█		█	█		█
Tecoma stans													Yellow		█		█	█	█		█
Thevetia thevetioides													Yellow	█			█	█	█		█
Tipuana tipu													Gold			█		█	█		█
Tristaniopsis laurina			█										Yellow		█		█	█	█		
Vitex agnus-castus							█	█					Lavender	█				█	█		█
Vitex lucens							█	█					Pink		█		█	█	█		
Yucca elephantipes													Cream		█		█	█	█		█

Trees of Quail Botanical Gardens

Quail Botanical Gardens has over 3,000 species of plants on over thirty acres of gardens, landscapes, and natural areas. This map shows locations of larger specimen trees, although most of the trees in this book grow in the Gardens.

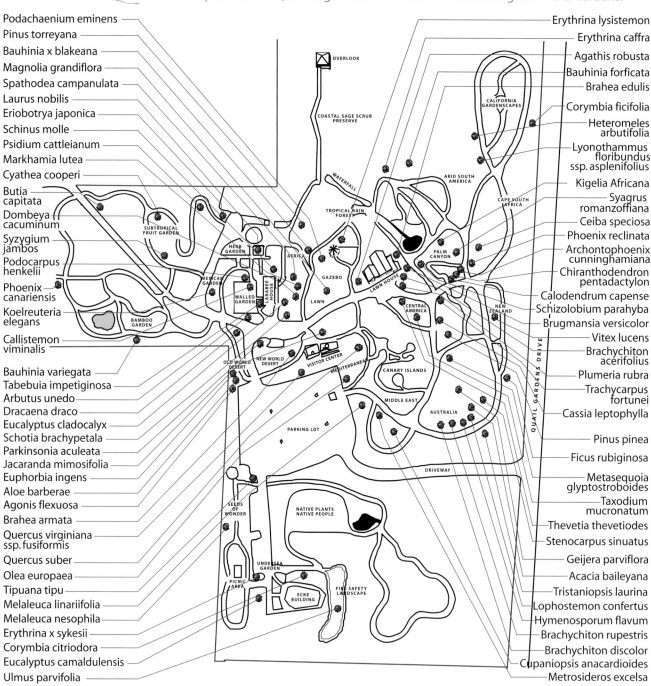

Podachaenium eminens
Pinus torreyana
Bauhinia x blakeana
Magnolia grandiflora
Spathodea campanulata
Laurus nobilis
Eriobotrya japonica
Schinus molle
Psidium cattleianum
Markhamia lutea
Cyathea cooperi
Butia capitata
Dombeya cacuminum
Syzygium jambos
Podocarpus henkelii
Phoenix canariensis
Koelreuteria elegans
Callistemon viminalis

Bauhinia variegata
Tabebuia impetiginosa
Arbutus unedo
Dracaena draco
Eucalyptus cladocalyx
Schotia brachypetala
Parkinsonia aculeata
Jacaranda mimosifolia
Euphorbia ingens
Aloe barberae
Agonis flexuosa
Brahea armata
Quercus virginiana ssp. fusiformis
Quercus suber
Olea europaea
Tipuana tipu
Melaleuca linariifolia
Melaleuca nesophila
Erythrina x sykesii
Corymbia citriodora
Eucalyptus camaldulensis
Ulmus parvifolia

Erythrina lysistemon
Erythrina caffra
Agathis robusta
Bauhinia forficata
Brahea edulis
Corymbia ficifolia
Heteromeles arbutifolia
Lyonothammus floribundus ssp. asplenifolius
Kigelia Africana
Syagrus romanzoffiana
Ceiba speciosa
Phoenix reclinata
Archontophoenix cunninghamiana
Chiranthodendron pentadactylon
Calodendrum capense
Schizolobium parahyba
Brugmansia versicolor
Vitex lucens
Brachychiton acerifolius
Plumeria rubra
Trachycarpus fortunei
Cassia leptophylla
Pinus pinea
Ficus rubiginosa
Metasequoia glyptostroboides
Taxodium mucronatum
Thevetia thevetiodes
Stenocarpus sinuatus
Geijera parviflora
Acacia baileyana
Tristaniopsis laurina
Lophostemon confertus
Hymenosporum flavum
Brachychiton rupestris
Brachychiton discolor
Cupaniopsis anacardioides
Metrosideros excelsa

DIRECTIONS: Off the I-5 freeway, exit at Encinitas Boulevard. Go east 1/4 mile to Quail Gardens Dr./Westlake Dr., then north to the entrance.

230 Quail Gardens Drive, Encinitas, CA 92024
760 436-3036 • **www.qbgardens.com**

144

Balboa Park Location Codes

Balboa Park is maintained by the City of San Diego Parks and Recreation Department and consists of 1100 acres that includes nearly 20,000 trees and 400 species. The San Diego Zoological Garden collection is contained within the Zoo and if included would nearly double those figures. The Balboa Park Location Codes will direct you to the general area where the tree is growing. To learn more about Balboa Park trees, refer to *Trees and Gardens of Balboa Park* or join Offshoot Tours which meets at the Visitor Center at 10 a.m. each Saturday for a free one-hour tour. Visit online for a map and more information at www.balboapark.org or www.sandiego.gov.

WEST MESA—Area bounded by Highway 163 on the east and south, Upas Street on the north and Sixth Avenue on the west. This area includes the Marston House and gardens

B1	Marston House Gardens	B7	North of Lawn Bowling Greens
B2	Upas St. & Balboa Dr.	B8	Sefton Plaza (El; Prado & Balboa Dr.)
B3	Quince St. & Balboa Dr.	B9	6th Ave. south of Laurel St.
B4	South of Marston House, east of Balboa Dr.	B10	Balboa Dr. southeast of Sefton Plaza
B5	Balboa Dr. south of Quince St.	B11	Balboa Dr. & Juniper St.
B6	6th Ave. north of Laurel St.	B12	Marston Point

CENTRAL MESA—Area bounded by Highway 163 on the west and south; Upas Street on the north and the edge of Florida Canyon (along Park Boulevard) on the eastern edge. This includes most of the museums, formal gardens and Inspiration Point

B13	War Memorial Bldg	B25	Australian Garden (southeast of the Organ Pavilion)
B14	S.D. Zoological Gardens	B26	Desert Garden
B15	Carousel	B27	Inez Grant Parker Memorial Rose Garden
B16	Village Place	B28	House of Hospitality
B17	Behind Palisades Building (Puppet Theater)	B29	Houses of Pacific Relations
B18	Botanical Building	B30	Federal Building /S.D. Hall of Champions
B19	S.D. Museum of Art	B31	Municipal Gym
B20	Old Globe Theater	B32	S.D. Aerospace Museum
B21	El Prado	B33	S.D. Automotive Museum
B22	Alcazar Gardens	B34	Japanese Friendship Garden
B23	Palm Canyon	B35	Casa del Prado
B24	Zoro Gardens	B36	Pepper Grove Playground
		B37	Inspiration Point

EAST MESA—Area on the east side of Florida Canyon Drive, bounded on the north by Upas Street and on the south by Russ Boulevard. This area includes Golden Hill Park, Grape St. Park and Morley Field

B38	Morley Field	B41	Grape St. Park
B39	Native Plant Demo Garden	B42	Golden Hill Park
B40	Florida Canyon Native Plant Preserve	B43	28th St. and A Street

Selected Bibliography

In addition to the trees presented in this book, there are many more kinds of beautiful trees which can be and should be grown in San Diego County. We wish we could have showed you them all, but considerations of space and time plus the inability to find mature public specimens has unfortunately left them out of this publication.

Although the Internet is an invaluable source of information and in fact was used quite a bit in researching the information we have presented, there is still nothing like a good book. The following reference books have been extremely useful in preparing our text, and we highly recommend them both as general references and guides to the full range of trees that can be grown in Mediterranean-type climates.

Bailey Hortorium, *Hortus Third*. New York: Macmillan Co., 1976.

Beittel, Will, *Santa Barbara's Trees*. Santa Barbara Horticultural Society, Santa Barbara, California, 1976.

Brenzel, Kathleen Norris, editor, *Sunset Western Garden Book*. Sunset Publishing Co., Menlo Park, California, 2001.

Citron, Joan, editor, *Selected Plants for Southern California Gardens*. Southern California Horticultural Society, Los Angeles, California, 2000.

Elliot, W. Rodger, and David L. Jones, *Encyclopedia of Australian Plants*. Lothian Publishing Co., Melbourne, Australia, 1982-2002.

Hodel, Donald R., Exceptional *Trees of Los Angeles*. California Arboretum Foundation, Los Angeles, California, 1988.

Hogan, Sean, chief consultant, *Flora*, Timber Press, Portland, Oregon, 2003.

Hoyt, Roland Stewart, *Ornamental Plants for Subtropical Regions* (revised edition). Livingston Press, Anaheim, CA. 1998.

Jones, David L., *Palms Throughout the World*. Smithsonian Institution Press, Washington, D.C., 1995.

Mabberly, D.J., *The Plant-Book* (second edition). Cambridge University Press, Cambridge, United Kingdom, 1997.

Macoboy, Stirling, *Trees for flower and fragrance*. Lansdowne Press, Sydney, Australia, 1982.

Macoboy, Stirling, *Trees for fruit and foliage*. Lansdowne Press, Sydney, Australia, 1982.

Mahoney, Michael T., et al., editors, *Street Trees Recommended for Southern California* (second edition). Street Tree Seminar, Inc., Anaheim, California, 1996.

Mathias, Mildred E., editor, *Flowering Plants in the Landscape*. University of California Press, Berkeley, California, 1982.

McClintock, Elizabeth, and Andrew T. Leiser, *An Annotated Checklist of Woody Ornamental Plants of California, Oregon, and Washington*. University of California, Berkeley, California, 1979.

Menninger, Edwin A., *Flowering Trees of the World*. Hearthside Press, New York, 1962.

Metcalf, L.J., *The Cultivation of New Zealand Trees and Shrubs* (revised edition). Reed Methuen Publishers Ltd., Auckland, New Zealand, 1987.

Osborne, Barry, Trish Reynoso, and Geoff Stein, *Palms for Southern California*. The Palm Society of Southern California, Thousand Oaks, California, 2000.

Palmer, Eve and Norah Pitman, *Trees of Southern Africa*. A.A. Balkema Co., Cape Town, South Africa, 1972.

Puplava, Kathy and Paul Sirois. *Trees and Gardens of Balboa Park*. City of San Diego Parks and Recreation Department, San Diego, California, 2001.

Riedel, Peter, *Plants for Extra-Tropical Regions*. California Arboretum Foundation, Arcadia, California, 1959.

Wasson, Ernie, chief consultant, *Trees and Shrubs*. Global Book Publishing Pty. Ltd., Willoughby, Australia, 2001.

Sources

American Horticultural Society
(703) 768-5700; membership@ahs.org; www.ahs.org. The American Horticultural Society is a national non-profit educational organization dedicated to "making America a nation of gardeners, a land of gardens."

Briggs Tree Company & Wholesale Nursery
1111 Poinsettia Ave., Vista, CA 92081; (760) 727-2727; sales@briggstree.com; www.briggstree.com

Buena Creek Gardens
418 Buena Creek Rd., San Marcos, CA 92069; (760) 744-2810; www.buenacreekgardens.com

Evergreen Nursery
7150 Black Mountain Rd., San Diego, CA 92130; (858) 481-0622; www.evergreennursery.com

***Horticulture* magazine**
(617) 742-5600 x327; bemerson@hortmag.com; www.hortmag.com

Hydro-Scape Products, Inc.
(858) 560-1600; alarsen@hydro-scape.com; www.hydro-scape.com

Nowell & Associates Landscape Architecture, Inc.
(619) 325-1990; mail@nowellassociates.com; www.nowellassociates.com

***Pacific Horticulture* magazine**
P.O. Box 680, Berkeley, CA 94701; (510) 849-1627; office@pacifichorticulture.org; www.pacifichorticulture.org. Pacific Horticulture, published by the non-profit Pacific Horticultural Foundation, is a quarterly journal dedicated to the art and science of gardening in the summer-dry climates of the West Coast. The Foundation also sponsors occasional lectures, symposia, and domestic and international garden tours.

Pardee Tree Nursery
(760) 630-5400; bwidas@pardeetree.com; www.pardeetree.com

Quail Botanical Gardens
230 Quail Gardens Dr., Encinitas, CA 92024; (760) 436-3036; info@qbgardens.com; www.qbgardens.org

San Diego County Flower & Plant Association
(760) 431-2572; info@flowerandplant.org; www.flowerandplant.org

***San Diego Home/Garden Lifestyles* magazine**
(858) 571-1818 x135; olander@sdhg.net. Beautiful monthly magazine dedicated to local coverage of architecture, interior design and gardens. Subscriptions available: 1 year/$18.

San Diego Natural History Museum
(619) 232-3821; administration@sdnhm.org; www.sdnhm.org. The San Diego Natural History Museum is passionate about the natural world—discovering it and sharing those discoveries with the hope of inspiring stewardship by all. Visit us in beautiful Balboa Park.

SeaWorld San Diego
500 Sea World Dr., San Diego, CA 92109; (619) 226-3900; www.seaworld.com ; www.seaworld.org

The Garden Conservancy's *Open Days Program*
(845) 265-5384; info@gardenconservancy.org; www.gardenconservancy.org

Walter Andersen Nurseries
12755 Danielson Ct., Poway, CA 92064, (858) 513-4790; 3642 Enterprise St.; San Diego, CA 92110, (619) 224-8271; www.walterandersen.com

Index of Common Names

149

Index of Botanical Names